International Economics

International Economics

Understanding the Forces of Globalization for Managers

Second Edition

Paul Torelli

BUSINESS EXPERT PRESS

International Economics: Understanding the Forces of Globalization for Managers, Second Edition

First published in 2013 by
Business Expert Press, LLC
222 East 46th Street, New York, NY 10017
www.businessexpertpress.com

ISBN-13: 978-1-63157-614-0 (paperback)
ISBN-13: 978-1-63157-615-7 (e-book)

Business Expert Press Economics Collection

Collection ISSN: 2163-761X (print)
Collection ISSN: 2163-7628 (electronic)

Cover and interior design by Exeter Premedia Services Private Ltd. Chennai, India

Second edition: 2017

10 9 8 7 6 5 4 3 2 1

Printed in the United States of America.

To my teachers

Abstract

Today's news media displays an intense fascination with the global economy—and for good reason. The degree of worldwide economic integration is unprecedented, and rising globalization has lifted living standards and reduced poverty. Foreign markets and new technologies continue to present opportunities for entrepreneurs and corporations. Still, economic shocks can spread across the world in minutes, impacting billions of lives. Citizens are understandably anxious in this age of macroeconomic turbulence and overextended governments.

Modern economics offers a powerful framework for understanding globalization, international trade, and economic growth. Many managers possess years of hands-on experience dealing with business cycles and foreign competitive pressures, yet these leaders may not have a solid grounding in economic concepts that shed light on the forces of globalization. This book explains economics in everyday language, using little or no math, giving businesspersons better tools to interpret current events as well as long-term economic and political developments.

Keywords

economics, human capital, financial crisis, macroeconomics, comparative advantage, absolute advantage, emerging economy, international trade, business strategy, economic growth, economic history, international economics, political economy, economic development, industrialization, labor market, convergence, New World, mercantilism, Industrial Revolution, productivity, technology, capital control, intellectual property, research and development, productivity slowdown, Adam Smith, factor proportions model, gravity model, infant industry, import substitution, Asian Tiger, trade policy, tariff, public choice, rent seeking, trade agreement, free trade, liberalization, information and communications technology, vertical integration, supply chain, poverty trap, big push, coordination failure, industrial policy, diversification, value added, managerial capital, skill biased technological change, population growth, wage inequality, middle income trap, tradable sector, offshoring, outsourcing, foreign direct investment, skill upgrading, immigration, wage structure, regulation, competitiveness, corruption, democracy, autocracy, socialism, communism, controlled capitalism, gold standard, natural resource curse, business cycle, collective bargaining, social insurance, safety net, labor union, Washington Consensus, multinational enterprise, exchange rate, sweatshop, spillover, human rights, labor standard, property rights, Dutch disease, extractive industry, negative externality, pollution haven, greenhouse gas, global warming, climate change

Contents

Preface xi

Chapter 1   A Brief History of Modern Economic Globalization 1

Chapter 2   Economic Growth, Convergence, and Trade....................41

Chapter 3   Theories of International Trade.......................................67

Chapter 4   Industrialization, Globalization, and Labor Markets........97

Chapter 5   Politics, Globalization, and the State 129

Chapter 6   Poverty, Progress, and Critics of Globalization 157

Epilogue 189
Postscript...199
Index 203

Preface

Now that world wide communications have been established thanks to the authority of the Roman Empire ... living standards have improved by the interchange of goods and by partnership in the joy of peace and by the general availability of things previously concealed.
—Gaius Plinius Secundus (Pliny the Elder),
Natural History, 77 AD

"Globalization" is the increasing economic interdependence of all regions of the world. Made possible through improvements in transportation and communications, globalization's driving force is the international movement of goods, people, capital, technology, culture, and ideas. Although silks and spices were traded between Asia and Europe at least as far back as Greco-Roman times, the process of intercontinental assimilation wasn't truly global until the 16th century, when the Americas became part of world trade and migration routes, uniting both hemispheres. Several centuries later, the "Industrial Revolution" opened up new production possibilities and wrought tremendous efficiencies, overturning the old "snail's pace" rate of economic growth that had previously ruled the civilized world. Globalization has played a central role in facilitating growth, consumption, and higher standards of living, above all when a major hegemon—such as the Roman or British Empire—has been in place to combat piracy and provide law and order. Historians commonly think of the "modern" Western world beginning around 1500, and this book begins with the follow-up to that date. World trade has grown mightily since then despite wars and depressions periodically slowing its expansion. The most recent "deglobalization" occurred during the period from World War I to World War II, when, after a prolonged period of peace and integration, cracks in the international economic order fissured, and tribalism and warfare reemerged. Today the degree of global economic connectivity is unprecedented, even greater than the previous watershed era prior to World War I.

To some extent, globalization reflects the progress of civilization and mankind. Whereas isolation breeds stagnation, cross-cultural contact brings new influences and technologies, which then vie against the old. And trade—whether short- or long-distance—yields mutual gains, a fact that has been understood and exploited since prehistoric times. It is revealing that the ancient city-state of Athens traded abroad vigorously and boasted a rich culture, whereas Sparta, its more introverted rival on the Greek peninsula, did not. Market economies in ancient Greece and Rome exchanged goods throughout vast regions of Asia and Africa. Far larger than the territories of any Greek city-state (or even the Macedonian Empire under Alexander the Great), the Roman Empire was partially funded by trade and tribute over an immense land network of roads. Its seagoing commercial ships carried Egyptian grain, Spanish copper, Greek wine, and Asian silks. Roman traders may have reached China by sea in the 2nd century AD, and at its peak around this time, the Roman Empire stretched across all sides of the Mediterranean Sea and most of Western Europe, ruling approximately 75 million people, with at least a million living in its capital city of Rome. Roman culture assimilated Greek ideas about philosophy, politics, art, science, and architecture, and then modified or sometimes improved upon them. The exceptional Roman capacity for administration—unmatched in the West until the British Empire more than a millennium later—provided order in an extremely violent ancient world, stimulating economic and cultural development.

Nevertheless, even the greatest and wealthiest civilizations may collapse. Toward its end, the Roman Empire had been weakening for more than a century, with ineffective governance and a disintegrating society. Rival generals vied for power and often required bribes to stave off coups. The Roman government had trouble raising funds and ultimately resorted to devaluing the currency, which caused a destructive hyperinflation. Wishing to evade the state's grasping hands, urban citizens and businesses fled to the countryside, helping to pave the way for feudalism. By the 3rd century AD, the Roman military began to suffer embarrassing defeats by Germanic forces—part of a rural society the Romans considered hopelessly barbaric—to the north and Persian armies to the east. The external threats worsened in the late-4th century, and in 410, Rome was famously sacked by an army of Germanic barbarians known as the Visigoths. The Empire continued to crumble in the 5th century as a number of Germanic tribes conquered Roman territories. The final act that has traditionally marked the end of the Western Roman Empire occurred in 476 when a Germanic chieftain, Flavius Odoacer, removed the last emperor, a teenager named Romulus Augustus, from power. (The Eastern Roman Empire, later known as the Byzantine Empire, survived until the 1453 conquest of Constantinople by Ottoman Turks.) For centuries afterward, during the period of conflict, disorder, and migration in Europe commonly known as the "Dark Ages," Middle Eastern merchants came to dominate trade routes along the crossroads region linking the Asian and European economies. Knowledge of many key technologies disappeared, and there were relatively few cultural achievements coming out of the West.

Written by an American economist, this book focuses on the experience of the West, albeit without ignoring the East. Based on the most recent academic research, it provides a brief readable introduction to the economic forces of globalization for an audience of modern managers and executives who may have little or no background in formal economics. By presenting key economic concepts that have withstood the test of time, this book offers valuable insights to business practitioners grappling with the effects of globalization, new technology, and international trade on their organization and work force. It is conscious of the present economic climate which follows several decades of rapid globalization, and its content can provide structure for an undergraduate or graduate course in business. Each chapter may engender classroom or workplace discussions, given the inherent complexity of the subject matter. Although this book is not meant to be historically exhaustive by any means, it endeavors to spark an interest in world economic history among readers. It can be supplemented with current materials from newspapers such as the *Wall Street Journal*, *New York Times*, and *Financial Times*, as well as insightful magazines such as the *Economist*. Relevant case studies from the Harvard Business School Press (which can be found online) are presented at the end of each chapter.

Economists commonly concentrate on international trade integration as the primary feature of globalization, as it is relatively easy to measure and analyze. This book is no exception: it emphasizes the effects of international trade as opposed to global financial liberalization and integration. Theoretical discussions of monetary issues—such as exchange rates, balance of payments, and optimal currency unions—are generally ignored. This is partly because financial and monetary theories remain controversial among economists, but more importantly—and in line with how economics is actually taught in universities today—this book reflects the philosophy that it is better to learn the fundamental structural factors driving economic events first, because complex financial and monetary factors can be studied later. Monetary theories of business cycle fluctuations and financial crises are traditionally based on behavioral theories of how money, credit, prices, and output interact. Interested readers are referred to the works of John Maynard Keynes, Charles Kindleberger, and Barry Eichengreen, among others, some of which are mentioned in "Further Reading" sections at the end of each chapter.

Further Reading

Amemiya, T. (2007). *Economy and economies of Ancient Greece*. New York, NY: Routledge.

Beckwith, C. (2009). *Empires of the silk road: A history of Central Eurasia from the Bronze Age to the present*. Princeton, NJ: Princeton University Press.

Bernstein, W. (2004). *The birth of plenty: How the prosperity of the modern world was created*. New York, NY: McGraw-Hill.

Bordo, M., Taylor, A., & Williamson, J. (2005). *Globalization in historical perspective*. Chicago, IL: University of Chicago Press.

Braudel, F. (1995). *A history of civilizations*. New York, NY: Penguin.

Davies, N. (2011). *Vanished kingdoms: The rise and fall of states and nations*. New York, NY: Viking.

Goldsworthy, A. (2009). *How Rome fell: Death of a superpower*. New Haven, CT: Yale University Press.

Hansen, V. (2012). *The Silk Road: A new history*. Oxford, England: Oxford University Press.

Jennings, J. (2014). *Globalizations and the ancient world*. Cambridge, England: Cambridge University Press.

Maddison, A. (2007). *Contours of the world economy 1-2030 AD: Essays in macro-economic history*. Oxford, England: Oxford University Press.

North, D. (2010). *Understanding the process of economic change*. Princeton, NJ: Princeton University Press.

Richard, C. (2010). *Why we're all Romans: The Roman contribution to the western world*. Lanham, MD: Rowman & Littlefield.

Stearns, P. (2009). *Globalization in history*. New York, NY: Routledge.

Temin, P. (2012). *The Roman market economy*. Princeton, NJ: Princeton University Press.

CHAPTER 1

A Brief History of Modern Economic Globalization

Introduction

The urge to exchange goods and services is a fundamental characteristic of
any economy, and human beings have traded across far-flung locales for
millennia. Archaeologists point to Mesopotamia, in modern day Iraq, as
the place where Western civilization began. The ancient Sumerians of
Mesopotamia were inveterate traders with a culture that featured writing,
mathematics, laws, and cities. Over the subsequent centuries, trade networks and economic integration grew to cover ever-greater regions of the
Eurasian landmass, depending on the stability and reach of existing political regimes. The 4,000-mile "Silk Road," a network of overland trade
routes connecting China to the Mediterranean, transferred goods and
spread ideas between the East and the West. Many scholars believe these
exchanges constitute the nascent beginnings of intercontinental economic
globalization within the "Old World."

The rise of the Mongol Empire under Genghis Khan in the early-13th
century—several centuries before the discovery of the "New World"—led
to the "Pax Mongolica" (or Mongol Peace). The Mongol conquests unified
Central Eurasia, promoting overland trade all the way from Western
Europe to East Asia. According to some contemporary accounts of this era,
the Silk Road was safe for travel and business. Under the Pax Mongolica,
Europeans such as the Venetian merchant Marco Polo came to China
for Asian silks and spices. Chinese silks sold in Italy for no less than three
times their purchase price in China, and the markets of Constantinople
contained all the wares of Asia. Because information flowed east to west
and vice-versa, Europeans took advantage of many Chinese inventions
and scientific concepts. Meanwhile, the Mongols—who lacked culture

and craft but possessed a taste for fine textiles and other riches—forcibly transplanted European artisans and Middle Eastern weavers back to Asia.

The Mongol Empire provided a conduit not only for trade but also for disease. In the mid-14th century, the Silk Road trade route aided the transmission of the plague from China to Europe. Economic integration declined, and the Mongols, possessing more skill in conquest than in governance, lost their grip on power shortly thereafter. As Europe's population recovered, feudalism gave way to nation-states, and seafaring adventurers discovered the New World, sparking an unprecedented globalization boom. Since then, the volume of world trade and degree of global economic integration has trended upward at an increasing pace. Few today believe that international economic integration will be reversed, although the period from World War I to World War II was the great exception, proving that disintegration is possible, and that taking part in globalization is a choice that nations face, not an imperative.

Mercantilist World View

Modern economists trace their field's origins back to Adam Smith's 1776 *Wealth of Nations*. This treatise examined trade's role in facilitating specialization and the division of labor, thereby increasing productivity and promoting prosperity. Its content was in opposition to the popular mercantilist beliefs that reached their apogee in the 17th century. Mercantilism of that era was a nationalistic doctrine promoted by a diffuse group of pamphleteers who advocated for specific interests and industries. Mercantilist writers were usually appreciative of international trade—just not unfettered free trade. In the 16th century, mercantilist pamphlets from England were the first writings that treated economic concerns as worthy of separate study, as opposed to remaining part of legal or moral concerns. For instance, one influential English thinker of this period, Sir Thomas Smith, emphasized the value of manufacturing raw materials at home and having a favorable "balance of trade," meaning that exports ought to be greater than imports.

Compared to later economic analysts such as Adam Smith, mercantilists did not focus on increased productive efficiency within or across nations. Instead, they concentrated on the importance of amassing factor inputs, such as land, labor, and raw materials, including bullion. Mercantilist principles prized national gold and silver holdings, made possible through heavy exporting with a minimum of importing. Because foreign colonies could supply raw resources and gold or silver bullion, mercantilists advocated a strong military with colonialist ambitions. Materials could be transported to the home nation and made into finished products for export. The militant mercantilist outlook was responsible for many tariffs and legal restrictions hindering international trade. It also required a robust navy to aid in navigation, enforce maritime laws, and deal with trade-related conflict.

Mercantilists emphasized the zero-sum aspect of economic development and trade. Viewing the gains from trade as fixed, they intended their own nation to capture the greater portion of them. In England and other parts of Europe at this time, imports were normally luxury consumption goods such as silk. Mercantilist writings regularly advocated for tariffs on these opulent imports because their purchase did not stimulate domestic production or increase national wealth. Yet mercantilists were in favor of importing raw materials to stimulate manufacturing. They desired high value-added processes such as manufacturing to be performed on domestic—not foreign—soil. Mercantilists advocated little to no restrictions on exports, and a few even called for export subsidies. They believed that higher exports stimulated domestic economic development, manufacturing capacity, and labor demand.

Often merchants themselves, mercantilist writers were altogether favorable toward trade and commerce, viewing state oversight as necessary to ensure trade enriched the nation, and not just tradespersons. On the other hand, specific mercantilist policies regularly benefitted narrow interests, such as the business owners within one domestic industry who were all too happy to block foreign competitors through high tariffs and other import restrictions. Although the influence of mercantilism has sharply declined over the past three centuries, mercantilist style policies exist in some nations today. China has been described as "neo-mercantilist" because of its strategic protectionism, forgoing of luxury spending to save and invest, amassing of foreign reserves, and, in lieu of military conquest, import of raw materials for manufacturing and investment, all under strong state administration. Other East Asian nations that have developed successfully (such as Japan and South Korea) expanded their export-oriented production capabilities in a manner broadly consistent with mercantilist principles.

Historical Background

The backdrop to mercantilism was an enormous drop in population due to the "Black Death," a plague caused by the *Yersinia pestis* bacterium. The most common form was bubonic plague, which infected the lymphatic system and caused swellings and discolorations, killing most victims within a week's time. Researchers have theorized that other types of the plague were present, including pneumonic (which infects the respiratory system), septicemic (which infects the blood stream), and enteric (which infects the digestive system). Following three centuries of strong population growth and expansion across arable lands, the Black Death of 1347 to 1353 swept through Europe and killed at least 25 million people from a population of 80 million. The Black Death ravaged the Middle East and Far East, too. Accounts of Egypt from that time describe depopulated towns, and between 1330 and 1420, the population of China fell from 72 million to 50 million. The plague then recurred for centuries in waves of decreasing intensity. Two of the last known major outbreaks in Europe were the Great Plague of London, which commenced in 1665, and the Great Plague of Marseille, which struck in 1720.

Unlike other disasters, the Black Death killed people but left property intact, meaning the remaining population had dramatically more resources to exploit. As a consequence, the Black Death brought about a huge drop in overall economic production with a simultaneous increase in *per capita* income and wealth. Because of the scarcity of labor, real wages increased—doubling in England over the next century—and peasant revolts became more common in Western Europe. Land was now abundant, so rents fell. With elevated incomes, there was an explosion in luxury goods such as high-quality wool textiles. Given the abundance of land relative to labor, land-intensive agricultural production such as sheep- and cattle-rearing experienced a boom as well. New "laborsaving" technologies, such as the printing press and firearms, may have been spurred by the relative scarcity of labor following the Black Death. After the plague, population growth favored cities, where there was more capital to complement workers. In Europe, it would take around 200 years for the population to return to pre-plague levels.

This period also saw the onset of the transition from feudalism to the nation-state in Europe. Despite its tendency toward disorder and conflict, feudalism was the dominant social structure of the later "Middle Ages" from the death of Charlemagne in the 9th century to the early Renaissance of the 15th century. In decentralized feudal economies, local lords retained administrative and judicial power over dependents who worked the land and paid homage by contributing taxes and performing military service. By rebalancing economic and social power in favor of labor over landowners, the Black Death contributed to the decline of the feudal system. Landlords were now forced to compete for labor because peasants were able to leave for more desirable circumstances. Those who failed to offer peasants better conditions or less onerous tasks could be faced with the prospect of labor shortages.

Elites were conscious of the difficulty of maintaining social control after the plague. In England, the 1351 Statute of Laborers attempted to suppress peasant wages and free movement, which ultimately led to social unrest and the Peasants Revolt of 1381. Modern economists have argued that the increased power and mobility of dependents—and the diminished authority of lords to tax them—sparked agricultural innovations and rural economic growth in Western Europe. A more prosperous and mobile peasantry shifted allegiance to the state, and centralized taxation and administration grew more common. Moreover, the inability of the Catholic Church to prevent the Black Death—along with the loss of many clergy to the plague itself—led to a loosening of the Church's grip on power in Europe. Some historians maintain that the Black Death was a primary catalyst for the eventual Protestant Reformation that began a century and half later.

The New World

As the population recovered in the 15th century, competing European powers grew interested in exploration. Tiny Portugal, with a population of barely one million at the time, sought a sea route around the southern tip of Africa and successfully made the voyage in 1488 under Bartolomeu Dias. Another Portuguese, Vasco da Gama, was the first European to make it to India around the Cape of Good Hope via the southern coast of Africa. He returned to Lisbon in 1499, 2 years after his initial departure. Most famously, Christopher Columbus—traditionally believed to be the Genoa-born son of a wool weaver—made four round-trip voyages from Spain to the New World of the Americas between 1492 and 1504. Columbus discovered a continent entirely unknown to Europeans (and Asians), whereas Dias and da Gama were aware that Africa and Asia existed before setting off on their journeys.

Within decades of Columbus's arrival, the Spanish had settled in parts of the Americas. New World crops were introduced to the rest of the world, fundamentally altering global agricultural and labor markets. Corn and sweet potatoes were spread all the way from the Americas to Asia, as were cocoa, tobacco, rubber, and tomatoes. Europeans brought horses, coffee, and sugarcane to the New World. They also infected indigenous populations with diseases from which they possessed no immunity, such as smallpox, cholera, measles, and typhus. As much as 95% of the native population was killed by these Old World diseases.

By the dawn of the 17th century, European navigators had made sense of Pacific and Atlantic Ocean wind patterns and improved upon long-distance maritime travel to such an extent that trade to and from the Americas occurred with relative ease. This period coincided with the middle of the "Scientific Revolution," when Galileo was in the prime of his career. It was the birth of truly global trade, as goods now regularly passed en masse across the Pacific and Atlantic Oceans—and thus, around the world. Spain founded Manila, its primary Asian trading post, in 1579. As part of the "Manila Galleon Trade," mammoth silver deposits in Mexico and Peru were shipped west to the Philippines to be exchanged for high-quality Chinese silk, at a time when the Chinese valued silver over gold. Threatened Spanish silk growers complained to the Spanish Crown, and in response, the Crown issued anti-trade edicts multiple times. Yet the trade was so profitable that the edicts were ignored, and the volume of trade only increased.

New World sugar cultivation quickly took off in the 16th century. The "Sugar Belt" extended from Brazil to the Caribbean, drawing many

Europeans in search of outsized profits. In northern Brazil, the Portuguese initially produced sugar with native slaves, though they eventually switched to West African slaves by the start of the 17th century. Holland, with its West India Company, attempted to break into the Brazilian sugar trade in the 17th century. The Dutch succeeded in capturing most of Brazil's northern coast for several decades, thereby controlling much of the world's sugar trade. However, by 1654 Holland had lost control of Recife to the Portuguese, and they eventually withdrew from Brazil in 1661. Outside of Brazil, Spain conquered nearly all the rest of South and Central America over the course of the 16th and 17th centuries.

East Indies Trade

During this "Age of Discovery," European long-distance trade also opened to the East, using the route that the Portuguese first made around the southern tip of Africa to India and Asia. Ever since pre-Christian times, the "Spice Trade" had brought cinnamon, ginger, cardamom, and turmeric from Asia to the Middle East to Europe, via camel transport along the Silk Road. Arab traders had a lock on the Spice Trade throughout most of the Middle Ages, an epoch when Central Asia—not Europe or China—was the economic and cultural center of the world. By the 14th century, the break-up of the Mongol Empire and the rise of the Ottoman Turks had closed off overland trade routes through Constantinople. The Europeans were initially beholden to Venetian middlemen who held a virtual monopoly on the Spice Trade with the Middle East. The enormous profits the Venetians made in trade were an incentive for other European powers (such as Portugal) to find maritime routes that would allow trade with Asia. Their search became all the more imperative after the 1453 fall of Constantinople to the Ottomans, followed by the 1479 Treaty of Constantinople which closed the Black Sea to the Venetians.

The Portuguese continued to dominate the East Indies Spice Trade throughout the 16th century during the zenith of the Portuguese Empire. Portugal established ports across the coasts of Africa, the Middle East, India, and Asia. Regular trade was even initiated with Japan after finding Nagasaki in 1543. Nevertheless, running an extended empire from Lisbon was always difficult. It could take 2 years for a letter to pass from Lisbon to

Goa, India, and the Portuguese Crown experienced difficulty monitoring the predatory activities of its many merchants, who were regularly inclined to plunder local populations. From 1580 to 1640, the Portuguese and Spanish crowns formed a union, which helped to promote trade and stability among their territorial possessions in the Americas and Asia.

Demand for European-made luxury goods lagged as spices and other goods from the East Indies and Americas flowed into Europe. Pepper from the East Indies was popular among Europeans but the Portuguese struggled to meet demand. The Dutch Republic, at war with the Spanish Crown, sent expeditions from Amsterdam to the East Indies at the very end of the 16th century. Some met with success, and in 1602, the Dutch East India Company was founded. They soon began raiding Portuguese territories in Indonesia and establishing outposts. Around the same time, England established its English East India Company. It made few inroads into Dutch-dominated Southeast Asia but was more successful in India.

Dutch Golden Age

The 17th century marked the decline of Portugal's control over Asian trade. The Dutch and English—with their respective East India Companies—ascended in power and influence. In practice, these corporations acted as sovereign nations when in Asia, thousands of miles away from the Crown. Their aim was to conquer ports, install processing facilities, and reap enormous profits via sea trade between Asia and Europe. These long-distance ventures were conducted under state-sponsored monopolies. Specifically, the Dutch and English governments regulated this trade by granting monopoly charters within a given foreign territory. Risk, maritime warfare, and profits went hand-in-hand for these East India Companies. They were frequently brutal to the native populations, though European diseases did not cause nearly the same amount of indigenous deaths in the East Indies as they did in the Americas.

It was the Dutch who came out ahead of the English, despite having a population of fewer than two million and waging a war of independence against Spain until 1648 (after which time, they fought trade wars against England). The Dutch far outpaced any other nation in the 17th century. They held the highest per capita income in 1600 and their lead only grew over the next century, as England did not overtake the Dutch until at least the late-18th century. Dutch finance was unquestionably the most sophisticated in the world. The Bank of Amsterdam supported financial stability and was the preeminent financial institution of the 17th and 18th centuries. The Dutch financial system featured relatively low interest rates, fractional ownership of commercial ventures, maritime insurance, and futures markets.

Over the course of the 17th century, the Dutch Republic sent 1,770 ships to Asia, more than twice as many as the English. Much of this advantage is attributed to advanced Dutch financial arrangements that promoted efficient risk-sharing. Dutch trading colonies in Asia were relatively centralized and well run as compared to the British. This maritime East Indies trade hastened the decline of the Republic of Venice—which had once been the main player in the Spice Trade—and their successors, the Portuguese. The British also overtook the Venetian textile industry by selling their poorer quality clothing on the Mediterranean market for much lower prices. The future of global trade lay in the Atlantic, so European power and influence shifted away from the Mediterranean toward nations seated on the Atlantic.

Slave Trade

One principal distinction between the West and East Indies trade was the employment of West African slaves. Although European colonists in the East Indies did not rely heavily on imported slaves, the British, Portuguese, and French each transported millions of slaves across the Atlantic to cultivate sugarcane, coffee, cotton, and tobacco in land-abundant North and South America. The farming of these crops (especially sugar) was highly labor-intensive, and slaves became the critical factor of production that drove profitability. Native American populations were the predominant source of slave labor at first before being displaced by African slaves, who were commonly bought for cloth before being shipped across the Atlantic. Coerced labor was endemic, as considerable numbers of Europeans who moved to the British territories of North America and the Caribbean were indentured servants or convicts. These migrants endured harsh conditions during their terms of service, but in exchange, they were able to secure small parcels of land and become subsistence farmers.

The volume of this slave trade picked up substantially during the 18th century. Most historians agree that at least 10 million slaves left Africa between the 15th and 19th centuries, with more than a tenth dying en route. As one example, historians have estimated that sugar plantations in 17th century Jamaica showed a rate of return of at least 10%, certainly greater than the standard interest rate in England at the time which averaged around 5%. To the British, Jamaica was an emerging market of great promise and risk. Jamaica eventually became the largest sugar exporter in the British Empire for the majority of the 18th century. Many British people who were of common birth made massive fortunes from these West Indies plantations powered by slave labor. These societies were based on "extractive" institutions where a small elite possessed legal rights and held power and wealth.

The mortality rate on the initial voyage across the Atlantic was very high among slaves. Once on land, slaves still experienced elevated mortality rates because of the grueling nature of the work, particularly on sugar plantations. Maintaining slave populations in the Caribbean "Sugar Islands" was difficult. Plantation owners did not place much value on slave children, since it would take at least a decade of care before they would be able to provide labor. In the United States and Canada—where sugar cultivation was less common—it was easier to sustain slave populations because, with a different crop mixture, there were lower mortality rates and higher fertility rates, meaning that fewer slaves were needed over time. The United States finally banned the import of slaves in 1808, so that by the Civil War, few American slaves had been born in Africa.

Age of Mercantilism

After 1500, European powers sought to acquire the territory and resources of the New World. The prevailing mercantilist doctrines of the age dictated that wealth accumulation was a zero-sum game, and that foreign colonies exist to provide raw materials for domestic manufacturing. Military force was a necessary instrument to support this trade. Uninterested in free trade, national corporations desired monopoly control over a given trade. With ample profit margins, earnings were used to maintain the military and state. Through trade and warfare, the English (with four times the population of the Dutch) were driven to compete against the Dutch Republic. Four Anglo-Dutch naval wars were fought over commercial dominance during this era.

Britain's New World territories prospered. From 1650 to 1770, the population of British North America shot from 55,000 to 2.3 million, while the population of the British West Indies grew from 60,000 to 480,000. The British West Indies, with an economy based on sugar, had a population that was 90% of African origin compared to only 20% in British North American colonies. Financially supported by commercial growth, Great Britain's Royal Navy was the world's most powerful by the end of the 17th century. British legislation certainly made use of the Royal Navy to further business interests. The Navigation Act of 1651 ordered that goods imported into England must be carried in ships that were either British or from the country that originated the goods. Consequently, American tobacco transported to England had to be carried in either English or American ships. This legislation was intended to destroy Dutch dominance in shipping and to protect Great Britain's market share in maritime transport and middleman commerce.

France was the third player seeking to control world trade. A land power with more than 10 times the population of the Dutch Republic, France resented Dutch commercial dominance in the 17th century. The French lacked a strong navy but they fought back through tariffs on Dutch goods shipped to France. In 1664, the French West India and East India Companies were chartered. A trade war between the French and the Dutch broke out, and soon a real war did as well. The French sided with the Dutch during the Second Anglo-Dutch War of 1665 to 1667, where England was defeated. Afterward France and England were more concerned with Dutch supremacy, and they sided together against the Dutch during the Third Anglo-Dutch War of 1672 to 1674. The alliance did not last forever, as France and England were intermittently at war with each other from 1689 to 1815, in a battle of two aspiring world empires. However, the English were better able to secure debt funding for warfare, giving them a decisive advantage over the French in the long run.

United States of America

Warfare, always expensive, strained the finances of the imperial powers, even rich ones like Great Britain. Between 1680 and 1780, the British army and navy tripled in size. By 1760, its military spending was nearly 15% of national income. British fiscal problems worsened with the world-wide recession that followed the Seven Years War of 1756 to 1763. The North American theatre of that war came to be known as the "French and Indian War," after the two main enemies of the British colonists. Great Britain attempted to shift some of its burdens—including the cost of defending the colonies with a standing army—to the North American colonies themselves, where residents were among the wealthiest in the world, having achieved an even higher standard of living than British subjects back on the home island. To extract revenue, the Stamp Act of 1765 was passed, taxing newspapers, pamphlets, and legal documents. After an outcry, it was repealed a year later. Next the Townshend Acts of 1767 were passed, raising customs duties and transferring customs power from the colonies to the Crown. Even after the new tax hikes, American colonists faced tax burdens that were less than a tenth of what the British government imposed on its own subjects at home.

Pressures mounted as the Americans resisted the Crown's encroachment on their political rights. The colonial subjects—increasingly forced to quarter British troops—demanded political representation if they were to be taxed by the Crown. In 1773, the Tea Act was passed. Interestingly, the law allowed the British East India Company to import tea directly from Asia to the colonies for the first time, undoubtedly leading to lower prices for colonial consumers. American merchants and smugglers, who were now cut out of the tea trade, masterminded a public relations outcry that successfully galvanized the public (despite the cheaper tea). After the Boston Tea Party of December 1773, a greater conflict was inevitable. The British Parliament responded with the Intolerable Acts of 1774, and in 1775, war broke out. The Battles of Lexington and Concord were fought on the outskirts of present day Boston. The colonies had already been at war with Great Britain for over a year by the time the Declaration of Independence was approved at the Second Continental Congress on July 4, 1776.

British Cotton Industry

Like silk, cotton was a high-end good at the beginning of the 17th century when the English East India Company was chartered. Although easy to grow, cotton required a great deal of manpower to process. Seeds needed to be removed from bolls. Fibers had to be arranged and packed. To produce thread, cotton wool required spinning in a process that took many days. India, with centuries of experience in cotton-processing and an inexpensive workforce, had the lead in producing cotton textiles, especially cloth, which was commonly exported to Europe. In England, cotton clothing styles signaled social class. The English East India Company gave Indian cotton freebies to the monarchy and they began to catch on among aristocrats, and later, the middle class. By the 18th century, British fashion held cotton in higher regard than silk or wool.

After the European market for spices became saturated at the end of the 17th century, the English East India Company increasingly specialized in the cotton trade with India. Within Great Britain, this generated controversy. According to standard mercantilist reasoning, cotton textile-processing ought to be performed in England, not India, to stimulate English labor demand. Furthermore, England should not trade its wealth for pricey Indian textile products. But the English East India Company did not follow this logic in practice. It brought some English textile manufacturing technologies to India, and Great Britain continued to establish fortified trading posts throughout India, including in Madras, Bombay, and Calcutta.

English textile workers, mercantilists, and moralists were concerned Great Britain was facing social disruption and loss of employment and bullion, all for the sake of clothing. They pressured the English Parliament to pass protectionist legislation, sometimes successfully, as in the case of laws passed between 1666 and 1680 that required the dead to be buried in wool. In addition to political lobbying, the domestic textile industry fought back against Indian competition by developing technological breakthroughs. In 1733, the flying shuttle was invented, doubling the productivity of weavers. A small mechanical device called the spinning jenny, invented by an illiterate artisan, became available commercially starting in the late 1760s. It was followed by the spinning frame, spinning mule, and power loom, all creations of British inventors. These break-throughs increased English demand for raw imported Indian cotton. Output of finished English cotton clothing grew, and prices fell. It was the dawn of the Industrial Revolution.

The cotton industry controversy sparked many pamphlets written by English mercantilists and, opposing them, free traders. As the debate evolved in Great Britain over the course of the 18th century, economic thought advanced. In one notable contribution that ran contrary to the perceived mercantilist wisdom of its day and expounded many ideas to be affirmed by *The Wealth of Nations*, Henry Martyn published *Considerations Upon the East India Trade* in 1701. A British free trader who would later become Inspector General of Imports and Exports in 1715, Martyn argued against restrictions on manufactured imports from India. He criticized monopoly protection of the East India trade, discussed the division of labor, and analyzed the gains from trade that result from laborsaving technological advances. Far ahead of his time, Martyn stressed that a country's wealth was properly measured by its level of *consumption*, not its store of bullion.

Great Britain's trade had truly globalized by this time. British foreign trade was increasingly driven by newfound consumer mass markets in tobacco, tea, and sugar. Encouraged by falling prices, the people of Great Britain developed a taste for these stimulating goods during the 18th century. By the mid-18th century, Chinese tea had become a working-class beverage in England. British manufactures, such as nails, clocks, and firearms, were exported to continental Europe and the Americas in larger quantities. Although France's volume of foreign trade nearly matched Great Britain's by the 1780s, French volumes were much smaller in per capita terms because of its greater population (which was roughly double Britain's). The British economy took the lead during the period from 1700 to 1820. As the total size of Great Britain's economy more than tripled, France's economy almost doubled, and the Dutch economy was generally stagnant.

India, China, and Europe

According to the best historical statistics available, from 1 AD to 1500, the world population doubled from 220 million to 440 million, with India and China combined accounting for half of the total. Throughout that millennium and a half, India and China each contained between a quarter and a third of the world's population and income. Because earnings were at subsistence levels in those days, a region's income corresponded closely to its population. Then, over the three centuries following 1500, China's population and output surpassed India's, and Europe's economic and technological development exploded. By the 16th century, per capita income in leading Western European economies had risen above subsistence levels, and after the 18th century, huge disparities arose between Europe and Asia owing to Europe's incalculable technological advantages. The intracontinental competition between European powers—resulting in expansionism and the inevitable sharing of information and technological progress—contributed to the European economic edge. The same process did not occur in India or China during the 16th to 18th centuries. In fact, like much of Asia, China resisted outside influences and was slow to globalize.

Ming and Qing Chinese Economy

As of the 14th century, Western Europe and China were broadly equal in terms of living standards, with Chinese technology, the product of a rich history, clearly superior. In power from 1368 to 1644, and following the Mongol rule of the Yuan Dynasty, the Ming Dynasty was the final reign by Han Chinese. The Ming period exhibited stability, with an agricultural economy dominated by independent peasant landholders. The third Ming emperor, Zhu Di, fortified China's power and was aggressive in his foreign policy, particularly against the Mongols. He ordered the 15th century "Ming Voyages," led by a physically imposing eunuch named Zheng He. Consisting of seven extravagant ocean expeditions, with hundreds of enormous ships and tens of thousands of sailors, the travelers reached India, the Persian Gulf, and Africa. A backlash against the explorations resulted, even though South China Sea trade prospered during the late Ming era. Some large-scale industrial organizations, such as southeastern textile centers, emerged during the Ming rule as a precursor to modern capitalism.

To the north and east, the Ming constantly worried about Mongol, Japanese, and Korean threats. Most of the existing Great Wall was built during Ming rule. Nevertheless, the Ming were eventually overthrown by domestic rebels who conquered Beijing in 1644. At that time, Manchu raiders—part of a northeastern ethnic minority—were invited to stem the uprising in China. Yet they ended up taking control of Beijing themselves, and then within a few decades, the rest of China as well. Called the Qing and led by the Manchu, it was China's last dynasty, reigning until 1911. During the Qing Dynasty, China's population grew from about 125 million in 1680 to 157 million in 1710. It then took off in the 18th and 19th centuries, reaching 412 million by 1850. During the 18th century, New World crops such as sweet potato, maize, and peanuts were introduced to China on an immense scale as part of the "Columbian Exchange" of animals, plants, culture, and disease. As Chinese yields per acre rose, greater populations could be supported.

Beginning in the 16th century, New World silver mined in Peru and Mexico was sent to China. Up to a third of the American silver ended up in China, and because of such massive inflows, silver gradually replaced copper and paper notes as the dominant currency in China during the Ming Dynasty. The Spanish eight-reale silver coin became ubiquitous in world trade, and by the 18th century, it was the world's first global currency. Technology continued to be transferred between European and Chinese statesmen and scientists. Fascinated by Chinese methods, Europeans visited China, helping to stimulate Chinese innovations. Chinese foreign trade during the Qing Dynasty was regulated by a wary government. The Qing restricted foreign trade to a single southern port city, Canton. This arrangement, which came to be known as the "Canton System," lasted until 1842, when the Treaty of Nanking marked the end of the First Opium War with Great Britain.

Breakdown of the Canton System

The British East India Company was the largest foreign player in the Canton trade. The Company's demand for Chinese tea (which primarily came from Fujian province) took off in the early-18th century. The tea came to be shipped on special tea clipper ships that made no stops on the return voyage to England in order to keep the tea fresh. At first, the British paid for the tea with silver. Later, as Europeans became more reluctant to part with silver (which they used to fund wars), Indian cotton and opium were traded for the tea. The Canton trade between China and Europe developed rapidly, although the British East India Company grew increasingly frustrated with Qing restrictions, especially on opium. Holding to a mercantilist outlook, the Chinese desired a positive trade balance. In 1796, they banned the importation of opium, but the British resorted to smuggling. China's "terms of trade" declined over time (meaning the price of Chinese exports such as tea went down relative to the price of foreign imports), and after 1806, the value of British opium imports exceeded the value of Chinese tea exports.

Free trade reformers succeeded in ending the British East India Company's chartered monopoly on trade to China in 1834. Private traders moved in and opium smuggling only grew, exacerbating tensions between China and Great Britain. China cracked down on opium, leading to the outbreak of the First Opium War in 1839. For years, Great Britain had possessed the most advanced merchant ships in the world, including artillery-wielding East Indiamen vessels measuring 40 meters long and weighing over 1,000 tons. China's military technology was very primitive by comparison. With steam-powered gunboats, Great Britain's overwhelming naval firepower gave it a decisive advantage during the Opium Wars. After losing the First Opium War, China agreed in the 1842 Treaty of Nanking to open major ports to trade (including Canton), limit tariffs on British imports, pay a large indemnity, and grant Hong Kong to the British in perpetuity.

The Treaty of Nanking—which China viewed as unfair—failed to resolve the contentious opium trade issue. Trafficking only escalated, and the Second Opium War broke out in 1856. This time France joined Great Britain in the hostilities against China, and by 1860, their technologically superior combined forces had invaded Beijing in a decisive victory over the Chinese. The October 1860 Convention of Beijing produced a treaty that legalized the opium trade, established foreign diplomatic representation in China, removed many restrictions on travel by foreigners within China, and granted another large indemnity to the European victors. Within China, citizens resented the ineffective response of their Manchu rulers to the gunboat-style diplomacy practiced by the Europeans. Consequently, the Qing Dynasty faced internal revolts and had difficulty governing. The most notable insurrection was the Tiaping Rebellion, a civil war in southern China that claimed over 20 million lives from 1850 to 1864. The crumbling of the Qing dynasty accelerated toward the end of the 19th century, and it finally fell in 1911.

Japan's Rapid Industrialization

Modern industry did not make its way into Asia until the late-19th century, when Japan was the first non-Western nation to industrialize prior to World War I. Japan's hasty industrialization and abrupt move toward globalization is the most remarkable story of 19th century Asian economic growth. Although Japan had intermittently exchanged goods, technologies, and cultural influences with Korea and China for centuries, the Japanese economy was poor, backward, and closed prior to the mid-19th century. It was linked to European trade routes after the 16th century through Portuguese and Dutch merchants (with foreigners confined to a Nagasaki enclave under threat of death). From 1603 to 1867, under the rule of the Tokugawa Shogunate, Japan maintained a refined feudal society dominated by rice farming, with some movement toward urbanization. During the 18th and 19th centuries, Japan intermittently suffered famines when successive years yielded crop failures, killing hundreds of thousands. Fearing the spread of Christianity, the Tokugawa allowed only a minimal amount of trade with Europeans for two centuries.

Foreign pressures to open Japan intensified as Europe and the United States industrialized, making them hungry for raw materials and new markets. The Dutch king unsuccessfully urged Japan to open its ports to world trade in 1844. Nine years later, the United States sent a quarter of its navy to Japan under the guise of a humanitarian mission to lift the death penalty on foreigners shipwrecked off Japan. Led by Commodore Matthew Perry, the Americans presented Tokugawa officials with the draft of a treaty that would open Japan to trade with the West. The Japanese had never seen such modern gunboats and did not wish to fight a war. A year later, the Kanagawa Treaty of 1854 was signed. It opened the Japanese ports of Shimoda and Hakodate to American trade and established a permanent American consul in Shimoda. Japan's period of seclusion was over. However, foreign influences quickly became a source of tension and conflict within Japan. Civil war eventually broke out between Tokugawa supporters and oppositional forces (aided by wealthy urban merchants) wishing to modernize and restore the emperor. The insurrectionists won, ushering in the Meiji Restoration era under Emperor Meiji that began in 1868. In spite of intense turmoil during this period, Japan's trade rose by a factor of 70 from 1858 to 1873.

The Meiji government set out to reconstruct Japanese society partly based on ideas and best practices derived from the Western powers. Under the "Iwakura Mission," the Meiji sent diplomats abroad to study foreign economic, political, technological, and educational systems. Armed with new information and aided by a steady trickle of visiting foreigners, Japan westernized its government and economy during an era of intense nationalism. The government abolished the caste system and promoted economic development through coordinated industrial policies. Eschewing foreign loans, state-owned enterprises (later privatized) adopted Western technologies, penetrated new industries, and produced increasing levels of value-added in goods. In the quarter century following the end of the Tokugawa era, Japanese agricultural output roughly doubled, supporting population growth, industrialization projects, and military modernization. Japan achieved a striking defeat of China in the First Sino-Japanese War, fought over Korea during 1894 and 1895, cementing Japan's status as an emerging global power.

British Industrial Revolution

Ascribed to mid-18th century England by most scholars, the birth of the Industrial Revolution was a watershed in human history. For thousands of years before this epoch, income per capita around the world showed no clear upward trend. For most of humanity in 1800, their 30-year life expectancy was no different from that of hunter-gatherer societies (and height was actually shorter on average). The wealthy lived well—especially in affluent nations like Great Britain and the Netherlands—but the majority working in the agrarian sector was not materially better off than their ancient ancestors. The period after the Black Death may have been something of an exception, for among the survivors, wage rates were high, and the population eventually recovered. By and large, however, income per capita around the world was essentially stagnant for several millennia prior to the Industrial Revolution.

Economic historians explain that before the Industrial Revolution began, economies around the world were in a "Malthusian trap," named after *An Essay on the Principle of Population* by the Reverend Thomas Malthus, published in 1798. Back then, technology-driven productivity growth was not sufficient to support improvements in living standards due to growing populations. Since technological advance was very, very slow, whenever incomes and living standards rose, higher rates of population growth provided a natural offset. Specifically, new affluence led to more births and a larger population, which in turn drove down wages and living standards. Malthus argued that this process resulted in higher death rates and lower birth rates. In equilibrium, the vast majority of the population would be living at essentially a subsistence level, with little or no per capita income growth. According to the Malthusian logic, events that increase death rates—such as war or plagues—cause a rise in material living standards, whereas shocks that lower death rates—such as the introduction of better sanitation—ultimately result in lower living standards.

So then, what changed at the outset of the Industrial Revolution? The answer is productivity growth: the rate of technological progress picked up by a large margin. Before the 18th century, technological advance happened, just at a much slower rate. Modern estimates suggest that prior to the Industrial Revolution, cumulative annual productivity growth from technological change was less than 0.05% per year, implying that an economy's productive capabilities (all else equal) would increase by less than 5% every century from technological improvements. In the "First Industrial Revolution," which spanned a century beginning in approximately 1760, the technological growth rate in England picked up to about 0.5% per year and was largely driven by textile efficiencies. During the "Second Industrial Revolution" that began around 1860 and lasted until World War I, the technological growth rate in England was at least as high, at closer to 1.0%. Combined with capital accumulation, such massive increases in productivity have allowed for both population growth and rising living standards over time.

Contrary to some popular impressions, the Industrial Revolution was not caused by several heroic inventors and entrepreneurs. Instead, it was a gradual process driven by a great number of inventors and merchants across many decades. Essentially, the supply of new innovations increased during the Industrial Revolution. Each incremental improvement led to excitement among other clever individuals on the same mental wavelength, who were then more likely to devise complementary improvements, sparking a virtuous cycle of innovation. Britain's favorable legal, cultural, and natural environment were a necessary prerequisite for this boom. Compared to continental Europe, labor was scarce in Britain, wages were high, and energy was cheap, making it all the more worthwhile to substitute machinery for labor. During the 18th century, civil engineering projects multiplied, and the number of books published in Great Britain tripled. Aside from cotton textiles, the British coal mining, iron, steel, canal building, and railroad industries all grew by leaps and bounds during the Industrial Revolution, leading to lower transportation costs, greater production, and lower prices for consumers, in England and abroad. Surprisingly, the plucky British inventors usually shared little of the great wealth their creations engendered, since in practice, the British patent system provided them weak protection and their inventions were quickly copied by others.

Rise of Great Britain

Driven by greater productivity, the population of Great Britain roughly tripled from eight million in 1770 to 23 million in 1860. In a Malthusian trap, this would lead to lower living standards. Yet British income per capita actually rose and real wages grew. In fact, after 1860 British per capita income began to grow at an even faster clip in spite of the sustained population growth. Urbanization and industrialization continued in Britain so by 1860, only about 20% of the population in England was employed in agriculture (as compared to 1% today). Given the British population explosion, the demand for food skyrocketed. But Britain did not possess a great deal of land, and productivity gains in the farm sector could not keep pace with the population increase. So Great Britain—the "workshop of the world" and an exporting powerhouse—imported food and raw materials that were exchanged for their own manufactured goods.

After the mid-18th century, land rent as a share of national income began its long decline in England. Before this time, the amount of land per worker had been a major factor determining per capita income growth among world economies. However, in the modern industrial era, economies typically grow through technological advance and increases in the amount of capital per worker. In fact, most economists today simply ignore land per worker in economic growth calculations, and from the experience of modern Hong Kong and Singapore, it is clear that economies with little land are not necessarily so disadvantaged. In Industrial Revolution England, as input demand shifted toward urban metropolises, rents on farm land declined and rents on urban land increased. Not coincidentally, the power of the British landed gentry waned.

As an interesting contrast to Britain, the United States was late to industrialize and instead concentrated on developing its massive land and resource endowments. The westward land expansion of the United States during the frontier 19th century greatly contributed to America's emergence as a 20th century economic powerhouse. In 1860, England had slightly over one acre of farmland per person compared to two acres per person throughout Western Europe. The United States, on the other hand, contained nearly 12 acres of farmland per person. The emergence of roads, steamboats, canals, and railroads throughout the 19th century allowed American farm products to be transported cheaply and then sold around the world at low prices. Agricultural products from the Americas increasingly helped to feed the global population, which was well over one billion by 1850. In 1820, the United States produced fewer than 2% of the world's total output. A century later, its share was nearly 20%.

Medieval England, along with the rest of Europe, featured interest rates that were commonly above 10%. Yet by the dawn of the Industrial Revolution, interest rates were down to modern levels of about 4% to 5% in Britain, which stimulated industrial investment. Furthermore, the fraction of the population living in cities in England was at least 20% by 1800. The increase in world trade during the 17th and 18th centuries fostered the movement to cities, although urban death rates were extremely high because of horribly inadequate hygiene and sanitation. Real wages continued to increase, even among unskilled workers, so popular goods such as tea, sugar, and tobacco were affordable to most 19th century British laborers. Breakfast shifted from a relatively heavy meal to a light serving that included tea or coffee. Other modern middle-class characteristics emerged. Literacy and numeracy were very rare in medieval Europe, but by the start of the Industrial Revolution, these skills became progressively more common in Britain. By the 19th century, most British men could read, and literacy rates in France and much of continental Europe were even higher than in Great Britain.

Diffusion of Industrial Revolution Technology

After the early-19th century, technological improvements led to rapid efficiency growth in the British economy. This did not escape the notice of other nations, since British military might and political power grew as economic output expanded. Luckily for competitors, copying technology is much easier than developing it anew. Within several decades, the United States and many countries in Europe had begun to utilize British inventions such as cotton mills and steam engines. England was busy building its internal railway system in the mid-19th century, along the way generating speculative investment frenzies (or "bubbles") like the "Railway Mania" of the 1840s. The United States quickly followed suit, and the first transcontinental railroad—extending to the Pacific Ocean near San Francisco—was completed by 1869. By the end of the 19th century, the United States had laid over 200,000 miles of railroad, far more than any nation in the world, and nearly 10 times the length of Britain's rail lines. From 1880, America's income per capita began to eclipse Britain's, and the difference would only grow during the 20th century.

The pace of information flows quickened at a dizzying clip over the course of the 19th century. As of 1800, information traveled over long distances at roughly the same rate as it had for centuries—no more than a few miles per hour. The introduction of the telegraph in 1844 allowed information to transmit at over 100 times the old rate. The first undersea telegraph cable between England and France was completed in 1851, and by 1866, telegraph cable connected the United States to Europe. Steam-powered railways and cargo ships traveled at least 10 miles per hour, and several innovations in the middle of the 19th century greatly lowered the cost and increased the speed of steam-powered ocean transport. Major canals also reduced transportation costs. The Suez Canal in Egypt opened in 1869, allowing sea transport between Europe and Asia without the need for navigation around Africa, while the Panama Canal, opened in 1914, created a direct maritime path between the Atlantic and Pacific Oceans. In the United States, the 364-mile Erie Canal was completed in 1825, dramatically cutting shipping costs from the Great Lakes region to the Atlantic. The "Pax Britannica," enforced by the dominant British Royal Navy across the world's seas, provided a safe environment for shipping and thus promoted inexpensive ocean transport prior to World War I.

The Second Industrial Revolution stretched to World War I, yielding many new consumer products based on scientific principles. The first gasoline-powered automobile was patented in 1886 by Karl Benz, a founder of Mercedes-Benz. Henry Ford, founder of the Ford Motor Company in 1903, is credited with developing mechanized assembly line production methods—powered by electricity—to mass produce Ford cars. Early telephone models were developed by the 1870s, and a number of inventors around the world patented radio transmission technologies during the 1890s. The tabulating machine—a precursor to today's computers—was used for the 1890 United States Census. These productivity-enhancing inventions, combined with a wealth of domestic natural resources utilized as material inputs, drove rapid American industrial growth during the final decades of the 19th century. By 1900, American manufacturing output exceeded the combined sum of its rivals Great Britain, France, and Germany.

19th Century Globalization Boom and Divergence

Economists often give a technical definition of globalization as the integration of markets across world regions. This characterization yields some testable propositions. For instance, as globalization increases, the price of a good should "converge" (or become the same) across locales. In addition, the amount of inter-regional trade should increase over time. Globalization can be contrasted with "autarky," where each economy is separate from another, meaning that each economy produces all the goods and services it consumes instead of specializing in products it makes best (like Swiss watches) and then trading. After one economy is aware of another and accessible via foot, camel, or sail, globalization may spread for a number of reasons, such as a fall in transportation costs, a decrease in tariffs, a lull in warfare, or a greater specialization into smaller production niches. This yields cost advantages and lower prices for consumers. The existence of an international hegemon—like Great Britain in the 19th century or the Mongols in the 13th century—can sustain overall commercial stability by reducing piracy and lowering transportation costs.

Although globalization and international trade picked up during the Age of Exploration, it was not until the 19th century that a giant world-wide globalization boom truly occurred. After the voyages of Columbus and da Gama, the volume of trade between continents grew by about 1% annually during the 16th to the 18th centuries. In the 19th century, this rate rose to over 3%, and it has averaged at least that level ever since. Prior to the 19th century, foreign exports to Europe were driven by European income growth and dominated by low-bulk luxury goods such as silks and spices, which few could afford. Goods needed to be valuable relative to their weight if the long, risky ocean shipping expeditions to trade for them were to be economical. But beginning in the 19th century, a mass market in inexpensive consumables developed in Europe, precipitated by falling transportation costs, rising middle-class incomes, and production-side economies of scale. Food, cheap textiles, and production inputs were increasingly exported to Europe. Some imports such as coffee and tea were not even produced in Europe. Their widespread consumption among the European middle classes signified greater market integration around the world.

Commodity prices also began to converge across the world in the 1820s during the peacetime recovery from the Napoleonic wars. Price convergence was caused by a 19th century revolution in transportation technology, as steamships, canals, and railroads cut shipping costs around the globe. Such technologies increased competitive pressures, and along with the growing influence of free trade schools of thought, these forces fostered 19th century trade liberalization policies. In fact, prior to the 19th century, nearly all intercontinental trade was accomplished via state-chartered monopolies—a coordinating system that raised consumer prices and reduced overall trade and output. England was a leader in trade liberalization after repealing the protectionist "Corn Laws" in 1846, some 30 years after they were passed. American and continental competitors often kept up tariff barriers to help nurture their own domestic manufacturing industries. Trade liberalization was uneven though growing until the 1870s when a globalization backlash arose, spurred by an economic depression and a collapse in farm prices.

After 1600, global inequality began to increase between nations. Economies that had escaped the Malthusian trap early on, such as Great Britain and the Dutch Republic, saw their income per capita and real wages outpace other nations. Their advantage only grew in the 18th century and afterward. Income divergence since the 19th century is especially clear when comparing rich versus poor economies. The former have grown swiftly while the latter have stagnated. Global capital markets were as well integrated prior to World War I as they would be nearly a century later. Capital accumulation in the United States was rapid, chasing after investment returns, and high wages drew millions of migrants from Europe to the developing Americas. Advanced economies in Europe and the Americas were especially efficient, producing more output per worker and per unit of capital. They drew added capital from global markets, leading to ever larger differences in per capita output and income. Then as now, poorer economies struggled to increase their productive efficiency per unit of inputs.

Adam Smith, David Ricardo, and the Corn Laws

Commercial policy in Europe was dominated by mercantilism through the 18th century, although its many critics in England and France were vociferous. A notable group in France called the "Physiocrats" argued for freedom to produce and trade, as they believed self-interest naturally led to the greatest amount of value creation. Yet until Adam Smith's *Wealth of Nations*, the many disparate arguments supporting free trade—and opposing the common protectionism of the day—lacked coherence. A bookish, absentminded, socially awkward systems builder with a reputation for giving excellent lectures, Adam Smith was able to put forth a tightly reasoned analytical framework for thinking about trade policy.

As a leading figure in the 18th century "Scottish Enlightenment" and a long-time professor of philosophy and political economy, Smith disagreed with the English philosopher Thomas Hobbes, who had argued a century earlier that self-interest was essentially destructive, and consequently, mankind required a social contract with a powerful state to protect people from one another. Smith contended that each individual's private interest leads them to employ their labor in the most profitable manner. According to Smith, individuals with differing interests will nevertheless cooperate through the mutually advantageous exchange of goods and services, a process that unintentionally creates the greatest social value, as if led by an "invisible hand." In terms of trade policy, Smith maintained that if a good can be imported more cheaply than it can be made domestically, it should be purchased from abroad. In such a case, home production would be inefficient because labor and capital inputs could be better utilized in creating other goods. Free trade also increases competitive pressures and facilitates the exchange of knowledge, processes that stimulate productive efficiencies and lead to lower consumer prices.

Smith's arguments in favor of free trade were tempered by his distrust of commercial interests and his belief that government had an essential role to play in any vibrant economy through maintaining law and order and providing public goods. He was critical of mercantilist trade policies because they favored special business interests at the expense of the general welfare. Protectionist policies, he argued, often advantaged producers in one industry while ignoring the benefits consumers would reap from allowing lower-priced imports. Disapproving of the British East India Company with its Crown monopoly, Smith warned of the collusive nature of business interests, which sometimes extend their pernicious reach into politics. Two centuries later, this art of obtaining wealth through political means was termed "rent-seeking" by economists. Smith was wary of protectionist legislation since such laws typically raise consumer prices and are influenced by the schemes of industry leaders.

Smith is credited with the theory of "absolute advantage," which proposes that countries should produce those goods for which they have an absolute cost advantage and trade for other goods produced abroad. The *Wealth of Nations* steadily grew in influence during the several decades following its publication, and its ideas were scrutinized by the most prominent intellectuals of the day. The next major innovation after Smith was the theory of "comparative advantage," attributed to David Ricardo from his *On the Principles of Political Economy and Taxation*, published in 1817. It explained why countries would import a good even if they possess an absolute advantage in producing it. According to Ricardo, a country's patterns of production depend on its cost structure and "opportunity costs" (meaning the amount of other goods that could have been produced instead). Even if it has an absolute advantage in many goods, Ricardo reasoned that a nation ought to specialize in producing those goods for which it possesses the lowest opportunity cost. The corollary was that even poor, backward economies should produce and trade based on their relative advantages in production.

During the first half of the 19th century, the British Corn Laws were a lightning rod of controversy. Introduced with the 1815 Importation Act, they created substantial tariffs on grain imported to Great Britain. Leading British economists such as Ricardo, James Mill, and Mill's son, John Stuart, were opposed. The beneficiaries were large landowners, but nearly all consumers—especially the poor—were forced to pay higher food prices. Opposed to agricultural interests, British industrialists were increasingly aware of the benefits from free trade. Their workshops were the world's vanguard, so opening bilateral trade would benefit them, given their comparative competitive advantages. Buoyed by ambitious capitalists and the growing free trade ideology of the day, the Corn Laws were repealed in 1846. Almost 15 years later, the Cobden-Chevalier Treaty between Britain and France lowered tariffs and averted another war between the two nations. Trade between England and France more than doubled, and France's industry was forced to modernize.

Long Depression and Resulting Backlash

Over the century following 1820, trade integrated the world economy. Helped along by lowered transportation costs and reduced tariffs, the intercontinental price gap in commodity markets dropped by 80%. From 1840 to 1870, an economic boom increased the amount of world trade by a factor of four, with trade expanding by about 5% every year. By 1870, international trade—measured as global imports plus exports—accounted for one tenth of all output around the world. Even so, the 1870s was a decade of economic turmoil. The years preceding 1873 saw a massive expansion in credit across continental Europe to fund construction, pro-voking an unsustainable bubble. Subsequently, the period from 1873 to 1896—called the "Long Depression"—was filled with "deflation" (mean-ing negative price growth) and crisis, beginning with the "Panic of 1873," which was triggered by the collapse of the Vienna stock exchange in May of that year.

In 1873, railroad construction in the United States had just absorbed an enormous amount of investment (often bundled into dubious financial securities). Under the weight of cheap American grain—transported from the heartland to ocean ports via railroads—the European agricultural sec-tor was in distress. As American farm and industrial products continued to flood foreign markets, land rents in Europe plummeted. The Panic of 1873 spread from the European financial sector to the United States, lead-ing to a severe 6-year economic slump. Unemployment in the United States peaked at 14% and the downturn was even worse in Europe. As nationalism surged, European landowners and agricultural interests called for tariff protection, which they often won, especially in France and Germany. During the 1880s and 1890s, the industrial economies of the United States and most of Europe turned against free trade in the face of economic turbulence. Deflation was commonplace, caused by technology-driven falling production costs, weak aggregate demand, lower asset prices induced by depression, and a gold shortage. From 1873 to 1896, prices fell by over 30% in the United States and 20% in Great Britain.

In the United States, a populist movement led by farmers (who commonly carried heavy debt loads) and energetic politicians such as Nebraskan William Jennings Bryan demanded the country go off the gold standard in order to devalue the dollar and end deflation. Yet instead of responding to the prolonged economic downturn and deflation with an aggressively expanded money supply—which would spark inflation and devalue farm debts—industrial nations united in favor of the gold standard and demonetization of silver. Such restrictive currency vehicles were not easily compatible with loose monetary policy, as would be demonstrated again during the "Great Depression" that began in 1929. At a time when the unemployment rate was 14%, the anti-gold Democrat Bryan lost the 1896 presidential election to Republican William McKinley, who sup-ported the gold standard. Aided by poor European harvests and fortuitous gold discoveries, the American economy began to pick up, and prices changed course as deflation turned to inflation.

Globalization at the Dawn of the 20th Century

Economic integration can grow in the face of rising protectionism if technology causes transportation costs to fall by an even greater degree. This is apparently what happened in the final decades of the 19th century, as world trade growth slowed yet still remained positive despite tariff retrenchments from a globalization backlash. Powered by the stream engine, there was growing price convergence in world commodity markets (including developing regions). Migration policy was liberal as millions moved from crowded regions such as Europe to land- and resource-abundant territories with higher wages such as the Americas. These labor flows were boosted by tragic events like the 1840s Irish famine and the poverty and unemployment engendered by the Long Depression. Capital also followed labor to cheap land, as investment flowed from the Old to the New World, facilitated by faster information transmission.

By the 20th century there was truly a global division of labor in place, with a substantial income disparity between advanced industrial regions and the developing world. Fostered by the twin prescriptions of economic liberalism—namely, an open international economy and an integrated currency system—the period from 1896 to 1914 was a high point of globalization and world economic integration. There were gold rushes in South Africa, Australia, and the United States, helping to generate inflation. From 1896 to 1913, prices increased by 41% in the United States and 16% in Great Britain. More states—including Russia, Japan, and Austria-Hungary—flocked to the gold standard, bringing stability to international trade and promoting investment among member nations. Yet just ahead, the 30 years of turmoil from World War I to World War II would yield a remarkable reversal in world trade and globalization trends.

World War I and the Great Collapse

On June 28, 1914, Gavrilo Princip, a Bosnian Serb student, assassinated Archduke Franz Ferdinand of Austria, the heir to the Austro-Hungarian throne, sparking a chain of events that ultimately led to World War I. The "Great War" was a prolonged conflict in which the economic resources of each side were fundamental to victory. Among belligerents, there was unprecedented government involvement in domestic economies. Among warring European nations, exports fell sharply, by design, because the military wished to stockpile goods that, in the past, would have been sold. Each side also tried to prevent adversaries from importing goods for the same reason. Blockades were an important tool designed to stop enemies from accessing goods and munitions. The British Royal Navy remained the foremost in the world, executing an increasingly effective blockade of Germany, and naval warfare was far-reaching, including submarine attacks on civilian ships.

European nations expanded industrial capacity in response to the war, and the United States ramped up industrial production and exports in spite of not officially joining the hostilities until April 1917. Primary goods-producing countries outside of Europe augmented their export capacities in order to meet wartime demand, a move that ultimately spurred their burgeoning industrialization. Japanese manufacturing boomed, as did industrial output in South Africa and Chile. Agricultural production shifted from Europe to other regions of the world, which would later lead to a large supply "overhang" in the 1920s. Shipping became more dangerous, and therefore, costlier. There was a consequent divergence in commodity prices around the world. While the effects of World War I on trade were uneven, the overall amount of world trade declined substantially during the conflict, probably by at least 25%.

After World War I, many European nations found it difficult to regain market share in sectors where developing nations had caught up because of their overtime war production. From 1913 to 1928, Europe's share of world manufacturing output slipped from 41% to 35%. Agricultural interests across Europe called for protective tariff barriers in the face of world supply gluts, leading to a wave of protectionism during the 1920s. Political developments led to the franchise being extended in many European countries, and trade unions rose in influence and power. Labor markets generally became more rigid and regulated, which would soon make the vexing problem of high and persistent unemployment during the Great Depression all the more difficult to solve.

American tariffs had been high during the second half of the 19th century, typically over 40% after 1860, largely to encourage domestic development and industrialization. As American industries became more competitive by the early-20th century, the need for protection diminished. Under Woodrow Wilson, average tariffs declined to a low of about 8% at the outset of World War I. The war increased the need for tax revenues, and a worldwide wave of protectionism led to double-digit tariffs in the 1920s. Commodity prices declined in the late 1920s, threatening American farmers, and during his victorious 1928 campaign, Herbert Hoover promised them protection with a new round of tariff hikes.

Great Depression

American economic growth was vigorous in the 1920s. During the "Roaring Twenties," electricity became a ubiquitous source of energy that powered new consumer products such as radios, telephones, irons, and refrigerators. Unfortunately, the electricity boom of the 1920s also helped to generate a frenzied stock market expansion, similar to the internet bubble of the 1990s. The Federal Reserve raised interest rates in 1928 and 1929 to combat excessive stock prices, but following several years of unsustainable speculation, the American stock market finally crashed in October 1929.

The Great Depression commenced in 1929 with the "Great Crash" on Wall Street. It was to be the longest and most severe depression experienced by the modern industrialized world. Between 1929 and 1933, American industrial production fell by almost 50% and America's total output dropped by 30%. Unemployment, which peaked at over 20%, would not fall below 10% until World War II. The magnitude of economic decline in other industrialized countries was similarly massive. World trade dropped off by over 50% from 1929 to 1932, recovering only slightly throughout the rest of the 1930s.

Protectionist barriers hindering trade increased amidst the enormous slack in aggregate demand across the world. In June 1930, the United States passed the infamous "Smoot-Hawley Tariff," which dictated a massive tariff increase on dutiable goods, averaging about 60%. However, tariff revenue as a fraction of total imports was only about 18% in 1931, which was far lower than late-19th century levels because fewer goods were actually dutiable in 1931. While the direct impact that Smoot-Hawley had on the world economic downturn is commonly exaggerated, it was clear that the United States, with the largest economy in the world, would not keep its markets open in the face of economic pressures. After a financial crisis in the summer of 1931, tariffs generally went up in Europe—partly as retaliation to Smoot-Hawley—and then across the world, especially on agricultural products.

After the Great Crash, a growing lack of confidence gripped the American public. Four massive banking panics swept through the nation from 1930 to 1932. The Federal Reserve did not respond to severe financial sector disruptions with credit, liquidity, and accommodative monetary policy. Instead, the money supply declined by 30% between 1929 and 1933, and many banks did, in fact, fail. In conjunction with depressed demand, this chain of events caused deflation in the United States. The gold standard had been prevalent among industrialized nations since 1879, and maintaining it in member countries required a monetary tightening to match the one that was transpiring in America. The result of the massive monetary contraction was a downward spiral that lowered demand and weakened financial sectors in gold standard countries.

An economy can expand its monetary supply by devaluing its currency, and in the dire circumstances of the 1930s, this required suspending gold convertibility, known as "going off" the gold standard. Great Britain went off the gold standard in 1931 and thereby devalued, regaining competitiveness and recovering relatively early, whereas countries that remained on the gold standard later—such as France, Belgium, and the Netherlands—resorted to tariffs, import quotas, and currency controls to a greater extent in order to shore up their domestic economies. The United States did not devalue until 1933, shortly after Roosevelt's election, and its recovery began later than Britain's. Between 1933 and 1937 the American money supply increased by about 40%, facilitating greater access to credit and stimulating demand. The United States also realized high tariffs were harming its recovery, so protectionism was gradually lowered throughout the 1930s. The overall global recovery was uneven, with Latin America and East Asia doing relatively well during the 1930s. While Western European output recovered to 1929 levels by 1935, it took North America until 1940 to reach its pre-Crash output.

World War II

American capital increasingly dominated the world economy during the 1920s as the United States took over Great Britain's pre-World War I role as hegemon. Nevertheless, the United States failed to provide the political and financial leadership that the British once had. The United States had traditionally been isolationist and protectionist, unlike Britain, and neither the United States nor Britain acted as a "lender of last resort" to prevent major commercial failures by offering liquidity to shore up the world financial system at the outset of the Great Depression. In addition, the European allies owed the United States billions in war debt. Many prominent analysts—notably John Maynard Keyes—predicted the massive reparations imposed on Germany in the wake of the Treaty of Versailles (which settled World War I) were likely to lead to great trouble in little time. The United States was unable to craft an acceptable political solution to these debt controversies despite expending substantial effort in the Dawes and Young Plans.

The Great Depression turned Germany's dire economic situation into a monumental disaster. Adolf Hitler and the National Socialists captured power in 1933, setting in motion events that would lead to the outbreak of World War II in 1939. Initially under the guidance of economic minister Hjalmar Schacht, the German economy was rebuilt and largely nationalized in the 1930s. Trade between belligerent nations collapsed during World War II as they focused on domestic industrial and war production. By 1942, there was almost no trade between German-controlled Europe, Japanese-controlled Asia, and the rest of the world. Submarine warfare along the Atlantic slowed trade and maritime transport. World trade fell, yet trade within allied blocs sometimes increased. American industrial production and exports boomed during the war. Allied advantages in population and economic production only grew larger after 1942, proving to be a decisive factor in their victory.

Aftermath and Reglobalization

At the conclusion of World War II, the American economy was robust and invigorated, in great contrast to the decimated economies of most other wartime participants. No longer a missing hegemon, the United States provided leadership in economic reconstruction and integration. The "Marshall Plan" gave financial assistance to European nations in exchange for agreeing to market reforms. The Soviet Union, along with its sphere of influence, declined to participate. As such, the "Cold War" had begun. In 1949, the North Atlantic Treaty was signed by Canada, the United States, and 10 Western European nations. It committed each nation to the armed defense of the others and brought the "North Atlantic Treaty Organization" (NATO) into existence. European colonialism in Africa and Asia was forever weakened by World War II, so that during the 1950s, the tide turned and decolonization movements grew. These newly independent nations were frequently hostile to integrating with the rest of the world economy, instead focusing on state-led industrialization programs.

Every nation remembered the political failures of the 1930s that had allowed protectionism to swell as the world descended into autarky, nationalism, and ghastly conflict. Looking toward the future, a 1944 Allied conference at Bretton Woods in New Hampshire set up an international monetary framework of fixed exchange rates tied to the American dollar—a currency that was, in turn, tied to gold at a fixed rate. The meeting established the "International Bank for Reconstruction and Development" (IBRD)—more commonly known as the "World Bank"—and the "International Monetary Fund" (IMF) as supporting institutions. The system cemented the shift in financial power from Britain to the United States. It would last until August 1971, when Richard Nixon—fearing an unsustainable run on Fort Knox's gold bullion—took the dollar off the $35 per ounce gold peg so that it could depreciate. Although announced as a temporary measure, this permanent move marked a new era of enhanced exchange rate flexibility among major world currencies.

International trade rules were also set up alongside the Bretton Woods system. Most important was the "General Agreement on Tariffs and Trade" (GATT) signed in 1947, which aimed to facilitate multilateral negotiations to reduce trade barriers. This agreement lasted until 1993 when it was replaced by the "World Trade Organization" (WTO). Nine rounds of negotiation have occurred since the first round in Geneva in 1947. The latest round commenced in Doha, Qatar, in November 2001, and over a decade later, it has not yet concluded. Initial rounds focused on lowering tariffs, particularly for industrial products, and later rounds have involved anti-dumping regulations, intellectual property laws, subsidies, and labor and environmental standards. Advanced industrial nations, especially in Europe and North America, have generally lowered their tariffs since World War II, whereas developing economies have been less likely to scrap their protectionist policies. In essence, the "periphery" of the world economy was closed during the first 35 years following World War II, while the wealthy "core" remained open. Since then, trade barriers have fallen, all the more so in the periphery.

Hyperglobalization

The 1980s sparked a renewal of trade openness and globalization (as discussed in later chapters). China initiated capitalist reform programs in 1978 under Deng Xiaopeng, triggering phenomenal growth. Communism collapsed in Eastern Europe and Russia, and "Third World" economies liberalized. Average tariffs in the developing world fell from 34% in the early 1980s, to 22% in the early 1990s, to 13% by 2000. There was no comparable decline in international transportation costs since the end of World War II. Thus, political factors stimulated the resurgence in economic integration and globalization in the late-20th century, whereas a century earlier, technology led the very same trend. World trade grew at a 6% annual rate during the second half of the 20th century, faster than any other period in history, although this was partly because of catching up after the destructive world wars. The division of labor within the global economy grew more vertically specialized as manufacturing became more complex, its processes performed in numerous stages, sometimes in multiple countries, as the Industrial Revolution percolated to the Third World. Large international corporations have facilitated such specialization, with sweeping supply chains that frequently span multiple regions of the world.

Conclusion

The world has transitioned toward greater economic integration and inter-national trade over the past half millennia, particularly since the Industrial Revolution. The dark period from World War I to World War II was the recent glaring exception, when deglobalization occurred amidst interna-tional capital market strains and immense conflict. The last 30 years have brought about a freewheeling international financial system that supports massive flows of capital at lightning speed. Many factors, including a lack of financial oversight coupled with a global savings glut in search of prof-itable outlets, contributed to the recent financial crisis that occurred some 80 years after the Great Depression. The crisis proved once again that no globalized financial system can provide an unassailable assurance of safety and dependability to participating nations. The ensuing decades will likely entail significant fiscal strains among European and American political and economic systems, alongside a continued strengthening of Asian economic and military power. As always, the direction and pace of globalization will remain critical to understanding future business developments around the world.

Further Reading

Allen, R. (2009). *The British Industrial Revolution in global perspective*. Cambridge, England: Cambridge University Press.

Allen, R. (2011). *Global economic history: A very short introduction*. New York, NY: Oxford University Press.

Bernstein, W. (2008). *A splendid exchange: How trade shaped the world*. New York, NY: Grove Press.

Chandler, A. (1993). *The visible hand: The managerial revolution in American business*. Cambridge, MA: Harvard University Press.

Clark, G. (2007). *A farewell to alms: A brief economic history of the world*. Princeton, NJ: Princeton University Press.

Crouzet, F. (2001). *A history of the European economy, 1000–2000*. Charlottesville, VA: University of Virginia Press.

Darwin, J. (2008). *After Tamarlane: The rise and fall of global empires, 1400–2000*. New York, NY: Bloomsbury Press.

Eichengreen, B. (1996). *Golden fetters: The gold standard and the great depression, 1919–1939*. New York, NY: Oxford University Press.

Eichengreen, B. (2008). *Globalizing capital: A history of the international monetary system.* Princeton, NJ: Princeton University Press.

Eichengreen, B. (2015). *Hall of mirrors: The Great Depression, the Great Recession, and the uses—and misuses—of history.* New York, NY: Oxford University Press.

Engerman, S., & Sokoloff, K. (2011). *Economic development in the Americas since 1500: Endowments and institutions.* Cambridge, England: Cambridge University Press.

Ferguson, N. (2004). *Empire: The rise and demise of the British world order and the lessons for global power.* New York, NY: Basic Books.

Ferguson, N. (2008). *The ascent of money: A financial history of the world.* New York, NY: Penguin.

Findlay, R., & O'Rourke, K. (2007). *Power and plenty: Trade, war, and the world economy in the second millennium.* Princeton, NJ: Princeton University Press.

Frieden, J. (2006). *Global capitalism: Its fall and rise in the twentieth century.* New York, NY: W.W. Norton and Company.

Hugill, P. (1993). *World trade since 1431: Geography, technology, and capitalism.* Baltimore, MD: Johns Hopkins University Press.

Irwin, D. (1996). *Against the tide: An intellectual history of free trade.* Princeton, NJ: Princeton University Press.

Kennedy, P. (1989). *The rise and fall of the great powers.* New York, NY: Vintage.

Kindleberger, C. (1973). *The world in depression, 1929–1939.* Berkeley, CA: University of California Press.

Kindleberger, C. (1993). *A financial history of Western Europe.* New York, NY: Oxford University Press.

Kindleberger, C. (1996). *World economic primacy: 1500–1990.* New York, NY: Oxford University Press.

Landes, D. (1999). *The wealth and poverty of nations: Why some are so rich and some so poor.* New York, NY: W.W. Norton and Company.

Mokyr, J. (1990). *The lever of riches: Technological creativity and economic progress.* New York, NY: Oxford University Press.

Mokyr, J. (2009). *The enlightened economy: An economic history of Britain 1700–1850.* New Haven, CT: Yale University Press.

Muller, J. (1995). *Adam Smith in his time and ours.* Princeton, NJ: Princeton University Press.

North, D., & Thomas, R. P. (1976). *The rise of the western world: A new economic history.* Cambridge, England: Cambridge University Press.

Williamson, J. (2002). *Coping with city growth during the British Industrial Revolution.* Cambridge, England: Cambridge University Press.

Williamson, J. (2011). *Trade and poverty: When the Third World fell behind.* Cambridge, MA: MIT Press.

Wrigley, F. A. (2010). *Energy and the English Industrial Revolution.* Cambridge, England: Cambridge University Press.

Harvard Business School Case Studies

Jones, G. G., & Fernandes, F. T. *The Guggenheims and Chilean nitrates*, 810141-PDF-ENG.

Jones, G. G., & Gallagher-Kernstine, M. *Walking on a tightrope: Maintaining London as a financial center*, 804081-PDF-ENG.

Jones, G. G., & Kiron, D. *Globalizing consumer durables: Singer sewing machine before 1914*, 804001-PDF-ENG.

Jones, G. G., & Vargas, I. *Ivar Kreuger and the Swedish match empire*, 804078-PDF-ENG.

Jones, G. G., & von Siemens, B. *Werner von Siemens and the electric telegraph*, 811004-PDF-ENG.

Jones, G. G., Egawa, M., & Yamazaki, M. *Yataro Iwasaki: Founding Mitsubishi*, 808158-PDF-ENG.

Jones, G. G., Koll, E., & Grendon, A. *Opium and entrepreneurship in the nineteenth century*, 805010-PDF-ENG.

Koll, E. *Enterprise culture in Chinese history: Zhang Jian and the Dasheng cotton mills*, 308068-PDF-ENG.

McCraw, T. K. *Jay Gould and the coming of railroad consolidation*, 391260-PDF-ENG.

McCraw, T. K. *Railroads and the beginnings of modern management*, 391131-PDF-ENG.

McCraw, T. K. *Samuel Slater, Francis Cabot Lowell, and the beginnings of the factory system in the United States*, 792008-PDF-ENG.

McCraw, T. K. *Work: Craft and factory in nineteenth-century America*, 391264-PDF-ENG.

Moss, D. A. *Constructing a nation: The United States and their constitution—1763-92*, 795063-PDF-ENG.

Moss, D. A., & Gownder, J. P. *Explaining the Great Depression*, 799067-PDF-ENG.

Moss, D. A., & Rotemberg, J. J. *German hyperinflation of 1923*, 798048-HCB-ENG.

Moss, D. A., Kintgen, E., & Rafalska, A. *The South Sea Company*, 708005-PDF-ENG.

Moss, D. A., Lee, M., Brennan, K., & Gorin, M. *Free trade vs. protectionism: The great Corn-Laws debate*, 701080-PDF-ENG.

Nicholas, T. *Trouble with a bubble*, 808067-PDF-ENG.

Rotemberg, J. J., & Lewis, L. H. *Birth of modern macroeconomic policy: Sweden and the Great Depression*, 704029-PDF-ENG.

CHAPTER 2

Economic Growth, Convergence, and Trade

Introduction

If there is one question in economics that dwarfs all the others in importance, it is this: Why are some countries so wealthy and others so poor? In 2011, per capita income was $49,000 in the United States, but only $1,700 in Bangladesh. Economists have been grappling with this issue for centuries. Adam Smith concluded that good governance and a well-developed division of labor were fundamental to economic growth. In the 19th century, Karl Marx argued that in modern capitalist economies, the owner class takes advantage of economies of scale in production and exploits labor, generating huge profits and a concentration of capital that will sooner or later spark a worker-led socialist revolution. Contra Marx, there is now a broad consensus around the world in support of market economies. This chapter discusses the main contemporary theory of long-term economic growth, paying attention to the vital forces that support economies.

Neoclassical Growth Model

Modern economics offers a long-run framework for thinking about economic growth across nations. Called the "neoclassical growth model," it has been developed and modified by economists ever since the 1950s. It serves as a framework for explaining economic growth over the long term (while ignoring short-term fluctuations), and has been primarily applied to the postwar era. The neoclassical growth model starts with a production function, $Y(K,L)$, where Y is the economy's output. Its level positively depends on factor inputs of capital, K, and labor, L. Capital is, by definition, anything that enhances the abilities of workers to perform productive labor in the economy. It is typically durable and depreciable, and includes the economy's buildings, equipment, tools, and other nonhuman resources used to produce goods. (Land is an input to production, but it isn't normally considered capital because it wasn't produced by people and its supply is fixed.) An economy's infrastructure is a type of public capital. The level of capital in an economy increases when firms or the government invest at a rate above depreciation. Labor is simply the amount of work-producing human resources within an economy. It grows with population size and declines according to retirements and deaths.

The chief characteristics of the neoclassical model's production function governing output Y are: (1) it exhibits positive and diminishing "marginal returns" to each separate input (capital or labor), and (2) it exhibits "constant returns to scale" overall. Diminishing marginal returns to each input means that the incremental effect of adding capital or labor to production is decreasing as the economy has more capital and labor. That is, holding all else equal within an economy, if a slight amount of capital or labor is added, its incremental productivity effect (though always positive) will be greater in an economy that is capital- or labor-poor, and lesser in an economy that is capital- or labor-rich. The figure below illustrates a diminishing returns production function. Labor is held constant (and ignored), and the x-axis represents capital. It shows that capital inputs yield greater incremental benefits in poor economies:

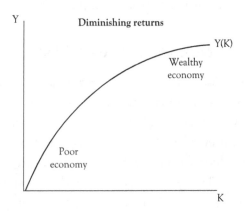

In other words, the advantageous effect of having more of a factor input declines as an economy matures and produces more. (Switching the places of capital and labor, the above figure would illustrate that, holding the amount of capital fixed, there are declining returns to additional labor.) This assumption seems reasonable: poor economies are relatively starved for resources, so increases in inputs should yield more "bang for the buck." Conversely, rich countries have already found all the "low-hanging fruit" in terms of productivity enhancements and efficient input usage, so marginal returns within them should be lower.

Constant returns to scale means that increasing every input by the same proportion will also increase output by that exact proportion. For example, if both capital and labor are doubled, output will double. It means that, by holding the technology of a production function constant, it is possible to replicate smaller economies or industries. The following table reflects a hypothetical constant returns to scale economy under four different sizes:

Economy	K	L	Y
Tiny	2	5	2.71
Small	4	10	5.43
Medium	6	15	8.14
Large	8	20	10.86

In this example, the "Cobb-Douglas" style production function (named after 20th century American economists Charles Cobb and Paul Douglas) happens to be $Y = K^{2/3}L^{1/3}$. In each case, the capital-to-labor ratio is fixed at 40%. Compared to the tiny economy, the small economy is double-sized, the medium economy is triple-sized, and the large economy is quadruple-sized. Total output increases in inputs, yet output per worker remains the same, at just over one half. If some capital is added to one of these economies, output will increase, as will output per capita. However, because the production function exhibits declining returns in each input, the marginal value of adding additional capital will decrease as more is added. The example can represent an entire economy, a growing industry, or a collection of industries. Think of the industries that you know best. It is probable that when both factors, capital and labor, are increased pro-portionately, output would increase by the same proportion, because the units within these industries are able to replicate their parts and scale up. This is generally true in the construction and health care sectors, for instance.

The constant returns property holds for any proportionate increase in inputs, not just a doubling. It implies that if capital and labor both increase by 1%, output would increase by 1%. It is an assumption about the *scale* of an economy. While it is a reasonable assumption for modern economies, not all economies exhibit constant returns to scale. For instance, a primitive agricultural economy with a fixed amount of land would not experience constant returns to scale: doubling the amount of labor and capital would lead to less than a doubling of output. In this case, because production is limited by the availability of a key resource, land, the economy would exhibit *decreasing* returns to scale. Manufacturing industries commonly display *increasing* returns to scale. Theoretically, a technology-intensive economy can exhibit increasing returns to scale in the aggregate, although it isn't clear that any economies today have this property.

The production function $Y(K,L)$ captures the aggregate output of an economy, holding technology constant at a given point in time. Within any economy, capital and labor are assumed to flow to their most productive usages, so that their marginal returns are roughly equal across industries. Therefore, the production function really consists of many small economies. Not every industry fits these assumptions precisely. For one, some "high-tech" industries, like software design, may exhibit sharply increasing returns to scale after the research and development of a product has been completed. In the case of Windows Vista, it supposedly cost Microsoft six billion dollars to develop the operating system, although the cost of producing a marginal copy is close to zero. Nevertheless, the two primary assumptions of this production function $Y(K,L)$ seem, on the whole, fairly reasonable in light of years of empirical research.

The basic neoclassical model includes a few other assumptions. Labor is assumed to grow at a constant rate, which is the rate of population growth. Workers are paid their marginal return to labor (equal to the wage rate). Each worker consumes part of their income and saves the rest. These savings are converted to investment via the financial sector. The interest rate is the marginal return to capital, which is, equivalently, the "cost of capital." Investment goes directly to capital improvements, and it is assumed that the economy's capital stock depreciates at a constant rate. With these assumptions, the neoclassical growth model can be solved with some algebra. However, interpretation is made easier by describing its critical results in words.

Steady-State Equilibrium

The model's central result is that any given economy—no matter where it starts from—will end up in a "steady-state" equilibrium where capital, labor, and output all grow at the same rate, which is the population growth rate in this simple world. Thus, output per capita will eventually be constant in equilibrium. Steady-state equilibrium occurs because: (1) the returns to capital and labor are decreasing due to the diminishing returns to each factor assumption, and (2) the economy can sustain indefinite growth along the steady state due to the constant returns to scale assumption. The more people save, the greater output per capita is. To optimize the well-being of citizens, it is best to maximize long-run consumption per capita, and to achieve this, a "Golden Rule" savings rate—which is neither too high, resulting in overinvestment, nor too low, resulting in overconsumption—can be found analytically. The inclusion of technology is one important modification to this model (discussed below). Technological progress causes output per capita to grow (instead of stagnate) in the long run.

Let's examine some examples of how economies reach the steady state in the neoclassical growth model. First, consider an economy with low levels of capital, such as an emerging or postwar economy (like 1950s Europe under the Marshall Plan). A little capital may go a long way here. The marginal return to capital is high, meaning that capital is very productive. With a reasonably high savings rate, output will grow fast and capital will accumulate quickly. As "capital-deepening" occurs, workers become more productive as each one has more capital to work with. As time goes on, however, the marginal return to capital will slow due to decreasing returns. Eventually, steady-state equilibrium is reached, so that the growth rate of capital, labor, and output will all be equal to the population growth rate. This example would also fit a New World frontier society, where population growth may be very slow at first, making migration from elsewhere necessary for robust growth.

Now consider what happens in the opposite case, where an economy has ample capital relative to its population. This is what occurred in economies afflicted by the Black Death of the 14th and 15th centuries that resulted in a very high capital-to-labor ratio. After the plague, wages were high—about three or four times subsistence—because labor was scarce and the marginal product of labor was high. The stock of capital was spread across fewer workers, signaling that the return to new capital investment was low. This depressed savings and interest rates, the latter falling in England from about 10% before the plague to 5% by 1500. In the model, the amount of capital per worker decreases as the population recovers, until the steady-state equilibrium—where capital, labor, and output grow at the same rate—is reached. This process, sparked by mass deaths, is the converse of the 1950s Europe scenario, which was kicked off by a massive destruction of capital. With some math, you would see that according to this model, an economy will eventually converge to the same equilibrium regardless of where it started out, although it may take a long time.

It should be noted that this growth model, as with all economic models, is a simplification. By their very nature, economic models focus on a select set of forces. The real world is complicated, so no model captures every relevant factor. Even so, economic models can provide tremendous insights by honing in on the interaction of key forces. In fact, Professor Robert Solow—Nobel Prize winner and one of the originators of the neoclassical growth model during the 1950s—later bemoaned the huge literature that his work spawned, since he thought most of it went beyond the appropriate confines of his original growth model, and thereby provided little value-added. Besides additional theory, some helpful empirical testing of the neoclassical model (discussed below) has been performed over the past half century.

Convergence

What does the neoclassical growth model imply for economic growth around the world? The most important prediction is that there is a tendency for economies to *converge*—or catch up—over time. Advanced industrial economies may lead the world in output and income, but if poorer economies have access to their leading technologies (and the general output possibilities that their superior production function implies), then these developing economies may very well catch up one day. According to the neoclassical growth model, poor countries have lower capital-to-labor ratios, so we may expect them to grow faster because their returns to capital are higher. They will catch up eventually, all else being equal. Globalized capital flows mean that leading economies can invest directly in developing nations, increasing the poorer country's level of technology, infrastructure, and output. In addition, information travels very quickly today, and not every country protects the intellectual property it uses, especially technologies that were developed abroad.

When economists dig into the data on economic growth, they usually test one of two convergence hypotheses that derive from the neoclassical growth model. The first is called unconditional—or *absolute*—convergence. The absolute convergence hypothesis is that poor countries experience higher economic growth rates than rich countries. Its logic is that if all economies possess the same steady-state equilibrium, and the primary difference between economies is their initial level of capital, then poor nations will grow rapidly as they accumulate capital and catch up. There is not much support for this notion in the data. In fact, the international data show that wealthier countries have usually tended to grow faster than poor countries. However, when a sample is restricted to a similar group of nations, such as only European countries, absolute convergence does show up in the data. This is because these countries are much more similar, and information, capital, and labor flow more freely within a relatively small geographical region. There are also vast differences in the growth experiences of continents. African countries have remained poor for many decades, so clearly, comparing them to European countries will not lend empirical support to the absolute convergence hypothesis.

Are there any reasonable adjustments to the absolute convergence hypothesis that fit the data better? Indeed, economists have tested a second convergence hypothesis known as *conditional* convergence. The idea behind it is that by controlling for factors that influence a country's steady-state level of output (such as savings rates), evidence of convergence will be found. For instance, a poor country with a low savings rate and undeveloped financial system may grow slowly and have trouble converging in spite of a high potential return to capital. By including appropriate control variables, it is possible to test whether very different countries converge to each other over time, all else being equal. These relevant controls include human capital levels, such as the average amount of education within a country's workforce; the quality of government (however measured) and infrastructure; and openness to international trade. It turns out that empirical analyses do lend support to conditional convergence (at least using data sets from the past half century, as data on appropriate controls generally aren't available before then). After controlling for important differences across countries, lower initial output strongly correlates with higher subsequent growth. As a result, there exists empirical support for the neoclassical growth model: poorer countries catch up to richer countries as long as basic discrepancies between them—such as education and governance—are accounted for.

Research on economic growth demonstrates that a number of other forces outside the basic model can facilitate or impede growth. To be sure, any student of history would contend that politics and government are important to growth, and stories about the impact of politics on economic growth are usually unhappy tales. For example, Argentina was one of the wealthiest countries in the world in the 1920s, but then endured a period of unstable governments (including military dictatorships) that exhibited poor monetary and fiscal policy and implemented other policies detrimental to growth. In an extreme case, Zimbabwe has suffered from poor growth, low investment, and hyperinflation under Robert Mugabe's rule since the 1980s. On the other hand, a number of East Asian nations have recently succeeded in coordinating export-driven growth as they integrated into the international division of labor and production. Most strikingly, at the end of World War II, North and South Korea were both very poor, though since then, under very different economic systems, the South has seen explosive growth compared to the stagnant North.

Contemporary research shows that although the size of government is not overly important to growth, its quality is. Huge deficits, hyperinflations, entrenched bureaucracies, and civil war all hamper growth. The institutions of governance are influential. Stable markets, property rights, and the rule of law all promote economic growth. Openness to trade and infrastructure—such as electricity-generating capacity, the amount of paved roads, and telephone usage—are positively related to economic growth. Given these empirical patterns, many have attempted to modify the neoclassical growth model in various ways, even by taking into account governance, which is arguably the most significant factor despite being difficult to measure or model with mathematics. Human capital and technology (discussed below) are two of the most important extensions providing additional elements of realism.

Human Capital

Human capital is the set of skills and abilities that each individual brings to their work and the labor market more generally. Human capital comes from education, training, experience, and talent. Economists often focus on education because schooling increases human capital, and data on educational attainment exist for many countries. The primary prediction of human capital theory is that increased education and human capital leads to higher wages and income, both for individuals and for nations. This is accomplished through higher productivity. Human capital is a complement to physical capital since it makes workers more productive under any given set of equipment and technology, meaning that workers with more human capital are better equipped to utilize physical capital efficiently. More human capital also implies greater research and development, yielding better technologies, which in turn leads to higher national output.

Consider the investment decision in the neoclassical growth model. Its basic version only allows investment in physical capital. Adding human capital allows for investment in education. Higher levels of education—or equivalently, greater human capital—can be included in the production function, which will now look like $F(K,L,H)$, where H is human capital. Economies with greater human capital produce more because human capital is complementary to labor and physical capital. Yet investing in human capital is costly for a society: the opportunity cost is consumption today or savings for later (with the latter option equivalent to investing in physical capital via the financial intermediation sector). In developing countries, families rarely have sufficient resources to pay for adequate private schooling, so public schooling is normally required to develop the national stock of human capital. Solving the extended neoclassical growth model with math demonstrates that countries that invest in human capital will have higher per capita income in equilibrium. It may also take longer for poorer countries to converge, since they will need to catch up to the higher levels of physical *and* human capital that richer countries have attained.

Human capital is both a cause and a consequence of economic growth. Skilled workers not only produce more, they also generate beneficial "spillovers" onto their local economy by achieving innovations, sharing information, and managing others. Experience shows that as economies progress from emerging to advanced status, greater investment in education is common. Some economists argue that a major reason why the United States was able to remain the dominant world economy throughout the 20th century was because of its relatively large investments in education during the earlier decades of that century, as public secondary education—meaning schooling through high school—became more accessible. Whereas the key to the 19th century industrial success was natural resources and machinery, human capital embedded in people grew more critical to national economic prowess over the course of the 20th century. The United States was the leader in providing mass secondary education in the early-20th century, when many European nations viewed the American system as wasteful precisely because it was not meritocratic. Under its egalitarian emphasis on general public education, full-time secondary school enrollment rates in the United States were much higher than in Britain and the rest of industrialized Western Europe throughout the first half of the 20th century. After World War II, the United States led in providing mass higher education. Combined with its world-leading universities, this factor contributed mightily to subsequent technological advances and productivity growth in the United States.

Empirical evidence shows that greater investments in education are associated with higher economic growth rates across nations, although the relationship isn't as strong as some economists had expected. This finding may be partly due to measurement difficulties, since educational quality is tough to gauge and compare across countries. Human capital not only makes workers more efficient, but it also enhances their ability to manage new technologies. Indeed, one important empirical finding is that economic growth is strongly related to the average level of schooling among adult males at the secondary and higher levels. Because workers with this educational background are likely to be most complementary to new technologies in emerging economies, it implies a vital role for the diffusion of technology in the development process. Other literatures show that education has many auxiliary beneficial effects such as the facilitation of political stability and the prevention of crime. Today, the internet is spreading educational information at little or no cost, improving living standards in ways that do not show up in national income statistics. Top universities are offering more online courses every year, and these new tools of learning may well contribute to global economic growth in the years to come.

Technology, Science, and Growth

Technology is the other main extension to the neoclassical model. It is defined as the modification and development of tools, techniques, and equipment to promote the economic productivity of workers and capital. In practice, it is the application of the functional sciences (such as engineering) to industry and commerce. Including accumulated technology, the production function becomes $Y(K,L,A)$, where A is the level of a country's technology, either assumed to grow at a specified constant rate or according to investments in research and development (possibly including human capital). The extended neoclassical model's main result is that the steady-state equilibrium growth rate of per capita income will be equal to the growth rate of technology. In other words, national wealth is driven by technological progress.

The fundamental mechanism is that new technology leads to productivity growth, allowing more goods to be produced in less time with fewer inputs and less effort. In the long run, growth and prosperity ultimately stem from productivity improvements, so technological progress is essential. Across countries, differences in technology lead to differences in productivity, and therefore incomes. Although poorer countries are expected to converge, they must accumulate technology—and the capabilities to utilize it effectively—in order to do so. And the larger the technology gap, the longer it takes them to converge. In some formulations, the technology factor is a catch-all for many different forces influencing economic growth in a region, including its degree of entrepreneurial spirit, its research and development spending, and its effective enforcement of intellectual property rights. The American city of Austin, Texas provides a good example of a region leveraging these factors—in conjunction with the resources of a large local research university—to become a bastion of technology-driven growth. Beginning in the 1980s, the coordinated efforts of local leaders in government, business, and academia led to a dramatic economic boom where thousands of tech companies were attracted to the Austin area. Given the private sector's intense demand for human capital, Austin has struggled to keep up at times, leading to periodic shortages of skilled labor.

Fresh examples of the power of technology come from computers and the internet, which are part of the scalable, knowledge-intensive high-tech sector. New software (like Windows) and web sites (like Google) have driven economic growth and generated immense wealth. The best ideas and best products are embraced globally, which has a "winner-take-all" multiplier effect on the payoff from being the absolute-best versus thousandth-best product developer. (Think of iPhone app sales.) One key difference between technology-driven improvements and physical capital accumulation is that, as opposed to capital investment, funding for high-tech research and development leads to breakthroughs that are "nonrival" (or sharable). Ideas can be transcribed or stored at no cost. This means that research and development can have an extremely beneficial effect on economic growth because ideas tend to spread quickly. In a healthy economy that innovates with scientific research, many sectors can operate at the "technology frontier" (or current limits of technology).

Intellectual Property Rights and Growth

The history of patent law demonstrates that nations are most concerned with intellectual property protection as a means to promote domestic economic growth. Venice originated the modern notion of patent protection with a 1474 statute granting 10 years of exclusive rights to inventors and entrepreneurs who had invented or brought new technologies to the Republic. In the 16th century, a system of patent monopolies developed in England under the Crown. Unfortunately, Queen Elizabeth I and King

James I frequently sold monopoly patent rights to raise revenue and reward political patrons. After decades of abuse, the 1624 "Statute of Monopolies" was enacted, providing the foundations for English patent law. It gave no protection to foreigners and clearly aimed to encourage domestic industrial activity, employment, and economic growth. During the early-19th century, the United States was very lax in protecting foreign intellectual property as it was drawing nearer to Britain, although it was actually a forerunner in enforcing the intellectual property rights of its own citizens. Following the 1836 passage of the "Patent Act," technically trained examiners began scrutinizing patent applications to make sure inventions were original advances, in a system that has endured to this day. By the mid-19th century, many observers attributed American technological savvy to its advanced system of intellectual property rights protection.

Today an organization may spend millions of dollars on developing the latest microchip technology, but if this information leaks, competitors may be able to utilize it at no cost. In general, if intellectual property is not well protected, investments in research and development could slow, hurting economic growth in the long term, both locally and globally. Practical perspectives on intellectual property rights depend on a nation's level of development and its distance to the technology frontier. A wealthy country with many new advanced technologies and heavy research and development spending (in both the private and public sector) may wish to enforce very strict intellectual property laws around the world. By contrast, it is much cheaper for developing nations to disregard intellectual property laws and instead copy (or reverse engineer) the technologies of other countries. Chinese intellectual property enforcement is still very loose today, which is common for a nation catching up to technological leaders. Borrowing foreign know-how can support economic growth today and spur the development of domestic technology-intensive sectors without requiring a lot of spending on research and development (at least in the early years).

Business Opportunities

The neoclassical growth model generates insights into potential business opportunities across nations. Sometimes called the cost of capital, the interest rate is understood to be a proxy for the profitability of business investments and the overall returns to investment within an economy. For a given economy, the interest rate is equal to the marginal product—or incremental output—of capital, which, all else equal, is likely to be decreasing as a country develops and amasses physical capital. Thus, returns may be expected to be higher in fast-growing emerging economies with many profitable business opportunities but scarce capital funds. In need of capital and expertise to catch up to advanced nations, emerging economies can be attractive regions for businesspersons and investors. On the other hand, emerging economies do not always have first-rate political institutions, contract enforcement, or infrastructure, so investing in them can be risky for foreigners.

To take this one step further, consider the neoclassical growth model with the technology factor A. Superior technology leads to higher interest rates because productivity and the returns to physical capital are an increasing function of technology. This implies that: (1) wealthier countries can sustain higher capital returns and interest rates over the long run if they are able to maintain their technological lead, and (2) in a globalized economy with international investment, capital can continue to flow to advanced economies instead of helping to build up emerging economies. Indeed, research shows that on net, capital tends to flow to wealthier countries. Although it is much more pronounced today, this finding of "wealth bias" was also observed prior to World War I, the last time that global capital markets were so well integrated. The phenomenon of capital flowing to wealthier countries rather than poorer ones has been labeled the "Lucas paradox" (after Nobel Prize-winning economist Robert Lucas) because it contradicts the notion that developing nations should be relatively more attractive places to invest due to higher expected returns on capital. Besides stamping out corruption and building political stability and infrastructure, emerging countries can import advanced technologies to help them compete for capital in the global investment market. Given their disadvantages, they should focus all the more on improving their overall human capital, technological, and institutional capabilities.

Large corporations from leading economies often try to break into emerging markets to achieve high returns on their investments, as there may be significant advantages to being the first company to successfully serve a new market and establish brand equity. Yet accomplishing this can be difficult in an increasingly globalized marketplace where information flows instantaneously. Entrepreneurs in emerging markets can be quick to copy business models devised in more advanced regions. One example is MercadoLibre, the Latin American eBay, which was started by an Argentine studying business in the United States. Emerging markets may pirate goods from advanced economies, such as Microsoft's software products, which are well known to be copied throughout China and many other regions. Even if a foreign company establishes a toehold in an emerging market, government-enforced barriers can hinder foreign firms, and domestic companies may spring up and attempt to compete with the advantage of subsidies or legal protections.

Productivity Across Nations

In the neoclassical growth model, the amount of physical capital per worker and the level of technology and human capital are the primary determinants of an economy's growth trajectory. When comparing countries around the world, richer countries compare favorably to poorer countries across all three dimensions: they have more physical capital per worker, greater stocks of human capital, and more advanced technologies. Empirical studies suggest that differences in physical capital explain no more than a quarter of per capita income differences across countries. The remainder is due to greater productivity in wealthier countries, caused by superior technology, greater efficiency, deeper human capital, and better institutions and governance. Economists call this residual "total factor productivity" (TFP), which represents how efficiently capital and labor are utilized within an economy.

Differences in labor quality are important in explaining productivity differences between nations. Measured human capital can explain some of the variation in labor quality, as can differences in the experience and quality of managers (called "managerial capital"). Better technology improves labor productivity and the productivity of capital. A strong political and legal environment facilitates labor productivity since in its absence, individuals and firms face considerable uncertainty, often have to pay bribes, and have less overall incentive to work hard and make productive long-term investments. In developing nations, workers are less productive partly because they lack access to modern medicine, adequate health care, and proper nutrition. The evidence also suggests that in poor economies, employing more workers per unit of capital does not increase output by much, which remains something of a puzzle.

The experience of economies decimated by World War II is instructive. Germany and Japan both grew at very high rates after their physical economies were destroyed by the war. Germany's work force possessed high levels of human capital, and its economy had access to foreign capital that was used to invest in industry. Japan improved its educational system after the war, emphasizing on-the-job training, and focused on understanding cutting-edge technologies used by foreign economies. Propelled by reverse engineering efforts and licensing agreements, it would emulate and then improve upon these technologies, so that the productivity of Japanese industry was among the best in the world by the 1970s. Such favorable growth stories contrast with India, a nation that turned inward after independence in 1947, and in its striving for self-sufficiency, failed to develop a thriving industrialized economy.

Productivity Slowdowns

As a matter of history, productivity growth isn't constant over time. It picked up considerably at the start of the Industrial Revolution in Great Britain, for example. More recently, productivity was strong in the postwar United States in the 1950s and 1960s before slowing in the 1970s and 1980s. This phenomenon was termed the "productivity slowdown puzzle" by economists at the time and it was heavily researched in the 1990s. Leading explanations were: (1) it was due to a lack of new technological improvements, because after the industrial heyday of the 1950s and 1960s, industry had finally caught up to the frontiers of science by the 1970s; (2) it was driven by the energy crisis in the 1970s, which caused cost inflation and retarded investment and productivity growth; and (3) it didn't really exist, as the supposed slowdown was simply a figment of the data's imagination. In hindsight, the first explanation is the most promising. Science leads to technological advancement which impacts productivity growth, but the timing at each stage is unpredictable.

Productivity growth in advanced nations started to pick up again in the 1990s, likely spurred by the information technology revolution and computerization. Evidence shows that in the United States, productivity growth from computers didn't really emerge until it surged in the late 1990s, and then stayed solid for the first half of the following decade, helped along by corporate cost cutting after the "Dotcom" bust. In Europe, productivity did not accelerate in the mid-1990s, even though new technologies were implemented (at least with a lag as compared to the United States). This may be due to other changes the United States implemented but Europe did not, such as laborsaving reorganizations, and the rise of big-box American retailers (notably Walmart) that were savvy about using new technology and supply chain management practices. Regardless, the debate continues. Measurement issues are always at the forefront since productivity is not directly observed and measures of technology utilization are never perfect, particularly in cross-country comparisons.

Socialism

Some of the greatest extended productivity slowdowns since the Industrial Revolution occurred in centrally planned socialist countries. Russia's socialist economy was governed by a series of 5-year plans until its dissolution in 1991. According to Western estimates, although the Soviet economy grew quickly in the first two postwar decades, it began stagnating in the 1970s and was in crisis by the 1980s (as Russian citizens could surmise themselves at the time). Russian living standards actually declined after the 1960s, as infant mortality rates increased and child and adult heights fell. To the extent that there was prosperity in late Soviet Russia, it was apparently not widespread. Centralized economic planning led to long-term imbalances in investment and industrial growth, so that the Soviet economy became increasingly unsound over time. In sum, it is difficult to restructure a command economy or develop and implement new technologies under socialism, as the great Austria-Hungary-born 20th century economists Friedrich von Hayek and Joseph Schumpeter reasoned. Nobel Prize winner Hayek focused on the insolvable problem of reorganization in the absence of market price signals, and Schumpeter recognized that capitalism's "creative destruction" process of continual restructuring was the essence of its dynamism.

China, the most populous socialist economy of the 20th century, provides a striking before-and-after comparison. Prior to 1979, China exhibited uneven growth for decades as it maintained a command economy that was isolated from the global economy. It relied on government directives and 5-year plans that were often disastrous. The second such plan, called the "Great Leap Forward," began in 1958. In an attempt to catch up to leading economies such as Great Britain, Mao Zedong collectivized agriculture and forced millions to move into industrial production. As a result, food production dropped sharply and tens of millions of rural peasants starved to death. Then, starting in 1966, Mao instituted the "Cultural Revolution," designed to purify Chinese society by purging it of all elitist bourgeois elements. The program devastated China's educational system, leading to a sharp decline in human capital. (Back in the 1940s, Hayek warned that authoritarian command economies would eventually lead to the collapse of civilization.) Beginning in 1979 under Deng Xiaoping, China slowly opened up to foreign trade and investment. With these reforms, China's real per capita "gross domestic product" (GDP) grew more than 13-fold from 1980 to 2010, and hundreds of millions were raised out of extreme poverty.

Growth Across Continents

The neoclassical growth model provides a valuable framework for measuring and analyzing how poor countries grow and catch up to the wealthiest economies. Emerging economies require active policies that foster economic diversification and summon a shift from low-productivity sectors such as agriculture to higher productivity activities. The rate at which this transition occurs depends in part on the economy's ease in absorbing knowledge from more advanced economies. Yet there is no automatic mechanism or policy recipe that allows any emerging economy to successfully transition to a wealthier state. Over the past half century, the growth experiences of developing economies across Asia, Latin America, and Africa provide some interesting contrasts.

Asia has been the biggest success. Hong Kong, Singapore, South Korea, and Taiwan led the way from the 1960s to the 1990s, exhibiting

GDP per capita growth rates that averaged at least 6%. These economies invested heavily, accumulating massive amounts of physical capital. Their populations and work forces grew, and they improved their educational systems so that human capital increased. These relatively small countries liberalized trade policies and promoted labor-intensive manufactured exports. Labor shifted from agriculture to manufacturing, and rapid export growth was a key feature of their success. After investigating the statistical evidence behind the "East Asian Tiger" experience, economists have concluded that most of their growth was due to massive factor accumulations as opposed to extraordinary technological progress. On the other hand, Japan, which was the original Asian Tiger, showed relatively greater technological efficiency in its postwar growth. It also had much higher human capital levels to begin with.

The two most populous nations in Asia, India and China, have both grown rapidly since 1980. India's growth has been similar to the East Asian Tigers, albeit slower. However, as opposed to growth in manufacturing, it has been fueled by a massive expansion in service industries. China's growth has been driven by greater amounts of physical capital accumulation and total factor productivity. Its service industries have expanded, but crucially, its industrial sector productivity and output have exploded, in lockstep with a major expansion in exports. India's industrial sector has not sustained such developments to date. Both India and China began liberalizing trade in the late 1970s. The share of China's output that is exported has remained much higher than India's, although both have more than tripled over the past 30 years.

Latin America, which was much wealthier than East Asia back in the 1950s, has been a disappointment. Savings and investment have remained weak, and education has not been emphasized to the extent that it was in East Asia. Although the region is rich in natural resources, this wealth has not always been directed to growth-enhancing investments like education and physical capital accumulation. Poor governance and explosive debt crises have historically been a problem, though today most of Latin America is ruled by democratically elected governments. In recent decades, the region has struggled to maintain high employment shares in industries that are liberalizing or undergoing productivity growth, so free trade has not been a blessing to the extent it was in East Asia. One bright spot is

Brazil, where economic growth, spurred by improving governance and high commodity prices, has been impressive over the past decade. Its experience is hopefully a harbinger of things to come for neighboring countries. In fact, while overall growth in Latin America slowed from the 1950s to the 1980s, it has picked up considerably since 1990.

Africa has been the worst performer. African economies have struggled to develop a modern industrial base in large part due to inadequate governance and institutions. Corruption in many nations is endemic and remains a major barrier to investment and growth. Civil wars have raged in many areas of Africa, making it difficult to attract physical capital investment, either domestically or from abroad. Wealth from natural resources often led to conflict instead of public sector improvements like enhanced schooling systems, and investors have resisted choosing Africa over other potentially profitable regions. In addition to low levels of human capital, worker productivity has been hampered by malnutrition, disease, and poor health care. Even when education has improved (such as in parts of North Africa), job opportunities and growth have not always materialized. Still, like Latin America, African political institutions have improved in recent years, and economic growth rates have increased since the 1990s.

Openness, Trade, and Growth

Conventional economic models of international trade suggest that trade promotes growth because it allows each nation to focus on the economic activities that it can perform most efficiently. In other words, it gives each country more opportunities, minimizes costs, maximizes output, and leads to a more finely tuned division of labor across the world. Trade also facilitates the transfer of new technologies and ideas, particularly from leading economies to developing economies. Then again, emerging economies may be wary of opening up their infant industries to import competition, and even among successful exporting industries, opening trade further can cause reallocations and social upheaval. For this reason, countries that have successfully liberalized trade, such as the East Asian Tigers, have been careful to watch out for dislocations. In recent decades, Latin American countries have not managed liberalizations with as much care and success, although Chile, assisted by subsidies to exporting industries, has achieved considerable export-driven economic growth.

According to postwar cross-country data, increased trade is correlated with higher incomes and greater economic growth. This does not necessarily mean that trade and openness cause economic growth, because, for instance, wealthy and fast-growing economies may have the most liberal trade policies, or, at the very least, they have been careful to time their openings to international trade in an optimal fashion. Recent research scrutinizing this relationship has generally concluded that trade facilitates economic growth and promotes investment in physical capital. Other studies, based on specific liberalizing experiences, suggest that when a country opens itself to trade, the most efficient plants expand and show efficiency improvements, exporting firms expand, and import-competing firms may contract. Consumers typically gain from an increased variety of goods, often at much lower prices. For example, a massive influx of low-priced Chinese imports has augmented the purchasing power of American consumers over the past couple decades.

Opening an economy to international trade often has an uneven distributional impact, meaning that some groups are harmed while others benefit or notice no ill effects. A classic example is weavers in India who were forced into unemployment by cheap textile imports from Britain in the 19th century. Even if skilled Indian weavers were eventually able to find employment at lower wages, they were hurt in the short and long term. Today, new international competitive pressures can deteriorate company margins, diminish the bargaining power of workers and unions, and necessitate capital and technology upgrading. Among nations that export a large fraction of their output, one downside risk to trade openness is a greater vulnerability to global business cycle fluctuations. Advanced economies that are the most exposed to international trade have also built up the largest public sectors and safety nets to protect workers from the inherent risks of openness. At one extreme are the United States and Japan, countries that do not rely heavily on exports, while at the other extreme are the Netherlands and Sweden, countries that do. Overall, the gains from allowing trade run into diminishing returns as fewer restrictions are in place, so that distributional considerations become more important.

Lowering tariffs and liberalizing international trade sometimes coincides with opening an economy to foreign capital flows. Unfortunately, economies that are open to international capital flows face the downside risk that capital may flow out of them very quickly, depressing prices, investment, and demand. For instance, during the 1990s, after years of brisk economic growth, increasing foreign investment, and rising asset prices, external shocks led to a fall in confidence and slowing growth in Southeast Asia, so that in July 1997, Thailand was forced to devalue its currency. The crisis soon spread to Indonesia, Malaysia, the Philippines, and other parts of the world. The poor are the most devastated by financial crises in developing economies. During the first year of the Thai crisis, the percentage of poor people in rural Thailand jumped by about 50%, and in Indonesia, manufacturing wages were nearly halved. Other Asian countries, such as China and India, made out relatively well due to their strict controls on capital flight. Historically, high levels of international capital mobility have led to international banking crises. The global financial crisis that began in 2007 is the most recent example, as investors fled foreign markets for the safety of home or prominent reserve currencies. Aided by smart capital controls or other restrictions, emerging economies that are liberalizing should balance the benefits from open capital flows with the downside risks that accompany capital mobility.

Conclusion

The neoclassical growth model implies that physical capital, human capital, labor, and technology all contribute to an economy's growth. What's more, emerging economies are capable of faster growth as they converge to advanced economies. China may be the best-known recent example of this phenomenon. Furthermore, since the 1990s developing economies have become more integrated with the world economy and have grown at a far brisker pace than developed economies. Globalization has undoubtedly contributed to technology transfer and enhanced productivity in emerging regions. Asia has been more successful than Latin America or Africa largely because Asian economies have better navigated structural change in expanding high-productivity, high-wage sectors. In the coming decades, high world demand for raw materials and commodities will provide extra financial resources to developing nations, which can potentially be used to support development through the provision of better educational opportunities and health care for their citizens. Hopefully emerging market governments will be up for the task, so that internal political conflicts are mitigated as these economies play to their strengths and increase exporting capabilities.

Further Reading

Acemoglu, D. (2008). *Introduction to modern economic growth.* Princeton, NJ: Princeton University Press.

Aghion, P., & Howitt, P. (2008). *The economics of growth.* Cambridge, MA: MIT Press.

Atkinson, R., & Ezell, S. (2012). *Innovation economics: The race for global advantage.* New Haven, CT: Yale University Press.

Barro, R., & Sala-i-Martin, X. (2003). *Economic growth.* Cambridge, MA: MIT Press.

De Soto, H. (2000). *The mystery of capital: Why capitalism triumphs in the West and fails everywhere else.* New York, NY: Basic Books.

Easterly, W. (2002). *The elusive quest for growth: Economists' adventures and misadventures in the tropics.* Cambridge, MA: MIT Press.

Galor, O. (2011). *Unified growth theory.* Princeton, NJ: Princeton University Press.

Goldin, C., & Katz, L. (2008). *The race between education and technology.* Cambridge, MA: Harvard University Press.

Gordon, R. (2016). *The rise and fall of American growth: The U.S. standard of living since the Civil War.* Princeton, NJ: Princeton University Press.

von Hayek, F. (1944). *The road to serfdom.* Chicago, IL: University of Chicago Press.

Helpman, E. (2010). *The mystery of economic growth.* Cambridge, MA: Harvard University Press.

Janeway, W. (2012). *Doing capitalism in the innovation economy: Markets, speculation and the state.* Cambridge, England: Cambridge University Press.

Jones, C. (2001). *Introduction to economic growth.* New York, NY: W. W. Norton and Company.

Leamer, E. (2010). *Macroeconomic patterns and stories.* New York, NY: Springer.

Lerner, J. (2012). *The architecture of innovation: The economics of creative organizations.* Boston, MA: Harvard Business Review Press.

North, D. (1982). *Structure and change in economic history.* New York, NY: W. W. Norton and Company.

Rodrik, D. (2008). *One economics, many recipes: Globalization, institutions, and economic growth*. Princeton, NJ: Princeton University Press.

Schumpeter, J. (1942). *Capitalism, socialism, and democracy*. New York, NY: Harper and Brothers.

Harvard Business School Case Studies

Cool, K., Seitz, M., Mestrits, J., Bajaria, S., & Yadati, U. *YouTube, Google, and the rise of internet video*, KEL403-PDF-ENG.

Cross, T. *Human capital strategy*, UV0648-PDF-ENG.

Edelman, B., & Eisenmann, T. R. *Google Inc.*, 910036-PDF-ENG.

Eisenmann, T. R., Bussgang, J. J., & Kiron, D. *Predictive biosciences*, 811015-PDF-ENG.

Hamermesh, R. G., Kiron, D., & Andrews, P. *Gene patents*, 811089-PDF-ENG.

Hardymon, G. F., & Nicholas, T. *Kleiner-Perkins and Genentech: When venture capital met science*, 813102-PDF-ENG.

Kumar, K., & Kumar, M. *Gold Peak Electronics: R&D globalization from East to West*, HKU857-PDF-ENG.

Lassiter, J. B., & Kiron, D. *Re-THINK-ing THINK: The electric car company*, 810105-PDF-ENG.

Lassiter, J. B., & Kiron, D. *Highland Capital Partners: Investing in cleantech*, 811009-PDF-ENG.

Lassiter, J. B., Nanda, R., Kiron, D., & Richardson, E. *1366 Technologies: Scaling the venture*, 811076-PDF-ENG.

Li, W. *Note on central planning*, UV0380-PDF-ENG.

Mayo, A. J., & Benson, M. *Bill Gates and Steve Jobs*, 407028-PDF-ENG.

Nguyen-Chyung, A., & Faulk, E. *Amazon in emerging markets*, W94C01-PDF-ENG. https://cb.hbsp.harvard.edu/cbmp/product/W94C01-PDF-ENG

Nicholas, T., & Chen, D. *Georges Doriot and American venture capital*, 812110-PDF-ENG.

Nohria, N., Mayo, A. J., & Gurtler, B. *Walt Disney and the 1941 animator's strike*, 406076-PDF-ENG.

Pill, H., & Mathis, D. *Bahtulism, collapse, resurrection? Financial crisis in Asia: 1997-1998*, 798089-PDF-ENG.

Pill, H., Tella, R. D., & Schlefer, J. *Financial crisis in Asia: 1997–1998*, 709004-PDF-ENG.

Rodriguez, P. *A note on long-run models of economic growth*, UV4282-PDF-ENG.

Scott, B. R., & Sunder, S. R. *Austin, Texas: Building a high-tech economy*, 799038-PDF-ENG.

Shih, W., Chai, S., Bliznashki, K., & Hyland, C. *Office of Technology Transfer—Shanghai Institutes for Biological Sciences*, 611057-PDF-ENG.

Shih, W., & Dai, N. H. *From imitation to innovation: Zongshen Industrial Group*, 610057-PDF-ENG.

Yang, W., & Kiron, D. *Cambridge NanoTech*, 610083-PDF-ENG.

CHAPTER 3

Theories of International Trade

Introduction

In the centuries following the voyages of Columbus and da Gama, European economic growth was concentrated within nations sitting just off the North Atlantic Ocean—namely, Portugal, Spain, the Netherlands, France, and Britain. This was no coincidence, as long-distance trade was vital to the prosperity of these states. The opening of Atlantic trade routes transferred economic power from the Mediterranean to Western Europe, and merchant classes became more influential. The development of advanced financial systems in the Netherlands and Britain sustained the commercial growth and relative dominance of the Dutch and British. The great powers could fund expeditions for raw materials, and domestic consumers grew to enjoy a variety of goods from around the globe. Before the 18th century, long-distance trade focused mainly on "noncompeting" goods (meaning products that must be imported because they are not produced domestically). This included Asian spices and textiles and South American gold and silver. As transportation costs declined and manufacturing efficiencies multiplied in the 19th century, long-distance trade grew at a far brisker pace, particularly in competing goods. As a consequence, the degree of diversification among internationally traded goods increased before redoubling during the 20th century.

This chapter presents essential economic theories of international trade, paying attention to the political factors underlying trade policies that governments actually choose in practice. As suggested above, countries trade with each other because economies specialize, consumers enjoy variety, and not all goods are produced (or are naturally available) in every region of the world. International trade barriers have declined since World

War II, in part due to a greater theoretical appreciation of the benefits of free trade, yet in the past decade, a backlash has also developed within many countries, including the United States and much of Europe. East Asian nations—most notably China—have implemented successful strategic trade policies protecting some domestic industries, although it isn't clear that every emerging nation would be able to do the same nearly so effectively. With the exception of comparative advantage, economic theories of international trade are controversial because no single model can successfully rationalize all data on actual trade flows. Measuring the precise welfare implications of alternative trade policies is even more difficult. Regardless, these canonical theories of trade are central to understanding why—and how—nations trade their goods in the modern globalized economy.

Absolute and Comparative Advantage

The earliest theory of international trade that modern economists freely reference is absolute advantage from the *Wealth of Nations*. Adam Smith argued that it was not possible for all nations to flourish by following mercantilist policies which favored exporting in exchange for bullion yet frowned upon importing, since one nation's exports were another nation's imports. Instead, he believed that an international division of labor was optimal, based on the productive advantages that each country possesses. If Switzerland can manufacture clocks with greater efficiency than France, and France can make cheese more efficiently than Switzerland, then Switzerland and France should specialize, and hence trade clocks for cheese. Each country's absolute advantage in production is determined by its cost structure; the country with the lowest costs and greatest efficiencies in making any good possesses an absolute advantage. Nevertheless, some countries—especially developing ones with little capital and technology—may have an absolute advantage in producing few, if any, goods.

The next major refinement of this theory came from David Ricardo, the great British political economist who developed the concept of comparative advantage in the early-19th century. Ricardo had a remarkable career, starting out as a stockbroker and achieving great wealth and success. He developed an interest in economics after reading Adam Smith's *Wealth of Nations*, though unlike today's academic economists, Ricardo did not write his first economics article until he was well into his 30s. Later he was elected into the British House of Commons. Developed in Ricardo's 1817 book *On the Principles of Political Economy and Taxation*, the theory of comparative advantage is based on a comparison of each nation's production possibilities and the opportunity costs they face. An economy has a comparative advantage if its opportunity cost of producing a good—in terms of other goods—is lower than elsewhere. Comparative advantage dictates that each economy should focus on producing those goods for which it faces the lowest opportunity cost of production.

While absolute advantage is intuitive and useful, comparative advantage provides insights in instances where absolute advantage does not. Consider two neighbors, Frederick and Joe. Talented Frederick is a successful plastic surgeon who also happens to be a fabulous carpenter—even better than Joe, who is a full-time professional carpenter. If Frederick has water damage in his home and needs a carpenter to fix it, absolute advantage would suggest that Frederick should do the work himself, because he is a faster and more competent carpenter than Joe. Comparative advantage, by contrast, takes into account Frederick's opportunity cost. He makes $1,000 per hour as a surgeon, so instead of taking off Wednesday to fix his house, he is better off calling Joe, who charges just $50 per hour. This superior decision comes from a comparison of Frederick's opportunity costs in deciding to spend Wednesday operating on patients or fixing his house.

Wine and Cloth

Ricardo's initial demonstration from Chapter 7 of his *Principles* involved wine and cloth production in England and Portugal. Based on Portugal's lower labor costs, he showed that the relative cost of manufacture was of primary importance. A concrete example may help to illustrate the gains from international specialization and trade. Suppose that in Portugal, it takes 1 hour of labor to produce a bottle of wine and 4 hours of labor to produce a unit of cloth. In England, the respective figures are 2 and 6, so that Portugal has an absolute advantage in producing *both* goods. The table below summarizes these production technologies, where costs are in hourly units of time.

Cost	Wine	Cloth
Portugal	1	4
England	2	6

Ricardo's theory of comparative advantage implies that the country with a smaller opportunity cost of producing a given good has the relative advantage and should therefore specialize in making that good. The logic is as follows. Consider the opportunity cost of making 1 unit of cloth in Portugal. It is 4 bottles of wine, meaning the Portuguese give up 4 bottles of wine for each unit of cloth they make. In England, this cost is just 3 bottles of wine. So, England should specialize in making cloth. Now consider the opportunity cost of making 1 bottle of wine in Portugal, which is a quarter unit of cloth. In England, the cost is a third of a unit, which is higher. According to Ricardo, Portugal ought to focus on producing wine.

It may be surprising that both countries can benefit from trade in spite of greater Portuguese efficiency in producing both goods (meaning Portugal has an absolute advantage). However, by extending the example above, we see that this is true. Suppose that, initially, there is no trade between Portugal and England. Portugal produces 100 units each of wine and cloth, at a cost of 500 hours of labor. Likewise, England produces 100 units each of wine and cloth, costing 800 hours of labor. Now, let's allow a tiny bit of trade and specialization: England shifts to more cloth production and Portugal shifts to more wine production. Let's say that England holds off on producing the last 3 bottles of wine it usually produces each year, at a cost saving of 6 hours of labor, and makes a unit of cloth instead. Likewise, Portugal decides not to make the hundredth unit of cloth it usually does, and instead produces 4 bottles of wine.

In this scenario, England can trade its extra unit of cloth for 3 bottles of wine from Portugal: England will be no worse off and Portugal will be better off by a bottle of wine. This slight, incremental amount of trade improves overall welfare, so we see that there are gains from trade. Now let's push this example a bit further. If England only makes cloth, it can make 800 / 6 = 133.3 units of cloth. Portugal can produce up to 500 bottles of wine, but assuming they don't want to overproduce (so that all

English and Portuguese citizens imbibe too much and can't work), let's assume they stop after 220 bottles of wine. With the remaining 280 hours of labor, the Portuguese can make 280 / 4 = 70 units of cloth. Adding up the total output of both economies, we have 133.3 + 70 = 203.3 units of cloth and 0 + 220 = 220 bottles of wine. Before opening trade, the total autarkic output was 200 units of cloth and wine each, so it turns out that there are significant gains from specialization.

England ought to be able to trade its excess cloth for wine. Say it wants to sell 32 units of cloth, leaving it with 101.3. (In Portugal, these 32 units would cost 32 × 4 = 128 labor hours to make.) In return, England wants 110 bottles of wine, which would cost the Portuguese 110 labor hours. Supposing (to simplify) that there is a common currency called the "yurow," such that 1 labor hour is equal to 1 yurow, Portugal would agree to the trade with England. Portugal now has 110 bottles of wine and 102.3 units of cloth. England has 110 bottles of wine and 101.3 units of cloth. Both countries are better off with specialization and trade. Even though Portugal has the absolute advantage in production of both goods, by specializing according to the theory of comparative advantage and allowing trade, both countries are wealthier.

Gains from Trade

True but not obvious, comparative advantage has withstood the test of time among economists. In fact, it is the basis for much of modern trade theory. It implies that, as a rule, increased trade between nations or regions will lead to greater total output and aggregate gains among all parties. As more areas become part of a trade network, there will be more specialization and efficiency gains; perhaps Ricardo was inspired by Adam Smith's praises of a finely tuned division of labor in the *Wealth of Nations*. Comparative advantage can be applied to individuals, firms, or cities: each unit's comparative advantage is their *competitive* advantage. In this light, comparative advantage implies that each person should follow the career path or line of work which they are best at, to maximize their production and well-being, however measured. Within an organization, each member ought to work according to his or her strengths; within each industry, every company has its own comparative advantage giving it a relative advantage. Even if there is a leading company that holds absolute advantages across every margin, other firms can compete by charging lower prices or differentiating their product or service.

Now think of the bigger picture. In the *Wealth of Nations*, Adam Smith advocated the theory of absolute advantage, suggesting that nations should focus on producing goods they can make at lower cost than other countries can. It's a valid point, but it doesn't explain why countries produce goods that other countries are more efficient at making. In other words, in the real world, production is more diversified across the world than absolute advantage implies. For instance, wine and cloth are made in many countries of varying efficiency today; in the example above, England produces cloth even though it's always cheaper to make it in Portugal. The answer to this puzzle is that the other country, Portugal, has an even greater advantage in producing another good, wine. Absolute advantage cannot explain such patterns, but comparative advantage can. Therefore, to figure out the optimal pattern of production for an individual or a country, one must focus on relative—not absolute—advantages, specifically opportunity costs.

The process of economic development can be understood in terms of shifting comparative advantages. In emerging economies, relative advantages are commonly related to lower labor costs and an abundance of raw materials. As these economies grow and mature, they make investments in capital and people, allowing them to incorporate more complex production processes that involve greater physical and human capital. Subsequently, labor productivity and wages increase. Put another way, the opportunity cost to producing and exporting low value-added goods increases over time as the economy transitions to higher value-added production. The economy's relative advantage will shift to middle or high value-added processes within global supply chains. Wealthy industrialized nations compete for the lead in complex industries with advanced technologies. For them, relative advantages are often driven by technological edges, superior design, or greater industry-specific experience. And with globalized production, a good may be successful due to multiple sources of comparative advantage. For instance, Apple has succeeded in combining outstanding product development in the San Francisco Bay Area with low production costs abroad.

Impediments to trade, such as transportation costs, tariffs, or quotas, can hinder the realization of gains due to trade. In the Ricardian example above, if transportation or tariff costs are sufficiently high, England and Portugal would not specialize, since trading their good of relative advantage is not economical. Although tariffs do not always exist, transportation costs surely do, so there is almost always some real world barrier to trade. Today, the cost of shipping imported goods is about three times higher than tariff duties (in the aggregate). Transportation costs are most relevant to products manufactured in multiple countries under "vertical specialization," which occurs when a country utilizes imported inputs or intermediate parts to produce a good that is later exported. Most trade between bordering countries takes place over land, while most trade between countries without a common border occurs via ocean transport. Air transport—especially for long-distance trade in lightweight goods—is increasingly common due to superior speed coupled with large cost declines in recent decades. Lower transportation costs undoubtedly facilitate greater trade, and global productivity growth and technological progress support greater specialization, and hence, larger international trade volumes.

Evidence on Comparative Advantage

The traditional Ricardian model is based on labor productivity differences between nations, and it takes as given the resources used in production. For empirical researchers, its principal prediction is that nations will produce goods in which their relative productivity advantage is the greatest, and as a consequence, they will export a greater share of goods from relatively more productive domestic industries. By and large, the evidence is favorable to the comparative advantage model. For instance, an early study from the 1960s by economist Bela Balassa compared the United States to Britain after World War II. It found that America had an absolute advantage in every industry, yet Britain exported just as much as the Americans did. This was because Britain exported goods from industries where it had a comparative—not absolute—productivity advantage.

Recent research shows that comparative advantage explains the general pattern of trade flows from poor to wealthy nations: poor nations specialize in lower value-added products (like textiles) since their productivity is about half as high in these industries as compared to advanced nations, whereas in technology-intensive industries, their productivity may be only a tenth (or less) as great as in more advanced nations. Some industries in certain countries (such as the Japanese automobile industry) are extremely productive, and as a consequence of this relative advantage, they generate large export flows. Still, the Ricardian model predicts a very high degree of specialization that is not observed in the real world. Some extensions, and other models of trade discussed below, help to explain why.

Globalization Extensions

The Ricardian model focuses on goods produced with one input, labor. Adding capital—an internationally mobile factor of production—may weaken the gains from international specialization. Consider the following reasoning. If capital investment is mobile, and technologies for the production of a good (like blueprints for a certain factory) can be utilized in any region, then capital may flow to low labor cost regions. Over time, these poorer economies will develop, and their wages and labor costs will increase, as according to the neoclassical growth model. Production costs for any given good will tend to equalize in the long run. In the example above, Portugal is less developed than England (at the time of Ricardo's writing) and has lower labor costs, which may make it an attractive area for capital investment. Over time, its absolute advantage over England may disappear. More generally, in the presence of capital mobility, absolute advantages may erode, and comparative advantages may become less pronounced as well.

Human capital is another factor that is not included in the basic Ricardian model. Differences in human capital levels are a critical aspect explaining why certain countries possess a comparative advantage in producing a product. Research and development and technology-intensive manufacturing are examples of activities where wealthier countries with more human capital possess a comparative advantage. Yet poorer economies with large agricultural and low-tech manufacturing sectors can invest in the human capital of their workers to lessen their disadvantage over time. Social capital and culture are important as well. For instance, the sustained dominance of the United States in the development of new internet technologies may be in large part due to its: (1) ingrained national culture that prizes entrepreneurial risk-taking, and (2) vibrant marketplace in new "pop culture" products reflecting the ever-changing tastes of American consumers (which are often followed abroad).

Factor Proportions Model

The canonical 20th century theory of international trade is called the "factor proportions" model. The name is based on the idea of fixed factor proportions that go into making goods. The model assumes that each economy has a given endowment of capital, labor, technology, and other resources. It emphasizes the relative abundance of production inputs and natural resources across nations. It was developed by Eli Heckscher and Bertil Ohlin in the 1920s, and for this reason, it is also referred to as the "Heckscher-Ohlin" model of trade. Heckscher was 20 years Ohlin's senior and had taught Ohlin economics at the Stockholm School of Economics. Both Swedes, they were intrigued by late-19th century globalization trends and intimately familiar with Sweden's experience as a small open economy. (Ohlin later won a Nobel Prize for this work, which Heckscher would have also shared but was unable to, as he had passed away earlier and the Nobel Prize is not awarded posthumously.) In essence, the factor proportions model is about comparative advantages in endowments and resources. Whenever a nation possesses a large quantity of some material or production factor, it will intensively utilize it, rent it out, or sell it. It predicts that the direction of trade between nations will be determined by differences in supply-side factor abundance.

The basic model presumes that there are two countries, two goods produced, and two factors of production: capital and labor. The two countries have the same tastes but differ in their relative supply of capital and labor. One good requires relatively more capital to produce, while the other requires more labor. Capital and labor are immobile, which means they cannot move from one country to the other if there are differences in interest rates or wages. There is free trade with no cost to the transportation of goods. Both countries have access to the same technology and utilize the same production function, which is constant returns to scale and has diminishing marginal returns for each factor. Relaxing these assumptions leads to some differences in the model's predictions, but this simplified version is a good start for analysis.

The model's main result is that each country will produce the good that makes greater use of the factor of production that it has in abundance. It is a relative comparison, so by definition, one nation has relatively more capital, and the other has relatively more labor. The "capital-abundant" country will export the capital-intensive good to the "labor-abundant" country, and the labor-abundant country will export the labor-intensive good to the capital-abundant country. In terms of applying this model to the real world, the capital-abundant country generally possesses the wealthier, more developed economy (think of the United States) and the labor-abundant country features a poorer economy with less capital (think of Mexico or India). In this model, a good is more profitable to produce if its production costs are relatively low, and production costs depend on the abundance of production factors. A good that requires much capital will be cheaper if manufactured in a capital-abundant economy. This insight drives specialization across countries. And so, the greater the disparity in the relative abundance of the factors of production, the more trade there will be between nations.

As opposed to the basic Ricardian model, where labor is the only factor of production, factor proportions theory explicitly considers the level of capital across countries, just like the neoclassical growth model. In factor proportions theory, the basic model assumes economies all have the same technology (although it can be extended to allow for technological leaders). For example, the wealthier economy with more capital will typically have better technology, so its advantage in producing capital-intensive goods is only strengthened when we allow for differential production functions. In both the Ricardian and factor proportions models, the relative opportunity cost of producing one good versus another leads countries to specialize. Moreover, in the Ricardian model there tends to be full specialization, but not in the factor proportions model. That is because the factor proportions model has diminishing marginal returns, which means that a country's relative advantage in producing one good will decline as it produces more. This ultimately results in a more balanced (and realistic) production mix between countries.

In the neoclassical growth model, poorer countries eventually converge to wealthier countries as they accumulate more capital per worker over time. Although the basic factor proportions model is static, it can be extended to allow for shifts in capital and labor over time. For example, if immigration between countries opens up, workers will move from the low-wage country with abundant labor to the capital-abundant country that is more productive and has higher wages. (In the 19th century, workers in search of opportunity moved to land-abundant regions that were usually capital- and labor-poor.) Likewise, if international capital markets open up, capital will flow to the labor-abundant country where it is cheaper to hire workers to operate capital equipment. Over time, these forces will lead to convergence across countries in their relative abundance of capital versus labor as well as their production mix. Still, capital is rarely perfectly mobile in the real world, and immigration comes with considerable costs. While the capital-labor mix across countries may equalize, countries will still specialize in producing certain products due to their natural resource endowments or history.

Distributional Issues

Similar to the Ricardian model, there are gains to trade in the factor proportions model stemming from specialization and enhanced productive efficiencies, so trade makes countries better off. However, this does not mean that every group will benefit from trade, as there are important distributional consequences to consider. It can be shown with some mathematics that in the basic factor proportions model, when a country is opened up to trade, owners of the abundant factor will be made better off, and owners of the scarce factor will be made worse off. (Once again, whether a factor is abundant or scarce depends on its relative abundance or scarcity as compared to the rest of the world taken as a whole.) Production in the international economy will shift to areas where it is cheapest, which will be the country with a relatively abundant supply of a given factor, according to the factor proportions model. For instance, in a capital-abundant nation, capital owners will thrive and the production of capital-intensive goods will boom. With international trade, capital-intensive goods will be increasingly made in capital-abundant countries, and labor-intensive goods will be increasingly made in labor-abundant countries. As a corollary, companies that use the abundant factor intensively will be better off, and companies that use the scarce factor intensively will be worse off. Trade causes greater specialization and enhances relative advantages.

The unequal effects that opening trade has on the return to various factors of production is often referred to as the "Stolper-Samuelson" theorem, named for the two economists who developed it in 1941, Wolfgang Stolper and Paul Samuelson, the latter a Nobel Prize winner. (Throughout the rest of this book, the Stolper-Samuelson theorem is understood to be synonymous with the factor proportions model.) Consider the effects of opening trade in the capital-abundant country. Its economy will shift toward producing more capital-intensive goods; it used to just produce for domestic consumers but now it makes exports for foreign consumers. Overall, this will increase demand for domestic capital, which used to be abundant and quite cheap, bidding up its price, the local interest rate. Therefore, capital owners, and businesses that use capital intensively, will gain. On the other hand, labor will lose, as production of the labor-intensive good shifts abroad. In theory, each group can be made better off with the appropriate government policies. Here it would mean transfers from capital owners to workers after trade is opened. Yet it is far from clear that such policies are enacted in practice as countries open themselves up to trade and globalization. Just as trade leads to winners and losers within an economy, it can cause domestic political cleavages that are difficult to overcome.

A classic example is what happens when a capital-poor developing country begins trading with a capital-rich advanced country. According to the factor proportions model, opening trade in the poor economy will lead to an expansion in its sector producing labor-intensive goods (such as textiles), implying an increase in labor demand and higher wages. All else equal, workers in the poor economy will be better off due to enhanced opportunities. If this country has a large agricultural sector, workers in it may leave and move to urban areas to find factory work. In the wealthy country, the opposite is true. Workers there will see a reduction in demand for their services, and according to the theorem, their wages will go down, leaving them worse off. Capital-intensive industries will expand and export some of their goods to the poor country, so owners of capital will be better off. Governments can arrange policies to lessen the distributional impact—such as transferring funds from capital holders to workers in the wealthy country via tax policy—but such responses do not always take place in fact. Still, there may be a boom in cheap consumer goods—generally produced in emerging economies—on the world market, which raises living standards everywhere and benefits workers in the wealthy country.

The factor proportions model also yields a key reason why smaller or less developed countries may benefit the most from opening their economy to free trade. Generally speaking, a larger and better-developed economy will have relative factor endowments that are closer to overall world relative endowments. Bigger economies likely have a more diversified set of industries. Without trade, a smaller, underdeveloped country may not have access to many goods, and even if it has access, goods may not be available at competitive prices. Think of the benefits which consumers in a small economy such as Singapore gain from imports. And as mentioned above, less developed economies typically have a relative abundance of labor, so allowing trade can help workers by strengthening labor demand and increasing wages.

Technology and Human Capital

Adding technology and human capital to the basic factor proportions model has important implications for modern trade. In such a model, each country's production in a given sector depends on the level of technology it possesses and the human capital of its work force. As in the neoclassical growth model, this can be modeled by adding human capital and technology factors—H and A, respectively—to the production function, which generates the equation $Y(K,L,H,A)$, where K is capital and L is labor. Greater human capital and better technology generate more productive possibilities for a given amount of physical capital and labor. In a sector requiring skilled labor and technology, new research and more education within a country lead to greater productive efficiencies, so that the domestic industry produces more at a lower cost. The economy will become more specialized in skilled labor- and technology-intensive products, which will be increasingly reflected in their exports. Foreign competitors within the same industry will fret, and to keep their long-run costs low, they may be forced to upgrade technology and labor skill. In this way, international trade can cause productivity growth in the global traded manufacturing sector to increase, benefitting consumers worldwide. In service sectors, which are usually local and based primarily on labor inputs, it is less realistic to expect competitive pressures from international trade to result in productivity gains.

Changes in technology will favor owners of physical capital depending on whether capital is a complement or substitute to technology. Typically, technology improvements complement physical capital. If so, demand for capital will pick up, and output and trade in sectors that utilize it intensively will expand, favoring capital owners. Technology can complement or substitute for labor, depending on the industry and type of labor. Many new technologies, such as personal computers, generally complement labor, especially skilled or educated labor, making workers more productive, so that the relative demand for labor increases and workers gain. However, computers and automation equipment can also substitute for some types of labor, particularly unskilled workers who may be made temporarily redundant. The practice of "offshoring"—where some of a company's business processes and jobs are moved outside the country—is made more feasible through technology. It can harm domestic workers while benefitting foreign workers who are utilized instead.

Consider a technology-intensive manufacturing industry like aircraft or scientific instrument production, where technology is complementary to physical capital. Better technology will enhance productivity, so that the sector expands. This benefits capital owners in the industry. If the technology is also complementary to labor so that it enhances labor productivity, workers in the industry may also gain. On the other hand, labor may be harmed when new technology substitutes for human labor, such as within modern manufacturing industries that prize automation. A classic example comes from the early-19th century textile industry in Britain. With the introduction of automated loom technology, skilled weavers started to lose their livelihoods to unskilled operators who were poorly paid. Some of these skilled artisans reacted by smashing machinery and threatening industrialists. They came to be known as "Luddites," after a youth named Ned Ludd who had purportedly destroyed textile machines to protest laborsaving technology.

Greater human capital within a workforce has similar effects. Improving the educational system will increase the supply of skilled workers. Sectors that utilize them—such as human capital-intensive industries—will expand and export more. Although factor proportions reasoning suggests that sectors not relying on human capital may contract, harming unskilled workers, economic research shows that skilled workers generate local spillovers by creating innovations, starting companies, and utilizing services provided by less skilled workers (such as food preparation), so that, on net, greater human capital can bring significant benefits even to unskilled workers. In addition, human capital is usually complementary to physical capital—such as in complex equipment manufacturing industries—so a skilled workforce typically benefits capital owners, too. By and large, with more human capital, the economy restructures so that human capital-intensive sectors expand, and the economy's relative advantage is in producing goods that are of increasingly higher quality or complexity. This has been a pathway to development and wealth for many countries.

The impact of technological change and greater human capital is often complex, and within any industry, its effects may be challenging to disentangle without a comprehensive analysis. In Silicon Valley, workers with high levels of human capital congregate and produce new technologies, attracting hefty capital investment flows to implement their ideas. Sometimes these technologies end up substituting for certain types of labor, usually not highly skilled (like travel agents, who have been largely replaced by the internet). Indeed, in recent years, technological change has generally favored skilled labor in the United States. Evidence shows that the price of educated labor has increased as its utilization has picked up. Based on a traditional supply and demand framework, this suggests that demand growth has outpaced supply growth. But not all sectoral demand shifts have favored educated workers. During the height of the recent housing bubble, 40% of American investment was in property, which benefitted construction workers (as well as capital owners) in that sector.

Finally, the future direction of technology's impact on the factors of production is difficult to predict. The well-known "Habakkuk hypothesis" (developed by the mid-20th century British economic historian John Habakkuk) claims that in the 19th century, technological progress was faster in the United States than in England because American labor was scarce. This gave American industrialists an incentive to invent laborsaving technologies, and more generally, labor scarcity led to enhanced innovation and increased mechanization in America. Government regulations can conceivably have similar effects. The "Porter hypothesis" (formulated by contemporary business economist Michael Porter) proposes that modern environmental regulations have sometimes triggered the discovery and implementation of cleaner technologies. While recent economic research has focused on technological change favoring skilled workers in advanced economies, it is possible that future technologies—such as intensive online educational programs, which are often inexpensive or even free—will have very different impacts, potentially favoring less skilled workers. Only time will tell.

Leontief Paradox

An early empirical criticism of the factor proportions model—commonly called the "Leontief paradox"—came from Wassily Leontief, a Nobel Prize-winning economist who pioneered input-output tables. In his work during the 1950s, Leontief examined all products the United States was importing and exporting, based on 1947 input-output tables. Leontief noticed that American exports were relatively labor-intensive compared to the goods it imported. (Specifically, he found that in the production of American exports, $14,000 of capital was utilized per man-year of labor, while the same figure was $18,000 of capital per man-year of labor among imports.) Given that the United States was the most capital-abundant economy at the time, this result was completely at odds with the most fundamental prediction of the factor proportions model: countries with abundant capital will export capital-intensive goods and import labor-intensive goods. Later analyses through the proceeding decades have affirmed this finding, to varying degrees, in American trade data.

Economists have discovered that when the human capital of a workforce is included with physical capital in the neoclassical growth model, the measured rate of convergence matches the real world data better. Likewise, the best apparent resolution to the Leontief paradox is to include human capital with physical capital in the factor proportions model. American

exports are particularly intensive in skilled labor, meaning they are produced with large amounts of human capital (which is relatively abundant
in the United States) and technology. Overall, American exporting industries utilize a high ratio of skilled labor to other types of labor. Goods that
the United States imports, like textiles, employ an abundance of unskilled
labor. Thus, a factor proportions model allowing for human capital and
technology differences across countries implies that a country with an
abundance of skilled labor and technology will export goods that take
advantage of their resources, even if, technically speaking, the amount of
physical capital employed is not any greater than among countries without
these endowments.

Empirical testing of the factor proportions model has been ongoing for
over half a century. Although controversial, the literature has found that as
the primary assumptions of the model are appropriately relaxed, its conclusions are better supported by the data on international trade flows.
Remember that the basic factor proportions model assumes that all countries have the same technology and production function, produce the same
goods, and have no costs to trade such as transportation expenses. Ideally,
differences in production technologies—as well as differences in output
quality—can be measured. For example, the world market for cars includes
many different qualities and types. In addition, transportation costs (which
can be precisely measured) are usually substantial and increase with trading
distance. When controls for these differences between countries are
included in empirical analyses, the factor proportions model seems to do
increasingly well (although the literature is certainly not settled).

Gravity Model

Consider the United States. Its top trading partners—Canada, China,
Mexico, Japan, and Germany—are very large economies with robust
exporting sectors, and Canada and Mexico are even right next door. Incor-
porating these two qualities—size and distance—into a simple model of
trade yields the "gravity model" of international trade. Recall Newton's law
of universal gravitation from physics: any two objects attract each other
with a force that is proportional to the product of their mass, and inversely
proportional to the square of their distance. The gravity model of trade is

based on an analogous equation. It states that the amount of trade (meaning imports plus exports) between any two countries is proportional to the product of their economic output, and inversely proportional to their distance from each other. The first economist to use this model was Jan Tinbergen, who was the winner of the first Nobel Prize for economics in 1969. Most economists agree that the gravity model has been the most successful modern empirical model of international trade since it fits the data on international trade flows so well.

The gravity model is elegant and based on solid intuition. Larger economies consume more, so they are likely to import more goods. They also produce more, so their output is likely to be diverse and take advantage of economies of scale. These factors lead to a greater volume of exports. And due to transportation costs and other distance-based barriers, the closer two economies are, the more trade they are likely to engage in. There are additional factors that can be included in the gravity model, such as language, culture, borders, and trade agreements. Countries sharing a common language are more likely to conduct business with each other, and effective trade agreements facilitate trade. Other research has shown that trade among rich countries is more often based on differentiated products, as opposed to differences in factor abundance, which better characterizes exports from poor countries. Finally, economists have demonstrated that a number of models of trade are consistent with the gravity model; in other words, there are many theoretical explanations of international trade that generate empirical trade flow patterns captured by the gravity model. Some of these theories that go beyond the traditional concepts underlying trade are discussed below.

Increasing Returns and Trade

The Ricardian and factor proportions models of international trade assume constant returns to scale. They predict that countries will export those goods that they specialize in producing. In these models, countries trade with each other because they are different, and industries can shrink or grow seamlessly. The constant returns to scale assumption (which means that a doubling of inputs results in a doubling of output) is realistic in many service industries where output strongly depends on the amount of labor (and less on capital). Yet in the real world, many countries, especially wealthy ones, trade in similar goods. For example, Japan, Germany, and the United States produce and export cars. They also import foreign cars. Comparative advantage models may not be the best explanation for this type of "intraindustry" trade. Instead, economists have found that increasing returns models of production, along with variety-preferring consumers, are a more realistic way to understand international trade in automobiles.

According to the technical definition of increasing returns to scale, doubling inputs (like labor and capital) leads to more than a doubling of output. It implies that incremental costs per unit produced are decreasing in output, so that production is more efficient if it takes place on a larger scale. Many manufacturing industries exhibit increasing returns to scale: after a major capital outlay for a production facility, they can produce large quantities of goods with decreasing labor costs per unit. This contrasts with constant returns to scale production, where labor costs are not decreasing and there may be many similar firms competing against each other, which drives down prices toward production cost. Increasing returns typically leads to imperfect competition, where fewer firms compete and each has some pricing power to maintain their margins. In these industries, technology and research and development are often important to the production process. Consider an extreme example: the market for large commercial aircrafts. It is a duopoly consisting of Boeing and Airbus, which are located in the United States and Europe, respectively. In this industry, the idea of many small firms producing large commercial jets is not realistic due to the immense economies of scale.

On the production side of increasing returns to scale industries, size leads to efficiencies, and firms improve as they learn over time. Sometimes the company that is first to become established is able to capture a large market share, a phenomenon called the "first mover advantage." In the 19th century, American companies such as Proctor and Gamble, Campbell Soup, and Quaker Oats developed scale economies in production and distribution. This allowed them to capture large market shares which they have retained to this day. Then again, a lead can erode over time, as competitors innovate and leaders struggle to manage their growth or become complacent. This has happened many times within the computer and internet industries over the past several decades. Google didn't invent internet search engines, but it has managed to dominate this market space for the past decade. On the demand-side, as long as consumers prefer variety, there may be room for many firms in an international industry (assuming scale effects aren't too strong, as in the large commercial jet sector). Companies can specialize in specific market segments, and international trade will benefit consumers around the world, due to the high degree of variety and increased competition that it facilitates.

External Increasing Returns and Geography

By definition, "external" increasing returns to scale means that a firm's average costs fall with industry—not firm—output. External increasing returns are generally a local phenomenon: the larger the local industry is, the lower the costs of firms operating within it. External increasing returns within an industry may arise from the need for specialized capital inputs (such as capital instruments used in manufacturing) or labor with niche skills or experience (such as software engineers); a deeper local supply of these specialized inputs may drive down their cost. The presence of knowledge spillovers—where ideas and information are transferred between firms and workers—can also lead to external increasing returns. For instance, a promising new idea from a software engineer may spread to other local companies, leading to a wave of innovation.

Given its spatial dimension, the notion of external increasing returns is important to understanding economic geography, particularly industrial clustering. Consider Silicon Valley, Hollywood, and Wall Street, each the center of an American industry that is highly clustered geographically. They require specialized equipment and workers, and there is no doubt that knowledge spillovers occur all the time within these three areas. In terms of international trade and competition, while every country wishes it had a Silicon Valley, there may only be room for a few—including Bangalore, known as the "Silicon Valley of India"—due to strong economies of scale. Industries with increasing returns to scale may also exhibit "quality ladders," where advanced economies innovate and make high-quality varieties of a good and developing countries produce lower quality variants. This, of course, is a type of specialization. The theory is that technological progress is disproportionately generated by firms in the advanced country. Lower productivity countries may develop more primitive production technologies on their own or copy outdated ones from elsewhere.

Infant Industry Protection

Since at least the days of mercantilism, economists have argued that certain "infant industries" need protection from foreign competition, at least temporarily, in order to launch and become established. Most commonly, these are manufacturing industries exhibiting economies of scale. Government support may come from monopoly grants, protective tariffs against imports, or cheap loans. The notion is that without such support, a country's foray into a new industry will fail either due to powerful foreign import competition or potential pitfalls in learning unfamiliar production processes on the fly. Although Adam Smith was dismissive of this argument, Alexander Hamilton, the first United States Secretary of the Treasury, strongly supported it. In 1791, Hamilton submitted to Congress his *Report on Manufactures*, arguing that the United States government must prop up its burgeoning manufacturing sector with subsidies and moderate tariffs. These policies were adopted despite opposition from Thomas Jefferson and the agrarian interests of the South. The United States kept rather high tariffs throughout most of the 19th century, particularly on finished manufactured goods. Protective strategies were likely a factor behind the emergence of the United States as an industrial powerhouse. The infant industry argument has waned in popularity among economists over the past several decades, yet many (if not most) developing countries craft protectionist policies based upon its logic.

A number of criticisms have been leveled against infant industry protectionism. Subsidizing or protecting certain industries and firms can lead to bribery and corruption, particularly in countries that already suffer from widespread graft. In the case of "import-substituting" industrialization, governments encourage the domestic production of goods that had previously been imported. Even if successful in the long run, these policies lead to higher prices for domestic consumers. The historical experience of some countries (such as India) that have protected infant industries reveals it is more likely to be successful for light manufacturing (like textiles) instead of heavy manufactures (like airplanes), partly because poor countries lack many necessities for complex production, including infrastructure, skilled labor (such as engineers and entrepreneurs), managerial capital, and cheap financing. It can also be difficult for governments to identify the industries which could be successful if shepherded along in the near term. For example, in the 1970s South Korea favored chemical, steel, shipbuilding, and automobile industries, yet after setbacks in the late 1980s and early 1990s, it shifted focus to high-tech industries. On the whole, the experience of the East Asian Tigers demonstrated that emerging economies can be successful under either finely tuned state direction (as in Singapore) or minimal government influence (as shown by Hong Kong's commercial success).

Most analysts agree that China's infant industry protection policies have been highly effective. China was able to get its domestic automobile industry off the ground in the 1980s by allowing joint ventures between experienced foreign companies and local Chinese partners. For instance, Volkswagen's joint venture within China was given a near monopoly on taxi sales for almost 20 years. The German company used to send obsolete factory production equipment to China to manufacture outdated models it couldn't sell elsewhere. The Chinese automobile industry—which produced about 5,000 cars in 1985—is currently the largest in the world. China has set ambitious goals for utilizing renewable energy resources, including the development of a large-scale solar energy sector which has received access to tens of billions of dollars in subsidized credit from the China Development Bank. Observing the increasing returns to solar panel equipment production, the Chinese government surmised that it is best to take the technological lead before other countries do.

Infant industry considerations have surely influenced China's tariff policies. Since China began its bid for GATT membership in 1986, its average tariff rate has steadily declined, from 40% in 1986 to 36% in 1993 to 10% in 2005, reflecting the greater maturity of many developing industries which no longer need help. In 1997, for example, China reduced tariffs to 25% and 35% on refrigerators and televisions (both mature industries), respectively, while holding automobile tariffs to 100% due to the industry's infant status at the time. China was accepted into the WTO in December 2001, and from 2000 to 2010, average tariffs dropped from about 17% to under 10%, as the Chinese economy further integrated into the international trade system.

Basic Instruments of Trade Policy

A tariff is a tax levied on imports. Tariffs effectively increase the cost of shipping goods to a foreign country. There are two types: "specific" tariffs level a fixed tax on imports (such as $100 per automobile) while "ad valorem" tariffs charge a percentage of the good's value (such as 10% on televisions). Tariffs drive a wedge between prices in the importing and exporting countries. In the importing country, they raise consumer prices. Domestic producers of the good are better off as they face less competition (and are thus protected). As opposed to other instruments of trade policy, tariffs raise revenue for the government levying them. In the United States, tariffs were a very important source of government revenue until the early-20th century. Compared to trade policies of the 18th and 19th centuries, modern governments are more likely to utilize nontariff instruments such as import quotas, which limit the quantity of imports of a certain good, or voluntary export restraints, which limit the amount of exports coming from a country (and are usually requested by the importing country). By restricting supply, import quotas raise the price that domestic consumers pay for the imported good. Export restraints are often the result of trade policy bargaining; in the importing country, they protect producers and harm consumers.

Export subsidies are government payments to exporting firms. Around the world, they are most commonly given to agricultural industries. Export subsidies benefit producers in the exporting country and consumers in the importing country, but they harm producers in the importing country. Economists typically view them as reducing overall welfare, meaning the total costs outweigh the benefits. While export subsidies can conceivably help a country launch an industry with substantial increasing returns (such as commercial aircraft production) so that the long-run benefits potentially outweigh the costs, most analysts consider export subsidies to be primarily driven by domestic special interests, specifically, producers receiving the subsidy. One of the largest (and most criticized) subsidy regimes today is the "Common Agricultural Policy" (CAP) maintained by the "European

Union" (EU). Consuming over a third of the European Union's entire budget, CAP distorts many global markets in food and produce. For instance, European sugar producers are subsidized, a practice that lowers the world price of sugar. In turn, low-cost sugar producers in developing countries like Ethiopia and Mozambique are harmed. In the United States, textile companies have long complained about competitors in China and India receiving export subsidies or other preferential treatment from their governments. Under WTO rules, export subsidies have been increasingly restricted, though there are significant exemptions for some developing economies (in particular, the least developed countries which are disproportionately located in Africa).

Trade-Offs in International Trade Policy

Economists generally favor free trade because allowing each country to follow its comparative advantages without tariff or protectionist distortions is more likely to yield efficient sectoral development and international competition, which drives global productivity growth and lowers prices, benefitting consumers in every country. Several important arguments for protectionism were outlined above; these considerations are usually more important for developing nations trying to nurture new industries. Still, even the United States, a nation that largely favors free trade, sometimes pushes for protectionism. In one famous example from the early 1980s, American automobile makers were struggling to compete against Japanese competitors who were able to squeeze efficiencies out of their advanced production systems. With a growing market share in the United States, Japan worried that the United States might provoke a trade war that would potentially hurt both nations, so the Japanese assented to an export quota on its automobiles. The restricted supply led to higher auto prices in America, harming American consumers who had to pay more for cars. American car companies were happy to have less competition, and the agreement bought them some time to catch up to their foreign competitors.

When a country pushes for a protectionist trade policy, it is commonly aimed to support the incomes of a specific group. Centuries ago, mercantilists argued for protection that favored certain commercial interests, positing that such policies were best for the country. Since then, the impetus has changed little. Interest groups traditionally consist of an industry at large, or workers or capital owners within a sector. Theoretical economic models show that while trade policies such as tariffs benefit specific interest groups, the costs to consumers are usually greater. In the automobile example, American car company workers and shareholders were helped by the Japanese export quota, but tens of millions of American consumers were harmed. In another example, sugar imports are restricted in the United States, which forces prices higher than they would be under free trade. Some may believe that these policies could never survive the American democratic process because consumers are able to vote out of office the politicians who support such protectionist measures. In truth, most Americans are unaware of the sugar support program that costs the average American an estimated $10 per year. Undeniably, it is difficult for consumers to know how specific trade policies affect the price they pay for a good; voters normally don't have the time (or incentive) to research these issues in any depth.

An important field in economics called "public choice" analyzes the political economy of these policies. A major insight is that there is a fundamental asymmetry between consumers and protected industries—namely, consumers are a large and diffuse interest that is often uninformed, while protected industries are a concentrated interest that is very well informed. Any single consumer faces a large cost to repealing a protectionist policy that costs him only $10 per year. Since the gains to protesting protectionism are so disparate, organizing consumer opposition is difficult to accomplish in practice. On the other hand, an interest group (such as Florida sugar growers) is relatively small, and by organizing, lobbying, and contributing to political campaigns, they may reap millions or billions of dollars in benefits from a certain policy. Therefore, interest groups are better able to overcome the problem of "collective action" to maintain protectionist policies. Critics point out that while politicians compete for office by offering attractive policies to voters, they also require money to market and advertise their campaign. In effect, to generate money for campaign television commercials, they may be willing to trade off some amount of voter welfare for the welfare of special interests. And as money becomes increasingly important to winning political campaigns, more voter welfare may be sacrificed in exchange for special interest welfare.

Concentrated industry interests disproportionately influence domestic trade policies, yet on the international stage, foreign exporters can serve as a powerful counterweight during trade negotiations. Consider two countries that are bargaining for a new bilateral trade agreement. Within each country, industries that are currently protected—through import tariffs, for example—will lobby to keep the status quo. But their foreign competitors now facing these tariffs may mobilize to repeal them. Since most nations recognize that free trade is usually beneficial to consumers—who represent the largest imaginable interest group—trade negotiations can be successful in reducing protectionism on both sides. In practice, lowering a tariff benefits exporters from numerous countries. For instance, if Brazil lowers the tariffs it charges on personal computers, China, Taiwan, Japan, South Korea, and Singapore would all benefit. This implies that it may be efficient to negotiate trade agreements among many countries at the same time.

Such "multilateral" trade negotiations under the GATT and the WTO have been ongoing since World War II. Due to the interwar protectionism retrenchment, tariffs were fairly high at first, but then during the early decades of the GATT, there was a stiff reduction in tariffs and other barriers. These reductions continued, and under the WTO today, trade barriers are generally low (especially in manufacturing as compared to agriculture). Negotiating marginal reductions, often in industries that have been protected for decades, is challenging. This difficulty has been illustrated by the current Doha Round, which began in 2001 and has proceeded intermittently for more than a decade. Its ostensible aim has been to reduce agricultural protectionism, with an emphasis on fostering the development of emerging economies.

Conclusion

Absolute advantage, comparative advantage, and the factor proportions model are key conceptual building blocks to understanding trade flows in a globalized world. A fundamental insight to the factor proportions model is that traded goods can be viewed as bundles of the supply-side input factors that produce them—namely, capital, labor, land, and technology. Regions of the world abundant in one factor will tend to export goods that intensively make use of it; this is their comparative advantage. Likewise, nations with certain raw materials may export them abroad, as according to their absolute and comparative advantages. History and culture also influence an economy's relative advantages. The experience of modern Asian economic growth suggests that export expansion based on comparative advantages can be an extremely effective development path. International trade led by enhanced export capabilities drives domestic employment growth, attracts foreign investment, strengthens the national currency, and improves terms of trade.

On the other hand, according to the Stolper-Samuelson theorem, the benefits of trade and specialization do not accrue equally within an economy, potentially leading to political cleavages. The effects of well-managed trade liberalizations percolate across many sectors, bringing employment and wage growth, yet in less successful trade openings, new international competitive pressures—particularly within competing goods sectors—lead to wage cuts, worker displacement, and the decline of some industries. In fact, international survey evidence reveals that whether individuals with high levels of human capital favor free trade depends positively on whether their nation is relatively abundant in human capital, a finding that is consistent with the factor proportions model. Furthermore, workers employed in sectors that do not compete with imports are more likely to support free trade. In the future, decreased communications and transportation costs will make globalized production and trade networks more pervasive. As such, anyone planning to do business internationally ought to understand how these forces of international trade affect their own occupation, industry, and nation.

Further Reading

Bhagwati, J. (1989). *Protectionism*. Cambridge, MA: MIT Press.

Feenstra, R. (2010). *Product variety and the gains from international trade*. Cambridge, MA: MIT Press.

Grossman, G., & Helpman, E. (1993). *Innovation and growth in the global economy*. Cambridge, MA: MIT Press.

Helpman, E. (2011). *Understanding global trade*. Cambridge, MA: Harvard University Press.

Hoekman, B., & Kostecki, M. (2010). *The political economy of the world trading system*. Oxford, England: Oxford University Press.

Irwin, D. (2009). *Free trade under fire*. Princeton, NJ: Princeton University Press.

Irwin, D. (2011). *Trade policy disaster: Lessons from the 1930s*. Cambridge, MA: MIT Press.

Krugman, P. (1997). *Development, geography, and economic theory*. Cambridge, MA: MIT Press.

Krugman, P., Obstfeld, M., & Melitz, M. (2011). *International economics: Theory and policy*. Upper Saddle River, NJ: Prentice Hall.

Leamer, E. (2012). *The craft of economics: Lessons from the Heckscher-Ohlin framework*. Cambridge, MA: MIT Press.

Lin, J. Y. (2012). *The quest for prosperity: How developing economies can take off*. Princeton, NJ: Princeton University Press.

O'Rourke, K., & Williamson, J. (2001). *Globalization and history: The evolution of a nineteenth-century Atlantic economy*. Cambridge, MA: MIT Press.

Olson, M. (1965). *The logic of collective action: Public goods and the theory of groups*. Cambridge, MA: Harvard University Press.

Porter, M. (1985). *Competitive advantage: Creating and sustaining superior performance*. New York, NY: Free Press.

Harvard Business School Case Studies

Abdelal, R., Tarontsi, S., & Jorov, A. *Gazprom: Energy and strategy in Russian history*, 709008-PDF-ENG.

Besanko, D., & Burgess, B. *Subsidies and the global cotton trade*, KEL348-PDF-ENG.

Bodily, S. E., & Lichtendahl, K. C. *Airbus and Boeing: Superjumbo decisions*, UV1312-PDF-ENG.

Devereaux, C., & Lawrence, R. *The eagle and the dragon: The November 1999 US-China bilateral agreement and the battle over PNTR*, HKS476-PDF-ENG.

Devereaux, C., Lawrence, R., & Watkins, M. *Food fight: The US, Europe, and trade in hormone-treated beef*, HKS434-PDF-ENG.

Devereaux, C., Lawrence, R., & Watkins, M. *International trade meets intellectual porperty: The making of the TRIPS agreement*, HKS432-PDF-ENG.

George, W.W., Palepu, K.G., & Knoop, C.-I. *Novartis: Leading a global enterprise*, 413096-PDF-ENG.   https://cb.hbsp.harvard.edu/cbmp/product/413096-PDF-ENG

Goldberg, R. A., & Hogan, H. *Can Florida orange growers survive globalization?* 904415-PDF-ENG.

Iyer, L. *To trade or not to trade: NAFTA and the prospects of free trade in the Americas*, 705034-PDF-ENG.

Jones, G. G., & Gendron, A. *In search of global regulation*, 805025-HCB-ENG.

Lam, P.-L., Yiu, A., & Wong, K.-F. *Rent-seeking behavior in the power market*, HKU332-PDF-ENG.

Lodge, G. C., & High, J. *World Trade Organization: Toward free trade or world bureaucracy?*, 795149-PDF-ENG.

McKern, B., Denend, L., Chang, V., & Reuk, K. *The competitive advantage of Russia*, IB73-PDF-ENG.

Moss, D. A., & Bartlett, N. *World Trade Organization*, 703015-PDF-ENG.

Moss, D. A., Appling, G., & Archer, A. *Creating the international trade organization*, 798057-PDF-ENG.

Nolan, R. L., & Kotha, S. *Boeing 787: The dreamliner*, 305101-PDF-ENG.

Roscini, D., & Marin, C. *The TTIP: Bridging the transatlantic economy*, 716026-PDF-ENG. https://cb.hbsp.harvard.edu/cbmp/product/716026-PDF-ENG

Rosegrant, S., & Kelman, S. *Standing up for steel: The US government response to steel industry and union efforts to win protection from imports (1998-2003)*, HKS075-PDF-ENG.

Shih, W., Bliznashki, K., & Zhao, F. *IBM China Development Lab Shanghai: Capability by design*, 611055-PDF-ENG.

Trumbull, G., Corsi, E., & Dessain, V. *Common agricultural policy and the future of French farming*, 707027-PDF-ENG.

Vietor, R. H. K., & Galef, J. *China and the WTO: What price membership?* 707032-PDF-ENG.

Vietor, R. H. K., & Thompson, E. J. *Singapore Inc.*, 703040-PDF-ENG.

Wheelwright, S. C., Pisano, G. P., & West, J. *Eli Lilly and Co.: Manufacturing process technology strategy*, 692056-PDF-ENG.

CHAPTER 4

Industrialization, Globalization, and Labor Markets

Introduction

In standard models of labor markets, wages are equal to the "marginal product" (or incremental output) of an additional unit of labor. In other words, the amount a worker earns is equal to the amount he or she can produce. Intuitively, firms take on workers until the productivity of their last hire is equal to the market wage rate. If the wage rate were below productivity, firms would find it profitable to hire more workers, whereas if the wage were above productivity, firms would have an incentive to shed workers. Under this reasoning, more productive workers get paid more, which implies that labor productivity growth ultimately leads to wage growth in the long term. Indeed, empirical evidence shows labor costs and labor productivity are strongly related across nations.

Now consider the neoclassical growth model, where economic growth is driven by physical capital accumulation, technology, and human capital. These factors all increase labor productivity, and hence, labor demand. In essence, as economies grow, more manpower is required, so labor demand increases. Provided the labor supply doesn't expand too quickly from population growth, economic growth leads to wage growth in a wide class of economic models. With the above primer in mind, this chapter investigates the impact of globalization on labor markets across developing and developed countries. It discusses common economic models of development, industrialization, and industrial policies, focusing on domestic labor market consequences, and it broadly analyzes the experiences of American, Mexican, Chinese, and Indian labor markets in recent decades.

Lewis Model of Development

After World War II, many nations were rebuilding from the war or had just won independence. This climate sparked a renewed interest in economic theories of development. At the same time the neoclassical growth model was being developed, in 1954 Sir Arthur Lewis devised what came to be known as the Lewis two-sector "dual" model of development, for which he later won a Nobel Prize. Born in St. Lucia, then a British colonial territory in the Caribbean, Lewis was deeply knowledgeable about economic history. He had a lifelong interest in practical development policy and spent years in the field, advising Ghana and developing Caribbean nations. As opposed to the broader neoclassical growth model, which describes long-run growth and the behavior of emerging economies as they catch up to leading economies, the Lewis model shows how a traditional agricultural economy transforms into a modern manufacturing and service-based economy. According to Lewis, an abundant supply of cheap labor allows underdeveloped agrarian economies to accumulate capital and industrialize.

While investigating the early Industrial Revolution in Britain, Lewis was puzzled that wages had stagnated while savings, investment, and profits multiplied. (Later research by other scholars challenged Lewis's reading of those trends; some have argued that, at least during the late Industrial Revolution, wages soared, spurring laborsaving inventions in England.) Lewis remarked that in standard economic models, a surge in investment should have resulted in rising labor productivity and wages, alongside declining returns to capital. He cleverly solved the conundrum by making several alternate assumptions. First, he assumed developing economies possess two sectors, agricultural, where most of the population initially resides, and urban, where industrial activity takes place. Second, reminiscent of the economics of Reverend Malthus, he assumed that in the agricultural sector, labor was effectively in unlimited supply. This implied that agricultural labor productivity was minimal and wages remained at a subsistence level. Third, he proposed that the burgeoning urban sector possessed higher productivity with substantial capital, akin to the neoclassical growth model economy. In the Lewis model, capitalists in the urban sector pay relatively low wages because it only takes a slight premium over subsistence wages to attract workers from the country to the city. Capital accumulation and technological advancement cause productivity to increase in the urban sector, yet urban wages stay relatively flat due to the rural labor surplus.

The upshot is that urban business owners are able to make ample profits and invest heavily in new capital. Over time, the urban sector expands and modern manufacturing and service industries emerge. Urban labor demand stays strong and workers from the agricultural sector keep moving to the big city. However, because urban growth steadily diminishes the amount of labor in the countryside, the economy eventually reaches a "turning point" (or labor supply constraint) when rural labor is nearly exhausted. After the turning point occurs, wages in the city begin to increase even faster, eating into industrialist profits. (Think of China today.) By this time, most of the population lives in urban areas, and going forward, the neoclassical growth model is broadly applicable. After the turning point, labor disputes and strikes increase, since workers have new-found bargaining power. Future generations become used to greater consumption levels and have higher workplace expectations, inviting collective bargaining and burgeoning regulatory regimes. Governments start financing more basic education, which increases human capital and enhances productivity. As the economy becomes prosperous and more advanced, it orients itself toward services and internal consumption, with an export sector that produces increasingly complex goods requiring substantial skill and technology.

Unlike traditional models, the Lewis model illustrates why: (1) megacities in developing nations have shantytowns on their outskirts, full of unskilled workers from the countryside looking for urban work; (2) in developing economies, workers typically prefer regular wage employment to self-employment but often cannot find it; and (3) many individuals work full time yet are still poor. These observations are consistent with the Lewis model. Due to the rural labor surplus, the model predicts that developing countries feature low wages that do not increase much initially as the population moves to cities. After the turning point, wages may grow much faster. Higher incomes can be saved, supporting investment and further economic growth. On the other hand, the financial sector in emerging economies is often dreadfully underdeveloped. Workers may find few safe havens to keep their savings, and it may be difficult to obtain loans for new business ventures, even at very high interest rates. Due to deficient financial intermediary institutions and a dearth of domestic savings, developing nations may require foreign capital to finance industrial investment and economic growth. In the 19th century, American states borrowed heavily from wealthier nations abroad—to build canals, for example—and sometimes ended up defaulting.

Poverty Traps, Big-Pushes, and Take-Offs

During the 1950s, around the time that Lewis was formulating his two-sector theory, another famous model dominated development economics. Called the "big-push" model of economic development, it arose out of a paper by Paul Rosenstein-Rodan in 1943. Its key insight was that some poor countries exist in "poverty traps" which require substantial investment to jump start economic growth. The big-push model of development is based on the idea that poor economies suffer from "coordination failures," meaning private sector organizations lack the necessary incentives to adopt modern production techniques and achieve economies of scale. Unless there is an expectation that other firms will similarly invest in industrialization, there is unlikely to be sufficient consumer demand and capital funding to make such costly investments worthwhile. Each company only kicks-off investment projects if the others do, yet it is difficult to get companies to start investing all of a sudden. (Some call this type of conundrum a "chicken or egg" problem, because it isn't clear how one can come into being without the other existing first.)

Consider the plight of a poor farmer in a traditional subsistence economy. He would like to improve the yield of his soil with fertilizers, so the economy requires either the construction of a fertilizer factory or the import of foreign fertilizer. However, a factory requires infrastructure (such as roads, electric power, and water supply), trucks, fuel, capital investment, engineers, and packaging. And importing requires a dock, roads, trucks, fuel, and credit from bankers. It isn't at all likely that any single farmer would be able to carry out either of these scenarios. Meanwhile, ordinary citizens do not invest in education and training because there are no jobs available that would make use of higher level skills.

Foreign engineers, bankers, and lawyers may be required to fill the domestic void. In this view, what is needed is a powerful entity—typically a national government—to coordinate the decisions of firms and households to overcome market synchronization failures. This coordinating entity would provide investment funding to the private sector to build: (1) an industrial base with new technologies and (2) education and training facilities for workers. The economy would then "take off," driven by consumer demand. One classic example of a big-push success story is Meiji Japan, when the Japanese government—propelled by Japan's "zaibatsu," or pyramidal business groups—coordinated a rapid industrialization in the final decades of the 19th century. Another instance is the postwar American South, which received a big-push catalyst from public capital investments to build schools, hospitals, roads, dams, and power plants during the Great Depression and World War II.

If the least developed economies are stuck in poverty traps and face massive coordination failures, they probably won't be able to solve their problems on their own since tax bases and state coffers are too small. Development economists have frequently argued that the least developed economies need foreign aid and loans (such as from the World Bank or International Monetary Fund) to get out of this rut. These funds could be used for private sector investment and public goods like infrastructure, education, and health care. If an economy is capable of supporting an increasing returns industry, then the case for massive injections of capital is all the stronger. Large-scale industries can support worker payrolls, drive export growth, and provide tax revenues to governments. With substantial foreign investment, an economy stuck in a poverty trap will hopefully begin to grow. Then, after it has left the trap, growth will be self-sustaining. Ideally the economy would obtain access to foreign technologies, build domestic universities, and eventually conduct its own research and development. Labor productivity would grow quickly, resulting in higher wages for both skilled and unskilled workers. The influential mid-20th century economist Alexander Gerschenkron argued that, driven by heavy state involvement—and the adoption of foreign methods and borrowed technology, as stressed by American economist Thorstein Veblen—backward countries could accelerate economic growth.

Big-push development theory was the leading concept in development economics throughout the 1950s and 1960s. It was thought that economies all went through the same stages of growth. The proper mix of savings, investment, and foreign aid was all that was needed to power them. International development aid was intended to catalyze emerging economies and ignite self-sustaining growth. Big-push thinking lost favor during the 1970s and 1980s, in part due to the apparent failure of foreign investment and aid to produce significant increases in economic growth and productivity in Africa. The theory was displaced by market liberalization and privatization policies, although big-push ideas—sometimes combined with market liberalization—have reemerged over the past couple decades, chiefly among economists in advanced nations who stress the importance of foreign aid.

By and large, modern empirical studies lend little clear support to the big-push model. If the poorest economies are stuck in poverty traps and a big-push effort is essential to kindling growth, then developing nations receiving aid should grow faster than economies receiving little or no aid. Yet if anything, the cross-country data indicate the opposite is true. Also, the handful of countries that successfully underwent major growth transitions—or take-offs—over the past half century were disproportionately in East Asia. Despite the fact that their governments were instrumental in fostering economic growth, these economies only received a small amount of foreign aid on average. Big-pushes require massive investment, but with the exception of Singapore and possibly Hong Kong, investment was not exceptionally high at the beginning of East Asian take-offs.

Some big-push proponents have remarked that over the past two centuries, the output gap between the richest and poorest countries has gotten much larger, meaning these two groups have diverged. By and large, the wealthiest economies prospered while the poorest stagnated. Although it is possible many poor countries (particularly in Africa) have been stuck in a classic poverty trap, the actual growth trends are, at best, only broadly consistent with the need for big-pushes. Recent studies suggest weak institutions are probably a better explanation for the lackluster growth of the poorest economies over this long time frame. Many critics of foreign aid to sub-Saharan Africa and other poor regions point to studies showing a negative statistical relationship between the volume of foreign aid and subsequent

economic growth. Based on this evidence, they argue that aid erodes institutional quality by increasing the power of kleptocratic elites and corrupt
government officials, and in practice, is really just a windfall for despots.
Proponents of foreign aid contend that such destructive outcomes can be
prevented through enhanced monitoring and accountability measures.

Industrial Policy

Big-push investment projects—whether financed with tax revenues,
domestic savings, or foreign credit—are a form of "industrial policy." By
definition, industrial policies consist of sector-specific initiatives that
enhance industrialization, productivity growth, and national competitiveness, all aiming to promote the national interest. These policies have traditionally involved economic restructuring in the industrial, manufacturing,
and agricultural export-oriented sectors. Half a century ago, in line with
big-push thinking, development economists believed that forceful government interventions were the key to industrial policy. Based on historical
evidence and theoretical developments, economists today are more likely
to stress the importance of industrial policy driven by private initiative,
albeit within a framework supported by the public sector. These concepts
are potentially relevant to all economies, whether advanced or developing,
and the optimal set of industrial policies differs according to the circumstances of each economy.

Although implementing industrial policies involves controversy and
risk, the rewards can be enormous. Government officials and private firms
can work closely together to implement efficient restructurings, though in
practice, these alliances may also increase corruption. One classic industrial
policy is the subsidization of a brand new industry: governments may provide infrastructure, low-cost capital, or even protection from overseas competitors in the form of trade barriers. For example, in recent years China
has given favored domestic firms free land, subsidized energy, low-interest
loans, insider information, and favorably rigged bids. If successful, new
industries take off, resulting in demand spillovers across other domestic
sectors, which generate even greater employment and output.

Critics argue that industrial policies are likely to be disastrous because
governments are poor candidates to predict which industries will thrive.

For one, the venture capital industry has trouble forecasting which projects will ultimately be successful, so it is difficult to see how a government agency, using taxpayer funds, could do better. Even if the bureaucracy in charge of an industrial policy project is honest and relatively efficient, critics contend that it probably wouldn't be able to execute ventures with nearly the same resourcefulness and drive as private sector businesses. Furthermore, once an industrial policy directive is underway, it is difficult to gauge the success of long-term projects or thwart the rent-seeking efforts of powerful private sector agents. There is certainly evidence from past industrial policy failures to support these charges. With its "Cassa del Mezzogiorno" (or Fund for the South) program to develop and industrialize its backward southern economy after World War II, Italy experienced tremendous waste and corruption. At least a third of the funds were estimated to have been squandered. Factories never became operational and sham enterprises existed only to collect government grants. In postcolonial Africa, bureaucracies have often been dominated by political, tribal, and family influence, leading to a long list of failed industrial policy projects across many nations.

Other countries have succeeded with their industrial policies in the past. Japan's "Ministry of International Trade and Industry" (MITI) coordinated industrial and trade policy after World War II, supporting the development of the petrochemical industry in the 1950s, the electronics industry in the 1960s, the computer industry in the 1970s, and the biotechnology and aviation industries in the 1980s and 1990s. China has picked a number of winners in its manufacturing sector. If not for generous public assistance, it is possible that some Chinese industries would be much smaller or not exist at all today. Chile is another example. Chilean grapes, forest products, and salmon are all successful export industries that were aided by government assistance and subsidies. Industrial policies may take different forms within an industry over time. In Mexico, the motor vehicle and computer industries were initially supported by import-substitution policies that encouraged local production to take the place of imports. Later they benefitted from preferential tariff policies under NAFTA. Finally, governments must monitor subsidized industries and quickly phase out the support of failures. This is difficult to do in practice. East Asian governments have been much more successful than Latin American governments at this aspect of industrial policy.

Restructuring, Diversification, and Development

Economic development requires a shift from subsistence agriculture to modern industries exhibiting higher productivity levels. At low levels of development, economic growth entails a decreasing degree of concentration—meaning production becomes more diversified across sectors. At this stage of development, sectors within an economy exhibit vastly uneven productivity and growth. Entrepreneurs and businesses are discovering their own cost structures and learning how to improve their bottom line.

Research shows that when economies reach per capita income of approximately $15,000 to $20,000 in today's American dollars, they reach a tipping point: their economies start to become more concentrated and less diversified. At this stage of growth, economies have found their comparative advantages, and they are leveraging economies of scale. Their export sector is usually well developed, concentrating on a small number of manufactured goods that are highly popular with buyers around the world. Historical patterns of production, resource advantages, superior entrepreneurship, and pure chance all play vital roles in determining the basket of goods an economy specializes in producing and exporting. As these economies grow and prosper, their production shifts to complex goods that exhibit complementarities in production—meaning high-quality labor and capital inputs are necessary—and provide greater value-added.

In economies that develop successfully, labor moves from less productive activities to more productive ones, raising output and wages. This can be achieved by sectoral reallocations, such as transitioning from agriculture to manufacturing. In fact, labor in developing countries is about three to four times more productive in manufacturing than in agriculture, and wages are consequently higher. By successfully expanding the manufacturing sector, a developing economy can raise productivity and output, even in the absence of major technological improvements. Over the past several decades, this is precisely what happened in developing Asian nations such as China, India, the Philippines, and Indonesia. These economies benefitted from labor productivity growth within certain sectors, stemming from more capital, better technology, greater training and experience, and increased foreign direct investment. Import-substitution policies to promote industrialization—which saw their heyday in the 1960s and 1970s—were also successful in many countries, including Mexico (discussed below), Turkey, and Brazil.

In recent decades, however, developing economies in Latin America and Africa have struggled to shift labor from less productive to more productive sectors—if anything, the reverse has happened. At least labor productivity within sectors has grown, though not as much as in Asian economies. Some unsuccessful trade liberalization policies also contributed to Latin American and African structural "devolution." In Argentina and Zambia, for example, many manufacturing jobs were lost following import liberalizations when fragile domestic firms had trouble competing. This "shock treatment" ultimately discouraged broad economic growth.

Managerial Capital

Managerial capital is defined as the organizational and managerial abilities required to run organizations and scale them up. It is a type of specialized human capital that developing nations lack. Managerial capital leads to greater efficiencies within companies, allowing firms to improve the productivity of their capital, labor, and technology inputs. Skilled managers are better able to: utilize equipment efficiently; motivate and train employees; deploy effective sales, marketing, and advertising campaigns; restructure organizations and deploy capital when necessary; and access capital funding necessary for expansion. Such skills can be honed through schooling and on-the-job experience.

In wealthy economies, upper-level managers are broadly skilled and amply paid. As business operations have globalized and become more complex, the demand for the services of top managers and executives has grown among large companies. Compensation has been bid higher and higher, with incentive pay increasingly tied to short-term firm performance. Critics argue upper-level executives and boards of directors are too close for comfort, so much of the compensation growth is actually caused by collusion due to poor corporate governance.

At the other extreme, the absence of managerial capital in emerging economies can impede economic growth and entrepreneurship. As emerging economies grow and develop educational institutions, their stock of managerial capital builds. To bridge the gap in the meantime, they can import foreign managers, copy the best practices of multinational managers, or hire consulting firms to increase managerial capital.

Industrialization and Population Growth

There is no doubt that industrialization is responsible for the massive increase in world population over the past two centuries. During the early Industrial Revolution, the British were able to maintain their living standards despite rapid population growth because industrialization and international trade created such robust demand for their domestic labor. In the early-19th century, after the Industrial Revolution ignited in Britain then spread elsewhere, there were one billion people on the planet, compared to over seven billion today. Just in the past 50 years, the world population has doubled (although world population growth rates have steadily declined after peaking in the 1960s). All developing nations go through the "demographic transition" process: first death rates decline due to better living conditions and medical care, and thereafter birth rates fall due to lower infant mortality rates and more work opportunities for women. Economic development also extends life expectancy. Today it ranges from about 80 years at birth in the United States, Japan, and much of Europe, to 50 years in parts of Africa, such as Zimbabwe and Somalia.

Theory of Globalization and Labor Markets

In canonical economic growth models, wages increase as economies develop. Emerging economies accumulate capital and improve their technologies, thereby increasing labor productivity and boosting labor demand and wages. At the same time, an increased labor supply resulting from population growth puts downward pressure on wages during the industrialization process. By and large, the evidence suggests development leads to higher wages in spite of population growth, at least after a Lewis turning point is reached. Accordingly, there is a strong positive relationship between labor productivity and wages across nations.

To analyze the distributional consequences of transitioning labor markets, economists typically study wage differentials between skilled and unskilled workers. Useful, hard-to-develop skills—usually derived from education and training—lead to higher wages in the labor market. Even in the face of high demand, these skills are in relatively short supply due to the barriers of acquiring them, which include inadequate educational systems and a lack of interest and financing among prospective students. Skilled workers fill out professional and managerial occupations, while unskilled workers perform manual labor and basic service occupations that do not require advanced education or training.

As a practical simplification, economists commonly distinguish skilled and unskilled labor by the completion of a college degree. Education increases a worker's human capital, and it also leads to higher productivity and earnings. As economies develop, they customarily improve their educational institutions and increase aggregate schooling levels. International empirical evidence shows a strong positive relationship between a nation's level of income and the average years of schooling its workers complete. As a consequence, advanced nations tend to be relatively abundant in skilled (meaning educated) labor, while developing nations are relatively short of it.

The factor proportions model and associated Stolper-Samuelson theorem predict that trade between developed and developing nations benefits owners of the relatively abundant factor of production and harms those in possession of the relatively scarce factor. Accordingly, opening trade would benefit skilled workers in advanced economies and unskilled workers in developing nations, though it may hurt unskilled workers in advanced economies and skilled workers in developing nations. In terms of wage inequality within nations, the factor proportions model implies that opening trade around the world would lead to increased inequality in wealthy countries and lowered inequality in developing nations, all else being equal.

Evidence on Globalization and Labor Markets

Traditional economic theories of international trade propose that the effect of globalization on domestic labor markets depends on whether an economy is developed or undeveloped. Many economists have attempted to test these theories in recent years, and the literature is ongoing. Before proceeding, two facts about developing nations are worth mentioning: (1) comprehensive micro data measuring labor market inequality in developing countries is less likely to be available for periods prior to the 1980s and (2) before the 1980s, most developing countries were not open to trade. Openness grew more popular beginning in the 1980s, so that the fraction of nations considered relatively open increased roughly three-fold over the next 25 years (particularly after the collapse of the Soviet Union in 1991). Because of these two factors, most of the empirical evidence on developing economies and the impact of globalization on their local labor markets is derived from trade liberalization episodes after 1980. For developed nations, higher quality data going further back in time exist, so there is more evidence on wage trends, and trade openness (already rather high in 1980) increased only gradually thereafter. To summarize, comparative economic research on globalization and local labor markets is largely based on evidence from the hyperglobalization era of the past 30 years.

The key finding is that since 1980, income inequality expanded in most nations and regions, especially in middle- and high-income countries. Likewise, the demand for skilled and educated labor generally increased relative to other groups, particularly in advanced nations. Although globalization and inequality have both increased over the past 30 years in most countries, correlation does not prove causation. Another factor, technology, has been implicated by most economic researchers as the force that primarily drove the increase in inequality globally. Many have argued that the proliferation of new information and communications technologies since the 1980s—such as personal computing and the internet—has resulted in strong labor demand for skilled and educated workers who best know how to utilize these tools.

Called the "skill biased technological change" hypothesis, it proposes that changes brought about by new technology have increased the relative demand for high-level skills. Its proponents point out that skilled professionals are the first to know about new economic opportunities and the best able to take advantage of them. Possessing superior training and resourcefulness, professionals also benefit from higher quality networks and greater access to capital and government policymakers. In addition, capital flows and financial openness both relate to technology. Capital has become more likely to cross borders, and since capital is usually complementary to human capital and skill, countries that attract the most capital may exhibit increasing wage inequality. And contrary to Stolper-Samuelson, globalization can benefit an elite group of skilled insiders in emerging economies if they are able to access foreign capital flows and the benefits of a transitioning economy while outsiders cannot, due to political corruption and weak institutions. This is what happened in Russia during the 1990s.

Recent empirical research is suggestive, with the caveat that it is challenging to disentangle the effects of globalization, technology, and capital accumulation on local labor market inequality. Based on an international panel of countries beginning in 1980, trade liberalization and export growth are associated with greater wage equality in developing economies, consistent with Stolper-Samuelson. In these nations, increased agricultural exports reduce inequality because they strengthen low-skill labor demand in economies with a large agricultural employment share. In developed nations, the results are mixed (as discussed below). Foreign capital investment and the enhanced use of technology are generally associated with increasing inequality. Skilled and educated workers (such as managers, entrepreneurs, designers, researchers, and engineers) have the knowledge and talent to make use of technology and foreign capital, so their productivity and wages are boosted.

While the incomes of both skilled and unskilled workers have grown over the past three decades in most countries, the returns to skill and education have increased, widening some disparities. In the United States and other advanced English-speaking economies (such as England, Ireland, and Australia), the share of income going to the top one or five percent of income earners has gone up, which is also consistent with enhanced technology favoring their skill sets. On the other hand, the share going to top earners has remained relatively flat in Japan and continental Europe, indicating that political and cultural factors are fundamental to explaining these trends.

The full effect of globalization on inequality in developing countries is not clear-cut because export growth typically reduces inequality to some extent, whereas technology and capital upgrading increase inequality.

Furthermore, export growth, technological progress, and capital upgrading frequently take place at the same time as trade liberalization or capital liberalization episodes. Research has demonstrated that exporting and import-competing firms tend to be larger, more skill-intensive, more productive, and pay higher wages. After liberalizations, efficient exporting firm expand and sometimes upgrade their technology and capital, while less efficient exporters fail. This occurred in Brazil and Argentina during liberalization episodes in the 1980s and 1990s. Likewise, import-competing firms become either more efficient or exit. Thus, if a developing economy is not quite ready for the competitive pressures of international trade, domestic firms may fold, and the benefits of liberalization may accrue only to the most productive firms with efficient, skilled workers. As a result, the overall wage effects of globalization are difficult to predict. It can favor skilled workers, due to technology and capital improvements from trade, or it can favor unskilled workers if labor-intensive exporting sectors, such as textiles or agriculture, expand. Studies have uncovered a variety of responses to specific trade liberalization episodes. In fact, contradicting Stolper-Samuelson, wage inequality increased or stayed the same in many developing countries after they opened trade during the 1980s and 1990s.

Research on the impact of globalization on wealthy country labor markets is broadly consistent with the factor proportions model. As international economic integration steadily progressed, wage inequality in most affluent nations has increased since the 1980s. Most of the change in inequality in these nations occurred at the top of the distribution, meaning skilled workers have done particularly well. Factor proportions logic implies that skilled and educated workers gain from globalization because their abilities are in relative abundance in wealthy nations. Opening their domestic market to international trade and capital flows creates more demand for their skills. Cheaper travel and telecommunications enable highly skilled workers living in affluent countries to cooperate more extensively in production with workers in emerging markets. The story is different for unskilled laborers in wealthy nations, as they are substitutes for unskilled workers in developing economies. Facilitated by technology, production has become more fragmented across borders, and globalization has caused certain low-skill tasks to move to developing nations. This has occurred through the growth of multinationals in developing economies, as well as through offshoring and the "outsourcing" of tasks to external contractors and suppliers abroad. Since the 1970s, these developments have reduced the relative demand for middle-to-low skilled labor in wealthy nations.

Finally, one major event, not to be repeated in the future, had an enormous impact on the global supply of labor and demand for capital: one and a half billion Chinese and Indian workers joined the world economy in the 1990s. This doubling of the global labor supply was an unprecedented shock to the world's factor markets. It applied downward pressure to the wages of unskilled workers around the world. It also affected global capital markets: since physical capital is needed to build factories and infrastructure, capital poured into emerging markets in the 1990s. The late 1990s Asian financial crisis marked a turning point, however. In its wake, capital flows shifted toward advanced economies. Interestingly, emerging economies, led by oil-rich regions and China, became net exporters of capital beginning in 2000, instead of net capital importers, as they had been before. Human capital complements industrialization and technological innovation, so these developments increased the relative demand for skilled labor, which is still scarce in most parts of the world. Because the integration of China and India was a one-time event, the degree of pressure globalization places on the wages of less skilled workers across the world's labor markets is likely to be lower in the future than it has been in the recent past.

Globalization, Influence, and the American Labor Market

Throughout the 1950s and 1960s, American industry led the world as Europe and Asia were rebuilding from the destruction of World War II. American output per worker was twice that of Europe and six times that of Japan. In the pre-microprocessor era, strong American economic growth rates complemented a large and growing manufacturing base, rapidly rising educational attainment, and high unionization rates. Yet by the 1970s, parts of Europe and Asia had begun to catch up. Japan and some East Asian nations had perfected technologically sophisticated production processes and closed the productivity gap with the United States in some industries. Production began to globalize, too. Global supply chains slowly emerged. Lower value-added processes, performed with unskilled labor, moved to emerging economies, and higher value-added processes, increasingly complex due to technology, remained in advanced economies. The comparative advantage of the United States evolved toward more difficult, technologically-intensive procedures, as emerging economies took over simpler tasks and began their gradual ascent up the value-added chain.

Over the past 40 years, as the United States further integrated with the world economy, new technologies profoundly impacted most sectors of the American economy. This is especially true in the "tradables" sector (which, by definition, produces goods that can be traded abroad). This sector has become more efficient, and labor productivity within it has grown rapidly due to accumulated capital and technology. Many low and middle value-added tasks have shifted offshore, and on net, employment in tradables has slowed. Employment growth has instead been concentrated in the much larger "nontradables" sector, which is dominated by local service jobs in government, health care, retail, and food service. It is more difficult for technology and capital to make workers more productive in the service sector, which is driven by labor inputs. (Think of the productivity of an elementary school teacher.) Overall demand shifts have favored educated and skilled workers in both the tradables and nontradables sectors. These higher income workers are better able to absorb and spread new technologies, raising aggregate productivity. As opposed to unskilled workers, skilled workers commonly perform nonroutine problem-solving tasks that are harder to digitize, automate, or outsource. Educated and skilled workers have done relatively well throughout the American economy, while less skilled workers have shifted from manufacturing to service jobs as the manufacturing sector has progressively declined in relative importance.

The American private sector led many global innovation trends. After struggling in the 1970s—a decade that offered negative stock market returns after adjusting for inflation—American corporate profits rebounded in the 1980s. Many corporations in the United States restructured, looking for efficiencies that would allow them to beat foreign companies that had caught up. The world-leading American information and communications technology industry has been a principal catalyst for technological change throughout the international economy. These developments attracted massive inflows of foreign capital, and not just during the late 1990s Dotcom boom. The United States is now the world's largest recipient of foreign direct investment. The share of American output traded internationally has grown gradually, and its new technologies have facilitated global supply chains and outsourcing. More and more imports come from developing nations, particularly China. In Europe, economic changes have been broadly similar, although they began later and have been less pronounced, especially in continental economies. The labor market impacts of technology and globalization have led to relatively less wage inequality and more unemployment in European economies, due to less labor market flexibility and greater regulation and collective bargaining there.

In the United States, globalization and changes in technology are interrelated, and have trended in the same direction in recent decades. An important literature examines whether technological progress, international trade, or other factors such as "deunionization" have caused the relative demand for skilled and educated workers to strengthen since the 1970s. Research has shown that demand shifts favoring educated workers—in a process called "skill upgrading"—were pervasive in the United States and other advanced nations, despite the fact that the price of skilled labor was increasing. Industries that undertook larger investments in computerization also exhibited greater skill upgrading. Another essential piece of evidence is that low-income countries account for only a small fraction of manufactured imports to the United States. This suggests that unskilled workers in emerging economies are not primarily responsible for the sluggish demand for unskilled labor in the United States.

These findings point to a commonly held view among labor economists that technological change played a central role in driving the observed expansion in wage inequality, with globalization and trade secondary. Although trade has harmed some groups of workers in certain industries, the aggregate gains from increased trade, while incrementally diminishing, have outweighed the costs. Trade with developing nations like China has helped keep the price of consumer staples low in the United States. In fact, trade has disproportionately increased the purchasing power of lower income Americans because they spend a larger share of their income on goods that have become cheaper due to low-priced imports, such as clothing and electronics sold at Walmart. This purchasing power effect goes a long way toward compensating certain unskilled American workers for any sluggish wage and employment growth caused by foreign competition.

The recent "Great Recession" reduced world trade by about 20%, including the foreign trade of the United States, an economy which accounts for a tenth of all international trade. American exports quickly rebounded to prerecession levels, though imports have taken longer to recover. American consumer demand has been slow to bounce back. In the corporate sector, companies have shed workers and restructured, upgrading capital equipment with investments in automation, digitization, robotics, and other machinery that substitutes for labor. With lingering anxiety about future growth prospects and capital equipment relatively cheap compared to labor, postrecession hiring has been slow. Taking their cue from Germany, some American policymakers have begun calling for a renewed emphasis on vocational training programs and apprenticeships because many American companies—including international powerhouses like Apple—complain about shortages of specialized, blue-collar niche labor in the United States.

A number of encouraging new trends have emerged. The capital investments American businesses are making will inevitably lead to productivity gains for many years into the future, whilst labor costs in China and India are rapidly increasing. Given vast American productivity advantages, work has started to shift back to the United States. There are also highly favorable tends in American energy supply capabilities and costs. Finally, the middle classes in India, China, Brazil, and elsewhere are growing rapidly, and their consumer demand will help boost American economic growth in the years to come.

Globalization, Industrialization, and the Mexican Labor Market

After World War II, Mexico sustained strong economic growth for over 30 years, transitioning from an agrarian society to a semi-industrial economy with most of the population living in cities. As part of Mexico's development strategy, the government protected infant industries and promoted import-substitution policies, where high tariffs encouraged consumers to buy products made in Mexico. To advance industrialization, the export sector was supported. As a prominent example, beginning in the 1960s, the government established the "maquiladora" sector in a special free trade and investment area for Mexican export-processing plants located in the north near the United States border. Maquiladora factories are able to import materials and equipment on a duty-free and tariff-free basis for processing, assembly, or manufacturing, provided the output is subsequently exported.

During the 1970s, the discovery of oil reserves—coupled with high oil prices—encouraged populist Mexican governments to spend heavily. They accumulated large debt loads, which eventually led to the Mexican debt crisis of 1982. The 1980s came to be known as a "lost decade" for the Mexican economy, in spite of growing efforts to modernize and integrate internationally, which included privatization and trade liberalization. The "North American Free Trade Agreement" (NAFTA) was enacted in 1994, the same year Mexico experienced a currency crisis precipitated by political turmoil. A recession followed. Mexican economic growth picked up during the 1990s and exports have continued to increase. Today, combined imports and exports represent more than half of Mexico's economic output. Maquiladoras produce about half of Mexico's exports, most of which are manufactured goods. The United States is Mexico's top trading partner, accounting for over 80% of Mexican exports and half of Mexican imports.

In addition to NAFTA, Mexico joined the GATT in 1986 and the "Organization for Economic Cooperation and Development" (OECD) in 1994, as Mexico's industrial policy shifted from heavy state intervention to a market orientation with open trade. Foreign direct investment, the presence of multinational corporations, and outsourcing inflows all shot up in Mexico following reforms initiated after the 1982 debt crisis. According to the factor proportions model of trade, because Mexico is relatively abundant in unskilled labor, trade liberalization and increasing globalization would lead to rising employment, wages, and production in unskilled labor-intensive industries, with the reverse happening in skilled labor-intensive sectors. Yet numerous studies have shown that in Mexico, wage inequality and the skill premium actually went up until the mid-1990s.

An alternative theory is that technological change—induced by privatization and foreign competitive pressures stemming from trade liberalization—caused the relative demand for skilled and educated labor to increase through the mid-1990s. In this view, during the first half of the postreform era, Mexican companies were adjusting to the new economic climate and moving up the value-added production chain by utilizing relatively more educated and skilled labor, especially in the northern border regions. This notion is supported by the data through the mid-1990s. Empirical research shows that many Mexican companies upgraded their technology and production quality during this period of increasing exposure to international competition and globalized production sharing.

The mid-1990s gave way to the NAFTA era. Following NAFTA, wage inequality trends reversed course, so that the skill premium started to decline alongside growing real wages and incomes. Overall Mexican income inequality has fallen—in part due to increased social transfers and remittances—and average real wages have grown. Under NAFTA, Mexico integrated with the United States and Canada, countries that are relatively abundant in skilled labor. Research suggests that NAFTA's effect on Mexican wages was consistent with the factor proportions model. It benefitted the multitude of unskilled Mexican workers, and wage inequality between skilled and unskilled labor decreased. Regions that were more exposed to international trade and had stronger links to the American economy—such as the northern and border states—showed greater declines in the skill premium and more overall wage growth after NAFTA. However, agricultural workers were more likely to be displaced after NAFTA, and total agricultural employment declined, though this was partly caused by other changes in the agricultural sector, including productivity-enhancing technological and capital improvements.

More than a decade after its implementation, NAFTA is viewed favorably by a majority of Mexicans. Although large income disparities remain across Mexico, most of its 115 million citizens consider themselves middle class. Demographers point out that Mexican immigration to the United States has declined after peaking in 2000, principally due to Mexican economic growth and falling birth rates. Mexico has managed to increase the educational attainment of its labor force, despite the inefficiency of its educational sector. Combined with capital upgrading and additional international economic integration, these developments are a sign that Mexico's middle class will continue to expand as the "Aztec Tiger" emerges.

Globalization, Reforms, and the Chinese Labor Market

The Chinese economy underwent profound changes after major reforms were authorized in 1978, following Mao's 1976 death. Most remarkably, China transitioned from a closed system based on central planning to a market-oriented economy that is a dominant force in international commerce. Beginning with the phasing out of socialized agriculture, China liberalized its market pricing system, gave more autonomy to state enterprises, and opened itself up to foreign trade and investment. Due to the reforms, instead of hewing to Soviet-style production, millions of Chinese workers began following economic incentives that encouraged effort, efficiency, and productivity. Trade-oriented "Special Economic Zones" (SEZ) were opened from 1980 onward to attract foreign investment and technology transfer. Tariff barriers were high in the 1990s before coming down substantially over the following decade.

The Chinese government was careful to design industrial policies that encouraged the development of import-competing firms and exporters, frequently in new industries. Rapid productivity growth in the nonagricultural private sector has driven much Chinese economic growth. China has accumulated ample capital, financed by a very high domestic savings rate as well as foreign investment, and shifted labor from the country to the city, resulting in productivity gains and growth. A large income gap between rural and urban areas has persisted historically. Today, a little over half of China's 1.35 billion residents live in cities, and urbanization efforts continue, leading to productivity growth coupled with social strife and endemic public policy challenges. Extreme pollution and corruption are widespread throughout China, though the government has begun major clean energy initiatives.

Exports have been an engine of Chinese economic growth, particularly since the 1990s. Government policy—such as the maintenance of an undervalued currency and the extension of cheap credit—has supported the export sector. Chinese households maintain very high savings rates of over 25%, among the highest in the world. These funds have been used for state-directed capital investment and infrastructure spending instead of personal consumption. China continues to build domestic infrastructure on a massive scale, intended to support future economic growth and urbanization efforts. The present challenge is to initiate the transition to an economy sustained by domestic consumption and innovation, as opposed to export growth and capital formation.

For decades, the Chinese industrial sector has been a low-cost producer unafraid to imitate (and then improve upon) foreign technologies, intellectual property, and best practices. China is known for its sophisticated supply chains, massive scale economies, and dynamic production lines that can ramp up output in a matter of hours. However, China does not have a track record of developing major innovations (at least in the modern era), so it has begun spending billions on research and development, including the retooling of its university system. Mirroring cities in wealthy industrialized nations around the world, Shanghai and other large urban areas are full of young, upwardly mobile workers hoping to find well-paying work and possibly finish college or even a Master of Business Administration (MBA) degree. Early reforms in the 1980s benefitted rural households engaged in agricultural work, while later reform policies since the 1990s have led to faster urban income growth and a large new class of ultra-wealthy Chinese in coastal regions. Still, China's financial sector is largely state-controlled, and a substantial portion of its manufacturing and service sector consists of state-owned enterprises.

China's greatest comparative advantage during its explosive growth phase of development has been its abundance of low-cost labor, which has made it globally competitive in producing inexpensive, labor-intensive manufactures. Although the Chinese labor cost advantage has narrowed considerably, it still remains vast compared to the United States. For instance, among manufacturing companies in 2010, the hourly cost of labor in China was less than $2, compared to $34 in the United States. As a result, manufactured products utilizing cheap unskilled labor constitute a significant share of China's trade, which is precisely what the factor proportions model of trade predicts. With the rise of offshoring and declines in trade barriers, a substantial portion of China's imports come from parts and components that are assembled into finished products—like consumer electronics and computers—and later exported. The value added to most of these products by Chinese workers is small compared to the total value of the product after it is shipped abroad. For instance, while Apple's iPhone is primarily manufactured in China, the cost of Chinese labor for components and assembly represents just 2% of an iPhone's final retail price.

Since the 1990s, China has been unique among developing nations in its extraordinary ability to move up the "product ladder," meaning an increasing share of China's production comes from higher quality goods that utilize capital-intensive, higher value-added processes. China contrasts with stagnated emerging economies at the bottom of the product ladder that primarily export raw materials (in Africa) or perform basic assembling of manufactured goods (in Central America). China's success may be largely due to savvy industrial policies and superior strategic timing and coordination. Overall, economic policymaking in China has been much more effective than in other developing regions. Economic research shows that in wealthier countries, firms that directly compete with Chinese companies have made greater investments in upgrading technology and innovation to lower their long-run costs by enhancing productivity.

Studies of the Chinese labor market have uncovered a number of valuable findings. Most importantly, Chinese workers have broadly experienced strong wage growth. Under periods of rapid economic growth and convergence, such a pattern is expected. Wage setting and employment policies, which used to be controlled by the government, have been gradually liberalized to reflect market forces. Rural incomes grew faster than urban incomes in the 1980s, largely due to agricultural reforms. Urban incomes then outstripped rural incomes from 1990 to 2010, particularly after China joined the WTO in 2001. In the 1990s, minimum wage, unemployment insurance, and worker injury insurance reforms were enacted, and the labor bureau stopped allocating jobs to college graduates. The skill premium for college-educated workers, which was very low in the 1980s, has risen so that it now matches the United States.

All segments of the population, including the uneducated poor in rural inland areas, have experienced income growth, although the largest gains have accrued to those with higher income and education in urban coastal regions. As a result, while poverty rates have declined, overall income inequality has increased since 1979 by most measures. The increase in wage dispersion stands in contrast to a key prediction of the factor proportions model of trade, which is that, due to its abundance of unskilled labor, China's integration into global markets would benefit its unskilled workers and possibly harm skilled and educated workers, with wage inequality generally declining. Indeed, taken as a whole, the evidence suggests that globalization and trade have not been the dominant factors behind changes in the Chinese wage structure. Instead, structural reforms and technological upgrading—undoubtedly spurred by international trade—have been more important drivers. And given recent news of strong wage growth, increasing demands by workers, and a surge in labor shortages and social unrest, a Lewis turning point has, in all likelihood, already been reached in China.

Many analysts point out that China's development strategies may eventually run out of steam. Moving the population from the country to the city causes large productivity gains, but half of the Chinese population is already in urban areas. The international evidence on economic growth shows that once fast-growing economies transition to middle-income levels, they are likely to experience slower growth, particularly if they previously maintained an undervalued currency to promote exports. Called the "middle-income trap" by economists, this slowdown has commonly occurred once economies attain per capita income in the range of $10,000 to $20,000 in current American dollars. (China is expected to reach the lower end of this level by about 2015.) To combat it, countries must accumulate ever more advanced technologies, perform higher value-added processes, ensure more workers complete college, and build a larger, more sophisticated services sector. However, a sizeable retired population relative to the work force tends to exacerbate the growth slowdown, and due to population control strategies such as the one-child policy instituted in 1979, China is one of the most rapidly aging nations in the world. This change in the age profile of the Chinese population will shift resources away from capital investment and lead to tighter labor markets, eroding China's cost advantages in production.

The health of China's state-dominated financial system—which is not as sound or advanced as Japan's was at a similar level of development—is also questionable. Households have little choice but to park their savings in accounts paying minimal interest. With these funds, the government provides cheap credit to support development. Capital has disproportionately gone to the state sector, yet research shows that returns to capital have been far superior in the private sector. Hopefully there will be no forthcoming financial sector meltdown, such as the one that occurred in Japan, a country which enjoyed decades of strong export-driven growth, helping to prop up a massive real estate and asset price bubble that peaked in 1991. After it collapsed, Japan faced two decades of minimal growth in spite of massive monetary and fiscal stimulus. China has unquestionably learned from the growth experiences of other nations, and it has strategically maintained capital controls and regulations on real estate purchases to help prevent such a scenario. The Chinese economy will ideally be able to maintain healthy growth by shifting investment to the non-state sector, transplanting successful economic policies to the poorer inland regions, and supporting a consumer culture that will power domestic demand for years to come.

Globalization, Development, and the Indian Labor Market

After independence from Britain in 1947, India achieved slow and steady growth for the next three decades. From 1950 to 1980, India's annual income per capita growth rate was 1.7%, a pace one Indian economist famously dubbed the "Hindu rate of growth," as it was far below East Asian nations outside of communist China. India's economic policy was protectionist, featuring import-substitution industrialization, heavy regulation of the private sector, and a colossal bureaucratic public sector. In 1980, Indira Gandhi returned to power for a fourth term as Prime Minister, this time with an orientation more favorable to markets, instead of hostile as before. Change was in the air in India during the 1980s. Market reforms were initiated, such as a curbing of price controls and corporate taxation, making it easier for businesses to grow. India did not initiate a massive accumulation of capital and technology at this time. Instead, the new policies allowed India to slowly tap into its latent potential and increase its productivity per worker.

India's output per worker grew more than four times as fast in the 1980s than it did during the 1970s. Protectionism increased somewhat throughout the 1980s before significant liberalization policies were enacted in the 1990s, facilitating India's entry into the world economy. The changes occurred when India's ability to pay a massive foreign debt load was called into question in 1991, which sparked a financial crisis. The IMF bailed India out, yet it required economic restructuring and liberalization policies as part of the deal. Trade was liberalized, foreign investment allowed, and the "License Raj"—one major source of red tape, corruption, and frustration throughout the private sector—was effectively abolished. After stagnating throughout the 1980s, Indian trade as a fraction of total output increased 50% during the 1990s.

India's growth since the 1980s has been driven by an immense expansion of the service sector. This contrasts with the traditional Asian path of development based on low-wage industrial production and export growth. In India, labor has shifted from agriculture to services and (to a lesser extent) industry. Its information and communications technology industry based in Bangalore, the Silicon Valley of India, has boomed. Yet India has failed to maintain high investment levels and its infrastructure remains very poor. In this respect, India contrasts with China, where growth has been driven by greater amounts of physical capital accumulation and new infrastructure.

India's industrial sector is relatively undeveloped, and the export share of its economy remains much lower than China. Trade constitutes a quarter of India's economy, compared to half of China's, and India has not benefitted from a savvy and far-reaching industrial policy. Although Indian and Chinese income per capita was roughly the same in 1990, over the last two decades, China's economy has grown much faster and it has experienced a slower rate of population growth. As a result, China's income per capita is now more than double India's. India's rural-urban transition lags China, as a third of Indians live in cities versus half of Chinese. India also fares less well according to most health and education measures. For instance, life expectancy at birth is 66 years in India versus 74 years in China; India's adult literacy rate is 74% versus 94% in China; and government spending on health care is nearly fives times greater in China than in India.

The factor proportions model implies that by opening up to world markets, globalization would help India's unskilled and poor workers and reduce income inequality. In addition, India's fast economic growth would help raise incomes for nearly all workers. Research shows that average incomes have risen throughout India since liberalizations began over 30 years ago, and India's poverty rate has been cut in half since 1980, despite substantial population growth. Nonagricultural workers have done the best. But contrary to the factor proportions model, there is evidence that, following the early 1990s reforms, income inequality increased, particularly in urban areas, in a manner consistent with a rising relative demand for skill. This is potentially due to greater technology utilization. Income growth has been more rapid among skilled workers.

Economic growth has brought greater benefits to the poor in regions of India with greater financial development and access to credit. In the rural sector, wage growth has been sluggish over the past decade despite strong economic growth, as the expanding supply of unskilled workers—most still operating in the informal sector—has overwhelmed demand. In regions with more stringent labor market regulations, the poor have done less well, as some laws have hindered manufacturing growth that would benefit unskilled laborers. Research also suggests improving education and infrastructure would help poor workers in India. Compared to China, India's labor force is much less structured and less likely to work in state-run enterprises. Over 90% of India's labor force remains in informal employment, versus about 50% in China. At the top end, a new class of super wealthy Indian entrepreneurs and businesspersons has emerged since the 1990s, similar to China. Today, India has about 50 billionaires, compared to roughly 100 in China and 400 in the United States.

As India integrated into the world economy alongside China, the global supply of labor effectively doubled. Based on standard economic growth models, whether wages in these two countries converge to advanced country levels in the long run depends on the amount of physical capital—in the form of machinery and computers—they accumulate, as well as their capacity to educate their workforce and absorb technologies. As these enormous developing countries amass factors of production, unskilled labor will become scarcer, driving up its wages. China has much more capital per worker than India, due to China's lower population growth rate and higher investment rate. China's capital per worker may eventually converge to wealthy nations such as Japan and the United States, though it would take decades longer for India to do so.

Since modern information technology allows work to move from wealthy countries with high labor costs to emerging markets like India and China, offshoring may grow in the future, particularly as India and China improve their educational systems. These forces may slowly shift the locus of global innovation in technology-intensive industries to cities such as Bangalore and Beijing. However, technology and growth can also be a recipe for income inequality and social unrest. Globalization can harm those in less productive organizations that struggle to compete internationally, while skilled entrepreneurs and employees working in ultra-modern, export-oriented companies benefit the most from integration with advanced nations. In the future, India will hopefully make better use of informal sector workers, reduce bureaucracy, and create structural reforms that lead to broadly shared benefits.

Conclusion

The factor proportions model of trade is a useful guide to understanding how trade impacts different types of workers and affects the relative demand for skilled versus unskilled labor within a given economy. But it is also imperfect. Experience demonstrates that economic integration can lead to economic growth benefitting most workers regardless of their education and skill set. Perhaps most importantly, globalization can help power the transition from agriculture to industry in developing countries, lifting millions out of poverty, as in the cases of post-NAFTA Mexico and post-Mao China. It can also benefit skilled workers in emerging markets, such as information technology professionals in India. On the other hand, globalization can harm domestic workers through inadequately managed trade reforms, leading to worker displacement and greater inequality, regardless of a country's level of development.

Overall income inequality between nations has declined in recent decades due to the rapid economic growth of developing nations such as China and India. At the same time, income inequality within most economies has proliferated, principally driven by technological factors favoring skilled and educated workers. Global supply chains and the impact of information and communications technologies have integrated production processes to an extent that few would have imagined a century ago, during the last pinnacle period of globalization. The result is an increase in the overall efficiency of the global economy, generating lower consumer prices in the long run. In the coming years, emerging economies will persevere in their efforts to move up the technology ladder and value-added chain. By increasing their national stock of human capital, building infrastructure, and reforming regulatory and taxation policies, developing nations can enhance competitiveness, leading to greater labor market opportunities for their domestic workers.

Further Reading

Banerjee, A., Benabou, R., & Mookherjee, D. (2006). *Understanding poverty.* Oxford, England: Oxford University Press.

Bell, D. (1973). *The coming of post-industrial society: A venture in social forecasting.* New York, NY: Basic Books.

Bhagwati, J., Blinder, A., & Friedman, B. (2009). *Offshoring of American jobs: What response from U.S. economic policy?* Cambridge, MA: MIT Press.

Brynjolfsson, E., & McAfee, A. (2012). *Race against the machine: How the digital revolution is accelerating innovation, driving productivity, and irreversibly transforming employment and the economy.* Lexington, MA: Digital Frontier Press.

Bulmer-Thomas, V. (2003). *The economic history of Latin America since independence.* Cambridge, England: Cambridge University Press.

Chandler, A. (1969). *Strategy and structure: Chapters in the history of the American industrial enterprise.* Cambridge, MA: MIT Press.

Chang, H.-J. (2003). *Kicking away the ladder: Development strategy in historical perspective.* London, England: Anthem Press.

Cohen, S., & Zysman, J. (1988). *Manufacturing matters: The myth of the post-industrial economy.* New York, NY: Basic Books.

Ehrenberg, R., & Smith, R. (2011). *Modern labor economics: Theory and public policy.* Upper Saddle River, NJ: Prentice Hall.

Feenstra, R. (2009). *Offshoring in the global economy: Microeconomic structure and macroeconomic implications.* Cambridge, MA: MIT Press.

Gershenkron, A. (1962). *Economic backwardness in historical perspective.* Cambridge, MA: Harvard University Press.

Haber, S. (1995). *Industry and underdevelopment: The industrialization of Mexico, 1890–1940.* Palo Alto, CA: Stanford University Press.

Haber, S., Klein, H., Maurer, N., & Middlebrook, K. (2008). *Mexico since 1980*. Cambridge, England: Cambridge University Press.

Moretti, E. (2012). *The new geography of jobs*. New York, NY: Houghton Mifflin Harcourt.

Lewis, A. (1955). *The theory of economic growth*. Homewood, IL: Richard Irwin.

Lin, J. Y. (2011). *Demystifying the Chinese economy*. Cambridge, England: Cambridge University Press.

Lin, J. Y. (2012). *New structural economics: A framework for rethinking development and policy*. Washington, DC: World Bank Press.

Naughton, B. (2006). *The Chinese economy: Transitions and growth*. Cambridge, MA: MIT Press.

North, D. (1990). *Institutions, institutional change and economic performance*. Cambridge, MA: Cambridge University Press.

Perkins, D., Radelet, S., & Lindauer, D. (2006). *Economics of development*. New York, NY: W. W. Norton and Company.

Ray, D. (1998). *Development economics*. Princeton, NJ: Princeton University Press.

Rostow, W. (1960). *The stages of economic growth*. Cambridge, England: Cambridge University Press.

Schultz, T. (1964). *Transforming traditional agriculture*. New Haven, CT: Yale University Press.

Todaro, M., & Smith, S. (2011). *Economic development*. Upper Saddle River, NJ: Prentice Hall.

Williamson, J. (2009). *Globalization and the poor periphery before 1950*. Cambridge, MA: MIT Press.

Harvard Business School Case Studies

Abdelal, R., & Tarontsi, S. *Russia: Revolution and reform*, 710030-PDF-ENG.

Alfaro, L., & Iyer, L. *Special economic zones in India: Public purpose and private property*, 709027-PDF-ENG.

Comin, D., & Vietor, R. H. K. *China "unbalanced,"* 711010-PDF-ENG.

Froot, K. A., & McBrady, M. *1994–95 Mexican peso crisis*, 296056-PDF-ENG.

Iyer, L., & Donovan, G.A. *Urbanizing China*, 713037-PDF-ENG. https://cb.hbsp.harvard.edu/cbmp/product/713037-PDF-ENG.

Iyer, L., & Vietor, R. H. K. *India 2012: The challenges of governance*, 712038-PDF-ENG.

Jones, G. G., & Bud-Frierman, L. *Weetman Pearson and the Mexican oil industry*, 804085-PDF-ENG.

Jones, G. G., & Gallagher-Kernstine, M. *The American challenge: Europe's response to American business*, 804057-HCB-ENG.

Jones, G. G., & Lefort, A. *McKinsey and the globalization of consultancy*, 806035-PDF-ENG.

Mathis, F. J., & Keat, P. G. *India: The promising future*, TB0265-PDF-ENG.

Musacchio, A., Tella, R. D., & Schlefer, J. *The Korean model of shared growth, 1960-1990*, 712052-PDF-ENG.

Musacchio, A., Vietor, R. H. K., & García-Cuéllar, R. *Mexico: Crisis and competitiveness*, 710058-PDF-ENG.

Oi, J., Bebenek, C., & Spar, D. L. *China: Building "capitalism with socialist characteristics,"* 706041-PDF-ENG.

Pill, H. *Mexican debt crisis of 1982*, 701111-PDF-ENG.

Pill, H. *Mexico: The tequila crisis—1994-95*, 702093-PDF-ENG.

Pill, H. *Mexico: From stabilized development to debt crisis*, 797096-PDF-ENG.

Pill, H. *Portfolio capital flows to emerging markets*, 796129-PDF-ENG.

Rithmire, M. *The "Chongqing model" and the future of China*, 713028-PDF-ENG.

Scott, B. R., & Matthews, J. L. *China's rural leap forward*, 703024-PDF-ENG.

Scott, B. R., & Matthews, J. L. *One country, two systems?: Italy and the Mezzogiorno*, 702096-PDF-ENG.

Scott, B. R., & Leight, J. *Chile: The conundrum of inequality*, 907411-PDF-ENG.

Shih, W., & Wang, J.-C. *Upgrading the economy: Industrial policy and Taiwan's semiconductor industry*, 609089-PDF-ENG.

Tella, R. D., & Vogel, I. *Inequality and the "American model,"* 703025-PDF-ENG.

Vietor, R. H. K. *Low-carbon, indigenous innovation in China*, 712061-PDF-ENG.

Vietor, R. H. K., Rivkin, J. W., & Seminerio, J. *The offshoring of America*, 708030-PDF-ENG.

Vietor, R. H. K., & Veytsman, A. *American outsourcing*, 705037-PDF-ENG.

Vietor, R. H. K., & Thompson, E. J. *India on the move*, 703050-PDF-ENG.

CHAPTER 5

Politics, Globalization, and the State

Introduction

For peaceful globalization to take place, much less succeed in the end, political will is necessary. Politicians, whether supported by ordinary citizens or vested interests, must believe they have something to gain by opening trade or liberalizing their economy and culture. Thereafter, restraints are lifted and their local area is awash in new goods and influences. Over the first major wave of globalization during the 100 years prior to World War I, many states made just such a wager. Capital and labor flowed to the New World where returns—and risks—were higher. Then, from World War I to World War II, barriers went up amidst economic turmoil and global warfare. Following postwar international accords like the Bretton Woods system, the Marshall Plan, and the GATT, the 1950s heralded a new age of economic growth, trade, and globalization. The pace only picked up after the 1970s, so that today, tariffs in many countries, including the United States and China, are minimal. Still, a recent backlash against globalization among many constituents around the world has prompted a rethinking of its rules. Few seem to desire a return to high tariffs, as workers in middle- or high-income nations have gotten used to buying cheap imports from developing nations at their local Walmart (or equivalent).

With unemployed teenagers leading protests and old regimes falling in the Middle East, recent events have highlighted trends that favor the expansion of political rights and economic freedoms in repressive states. Change can come quickly: a century ago, women had the right to vote in only a few nations. Technology such as cell phones and the internet have permeated most societies around the world, especially among the young. Modern information and communications technology was indispensable to the "Arab Spring" of 2011, where major protests occurred in Algeria, Oman, Iraq, Bahrain, Kuwait, Morocco, Lebanon, and Syria, and governments were overthrown in Egypt, Libya, Yemen, and Tunisia. These North African and Middle Eastern political movements began in December 2010 when Mohamed Bouazizi, a young street vendor in the Tunisian town of Sidi Bouzid, set himself on fire. He passed away from the injuries a month later. The human rights organization Amnesty International has argued that the leak of American diplomatic correspondence by WikiLeaks in 2010 was the necessary catalyst for the Arab Spring. The internet-based transmission of WikiLeaks documents shed light on the corrupt regime of Zine El Abidine Ben Ali in Tunisia, who would flee the country in January 2011 with his family, before being convicted and sentenced (in absentia) to 35 years in jail by a Tunisian court months later.

This sort of monumental political change had not occurred since the fall of the Berlin Wall in 1989, which paved the way for the end of the Cold War in 1991 when the Union of Soviet Socialist Republics (USSR) dissolved. Today all organizations face the reality, mandated by modern technology, that sunlight is the best disinfectant. Within minutes, photos and written documents can go viral worldwide, acting as powerful catalysts for social change. Combined with youthful populations, these forces may continue to topple other absolutist governments in the future; more than half the world's population currently lives under an autocratic regime, so there is plenty of room for progress. Yet the future of authoritarianism is hard to predict, and it is doubtful that modern information and communications technology spells ultimate doom for political repression in the long run. Insights from political and economic research are useful here. For decades, political scientists have grappled with globalization's impact on governance. Economists have now joined the debate, armed with cross-country statistical evidence that is increasingly sophisticated, as more indices measuring the political and institutional aspects of nations become available. Research shows that globalization clearly influences domestic political alignments, the likelihood of military conflict, and the size of governments around the world. The literature grows quickly, and many more findings will undoubtedly come to light in the coming years. This chapter, intended as an overview of important ideas and findings, discusses some political aspects of globalization from an economic perspective.

Democracy and Economic Growth

It's no secret that there is a strong correlation between national wealth and democratic rule. Economists and political scientists alike remark that all OECD countries are democratic and wealthy, while many nondemocratic states are in the poorest regions of the world, such as Africa and the Middle East. Over the past 40 years, democratic rule has spread across the globe. The number of electoral democracies grew from roughly 30 to 120 nations, so that over half of the independent states around the world are now democratic. At the same time, many nations have also gotten much richer. These patterns prompt a natural question: does democratic rule lead to economic growth? And conversely, does economic growth increase the likelihood of a democratic transition? Correlation does not prove causation, and over the past century, the statistical evidence that this correlation between income and democracy is causal is actually quite weak. At least there is some evidence that higher levels of education—which are more likely to occur in wealthy nations—lead to more democratic politics, although even this is contested.

Over the very long run, the statistical evidence supporting a relationship between growth and democracy is a bit stronger. At the start of the 19th century, after the Industrial Revolution had spread from England to other regions, very few countries were democratic. Since then, democratization has come together with growth. Some scholars have argued democracy requires a certain level of economic development—otherwise it will not last—and economic growth forecasts democratic rule. Going further back to some 500 years ago, countries that moved toward democracy also grew the most. At the time that Dias, da Gama, and Columbus were voyaging from Europe to faraway continents, there existed certain political constraints on monarchs in some European nations, whereas outside of Europe, absolutism still ruled. Some countries have embarked on paths embracing democratic rule and economic growth, while others have not, remaining absolutist and relatively poor. The empirical research is contentious and unsettled, though many prominent political scientists—including Robert Dahl, Samuel Huntington, and Seymour Martin Lipset—have maintained that the long-run link between democracy and income is indeed causal, perhaps best exemplified by the experience of Western European nations and their "offshoots."

Globalization and Democracy

Just as wealth and democracy have proliferated around the world over the past two centuries, globalization has also spread. The belief that globalization and democracy go hand-in-hand is very common among policymakers, scholars, and government leaders. It's easy to see why. Many economies in Central and Eastern Europe joined the global economy after Soviet authoritarianism collapsed. In Latin America, the twin forces of democratization and globalization have expanded since the 1970s. At the other extreme, despotic North Korea maintains a closed economy that is—not coincidentally—deeply impoverished and backward. Other nations present case studies that don't fit neatly into standard categories. Singapore is one of the most globalized and open economies in the world despite not being a full electoral democracy (at least according to most Westerners). Hong Kong, also an affluent globalization leader, is not a full democracy (though it does have a high degree of autonomy from mainland China). Globalization doesn't always bring democracy, either. The nondemocratic government in China has remained strong despite opening trade. Some even argue that economic growth powered by trade actually makes Chinese democratic reforms less likely—similar, perhaps, to Singapore's experience in some ways. And democracies don't always create pro-globalization policies. For instance, in Bolivia and Peru, democratization fueled populist measures opposing free trade.

Think of the distribution of political power in democratic versus absolutist governments. Democratic governments allocate political power broadly across the population, enfranchising ordinary workers and the poor. They distribute political power to most citizens, so that even those with minimal resources are represented. (In theory, communist governments do the same, claiming to represent workers and labor interests above all else, yet based on their track records, they are inefficient, repressive, and often fail to support the interests of common citizens, benefitting connected party members instead.) Progressive income taxes are common in democracies, as voters demand some redistributive aspects to their tax systems. Research shows that democratization leads to more social spending on education and health. Balancing the interests of many groups, democracies frequently enact policies regulating capital, landowners, natural resources, and workers. In the end, voter sentiment generally determines whether a democratic nation opens itself to free trade and foreign investment.

By contrast, absolutist regimes maintain power in the hands of a ruling elite, whether a single ruler (as in autocracy), a small clique (as in oligarchy), or a large class of party members (as in some socialist states). These systems frequently restrict trade and international influences. They feature concentrated political and economic power favoring the owners of nonlabor factors of production such as capital, land, and natural resources. For instance, the aristocratic landed gentry in pre-industrial England owned large tracts of land, living off their rental income, and possessed disproportionate political power for centuries. In China today, the ruling Communist Party has 80 million members, and most capital flows to state-owned enterprises which monopolize key industries and charge higher prices than would be possible under a more competitive economic environment. In Bolivia and Venezuela, wealth and power emanate from the possession of bountiful natural resources such as oil, natural gas, and lithium. Since absolutist governments may be expected to enact globalization policies consistent with the interests of the ruling class, if the factor of production that the elite control is relatively abundant, the state may push for free trade. If it is scarce—such as land in small, backward European nations during the 19th century—they may not. And compared to democracies, the interests of labor are likely to be given less weight in absolutist states.

The factor proportions model of international trade yields some predictions about governance in developing nations. Under democracy in poor developing countries that are full of unskilled labor, voters would support opening trade, since it would drive their wages up. However, capital owners may not support globalization, because capital is usually scarce in poor countries and foreign investment may drive down their rate of return. Thus, opening trade can reduce inequality, attract foreign investment, and generate growth, though not every powerful interest group would support it. Since democracies give relatively more political power to unskilled labor, democratic regimes should be more likely to foster globalization and trade in developing countries.

An important case—quite relevant to Africa, Latin America, and the Middle East—occurs when ruling elites control a domestic supply of exportable natural resources (like oil and gold) that is the country's abundant factor. The ruling government would support opening trade and then cash in. By supporting education and health spending in developing nations, resource wealth can be a blessing. Yet the possession of natural resources can also lead to friction, instability, and conflict among domestic factions, which retards economic and political progress. This situation is sometimes called the "natural resource curse," and it has afflicted a number of developing countries (such as Nigeria and Cote D'Ivoire, which are rich in oil and cocoa, respectively). Under democracy, voters might push for nationalization if they believe the benefits of their country's resources are not fairly shared. However, in a weak state, regardless of the type of political system, concentrated natural resources invite graft and corruption. Partly for this reason, democracy may be difficult to enact in the first place in these resource-rich developing nations. They are also commonly plagued by strong currencies, since foreigners buy large quantities of the domestic currency when they trade for the local natural resource, which hampers the export of other goods.

The empirical evidence supports the notion that democratic rule is more likely to promote globalization in developing nations, as openness would increase demand for unskilled labor. Potential exceptions are labor-scarce poor nations—such as frontier economies—or Latin American states where workers are worried about job losses from international competition. The case is less clear for affluent developed nations. Worried about low-wage competition abroad, rich state voters may not support free trade. Antiglobalization voices might hold more sway in a democratic regime, particularly in recent decades, as globalization has often come with an increased skill premium. On the other hand, rich nations are usually full of capital, and wealthy capital holders—who typically have a lot of clout under any type of government—would be expected to support globalization. Capital owners may be even better connected to ruling elites in wealthy nondemocratic states, giving them influence to help enact pro-globalization policies. There is also the issue of interest group pressure and protectionism. Narrow industry interests are frequently influential in democracies because voters lack information and politicians need funding. In wealthy absolutist countries, special interests can have influence if the ruling elites are aligned with them—or, without such an alliance, they may have no influence at all. Statistical research across developed nations yields mixed conclusions: wealthy countries are commonly democracies, but democratic governance does not necessarily make them more likely to globalize.

Reversing the causal arrow, there is also the question of whether globalization and trade foster democracy in nondemocratic nations. As discussed in the previous chapter, opening trade and liberalizing finance can enhance economic development and lead to a growing middle class, making a democratic transition more likely. Trade liberalization also brings new products and ideas which may increase the demand for democracy. However, trade can exacerbate income inequalities and cause significant employment dislocations. In some cases, openness may shift power to the wealthy and connected, strengthening the rule of an autocracy that clamps down on potential insurrections and democratic revolutionaries. A number of studies have yielded contradictory findings so far, indicating that there is no consistently measurable effect of globalization on democracy, at least according to international statistical evidence. Even so, there is probably some positive effect stemming from exposure to the cultural influences and ideas (including consumerism) of democratic societies. In fact, in the 18th century, Kant proposed that globalization spreads democratic ideals. Like developing a taste for blue jeans, trade and globalization—when combined with information and communications technologies—can lead to pro-democracy attitudes among the general public. And as societies get richer, citizens demand more political rights. Indeed, political scientists have long considered political rights to be a luxury good. These forces may eventually lead to greater democratic reforms in China.

Winners, Losers, and the Demand for Regulation

The logic of the Stolper-Samuelson theorem dictates that when a country opens up to trade, the domestic production of goods that intensively utilize the country's relatively abundant factor will go up. The price of the abundant factor of production will be bid up, and those who own it will gain from free trade. Using the reverse logic, owners of the relatively scarce factor of production will lose. The resulting prediction is that individuals whose income depends on scarce factors will fear free trade, and those controlling abundant factors will welcome it. An interesting 19th century example is the United States, a democratic developing nation with high tariff barriers to trade. It was labor- and capital-scarce, but it did have a lot of land. Many natives were skeptical about free trade and immigration because they feared it would drive down their wages. Agricultural interests welcomed both, as land was abundant and all the more profitable with additional immigrant labor. Organized labor was generally weak, so that, favored by business (capital) and farming groups (landowners), open immigration was allowed. (It wasn't until 1875 that the first federal law restricting immigration—the Page Act—was passed, aimed at Asian migrants.) After the United States had amassed an abundance of capital and the population had grown sufficiently, tariffs were eventually lowered, despite opposition from labor and capital. America's late-19th century agrarian competitors in Western Europe responded with a backlash that raised tariff barriers.

As the legendary Paul Samuelson, namesake of the Stolper-Samuelson theorem, liked to point out, although trade is beneficial in the aggregate and generates gains for certain interests, it will probably harm some other interests, and in practice, the winners may not compensate the losers, either because they cannot or they do not wish to. In theory, governments can take funds from the winners to compensate the losers. However, it can be politically difficult for the government to make such transfers. For example, if American sugar tariffs are abolished, American consumers would win, yet sugar workers might be devastated. In practice, sugar workers who lost their jobs might receive some public assistance, though probably not enough to make up for their troubles. Along these lines, economists commonly argue that modern mature economies have developed entrenched interest groups that lobby for inefficient policies, such as the maintenance of specific types of protectionism or the elimination of beneficial regulations. Like barnacles on an ocean liner, collusive political groups accumulate during prosperous decades. This notion certainly applied to the overextended British Empire prior to World War I. Political shake-ups, economic turmoil, and war can serve as catalysts for reform, but until such events transpire, the result can be "institutional sclerosis" which retards growth.

In the United States, during the 25 years preceding the Great Recession, the abundant factor capital did well in many sectors. The economy was further opened to trade and the financial system was liberalized, attracting billions of dollars in foreign investment. The size and profitability of the American financial sector increased dramatically. A handful of innovators in the information technology sector reaped millions (and sometimes billions) when their risky start-ups hit pay dirt. Labor struggled at times, especially lesser skilled workers who were substitutes for low-cost labor overseas, automated machinery, or computers. Overall income inequality in America returned to levels that had not been experienced since before World War II. The factor proportions model and Stolper-Samuelson theorem offer an insightful way to understand these trends leading up to the Great Recession. Relatively abundant in capital, technology, and skilled labor, the United States further integrated with the world economy. Owners of these factors of production favored globalization, for good reason. Influenced by lobbying, regulatory oversight of the financial sector became more lax. Heavy transaction volumes coupled with leverage-magnified bets generated hefty financial sector compensation. When bubbles burst to end the cycle, conventional strategies soured and the government was forced to intervene, supported by public funds.

The typical American family saw its wealth decline significantly in the wake of the Great Recession, and many voters have begun to question the fairness and adequacy of past policies. The situation in Europe is broadly comparable. International survey evidence suggests that since 2009, more citizens have grown to feel that economic benefits and burdens are not fairly distributed. Although most respondents firmly support capitalism, their call for retooled regulation has intensified. Some scholars, such as Nobel Prize winner Joseph Stiglitz, have gone as far as to argue that the benefits of capitalism and globalization have actually gone to the most skilled in rent-seeking, due to insufficient regulation in many countries. This argument suggests that, instead of progressing, the political process in many advanced nations has regressed. Recall the days of the English and Dutch Indies Companies from the 17th to the 19th centuries, when monopolies were granted by the state and benefits flowed to elites. Although democratic governments don't baldly sanction overseas trading monopolies by military force today, the end result may be similar because of moneyed special interests and polarized political systems. During Roman times, the historian Plutarch stated that "an imbalance between rich and poor is the oldest and most fatal ailment of all republics," so this challenge of governance is hardly new.

The period of hyperglobalization may have slowed for now as populist backlash pressures build. Survey evidence indicates that in the United States, Europe, and many other regions, voters and politicians are reevaluating the role of regulatory controls (such as banking supervision) that are designed to protect the public from downside risks caused by global market turmoil and international business cycles. The current age of fiscal strains and limited government funds makes it all the more important that the legal and regulatory aspects of market economies are improved and updated. Citizens are also reassessing their support for free trade and open capital markets. The trend even extends to China, a nondemocratic state where inequality has grown and a lack of environmental oversight has allowed pollution to explode (though top officials now acknowledge that these problems do pose threats to social stability). As part of China's effort to develop its capital markets and financial system, state authorities are enhancing regulation of the domestic stock market so that citizens feel comfortable investing in it. Fortunately, the world is much richer and less militaristic than it was a century ago, so popular discontent is less likely to turn outward and create military conflict. In poorer regions of the world, economic progress undoubtedly has the potential to bring shared prosperity and fund public sector budgets, as emerging economies accumulate physical and human capital stocks to complement their abundant supply of unskilled labor.

Popular Support for Free Trade

The factor proportions model is a rather accurate predictor of people's trade preferences. International survey evidence shows that in nations with plenty of skilled workers possessing human capital, individuals with more skill and human capital favor free trade. Yet in countries where human capital is relatively scarce, these same workers oppose free trade. In line with a given worker's self-interest, comparative advantage affects views on trade. Compared to those in nontradables sectors, workers in tradables sectors that do not possess a comparative advantage internationally are less likely to support free trade. Globalization is also worrisome for poorer workers; those who consider themselves of lower relative social standing and wealth are less likely to support free trade. Thus, an individual's place within their country's income distribution predicts their attitudes toward globalization. This is consistent with the evidence that, contra the factor proportions model, globalization can exacerbate inequalities even in developing nations, possibly due to the effects of technology and capital upgrading that favor skilled workers. Even in the free-trading United States, most citizens, including professionals and those with higher incomes, have become progressively more skeptical of globalization since the 1990s. They recognize the benefits but are concerned about the pressures it places on job security and compensation. And Europeans generally believe that globalization has benefitted corporations at the expense of domestic workers.

Survey respondents who have confidence in their nation's political institutions are more likely to favor free trade. This isn't surprising: a poorly governed or corrupt country will have trouble enacting trade policies that yield broad benefits. The experience of Latin America, where governments have not always managed economic integration well, illustrates this result. In many instances, elites have disproportionately benefitted, and the underclass has learned that, without sufficient market development in key industries, local economies may not be able to withstand competitive forces that come with trade and globalization. Subsequently, Latin American support for globalization has dropped. There has been a resurgence of leftist populist politicians in the region, including Chávez in Venezuela, Lula in Brazil, the Kirchners in Argentina, Morales in Bolivia, García in Peru, and Correa in Ecuador. Many of these politicians have vowed to redistribute natural resource wealth. The evidence suggests that these leaders have not so much reversed globalization as expanded the public sector and social welfare state to help labor cope with the risks that accompany globalization. Given the region's rich supply of natural resources (which Chinese and Indian economies crave), Latin American nations have plenty of incentive to maintain intercontinental economic integration and improve their infrastructure. With a bit of luck, perhaps Latin American entrepreneurial and creative talent will be better utilized in the future, once citizens are given a stronger political foundation for starting businesses and creating intellectual property.

History, Political Coalitions, and Trade

International trade can facilitate domestic economic growth yet it is not welcomed by every interest group. Motivated by their own economic concerns—as according to the factors of production that they own and control—domestic political factions have commonly fought international trade, calling instead for protectionist policies. The factor proportions model and Stolper-Samuelson theorem specify the incentives which each political coalition faces. Consider nations with a relative abundance of land—again, relative to international averages—like 19th century frontier societies in North America, South America, and Australia. Here landowners would support trade, allowing them to sell their inexpensive labor-intensive agricultural products globally. Labor and capital, both scarce (and pricey), are more likely to oppose opening trade. Landowners may also back infrastructure investments like railroads, which lower the cost of transporting agricultural exports, and approve of foreign capital inflows, which lower their cost of capital in making improvements. Of course, political coalitions are complex, and land is not as important as it once was, yet the example still generalizes. The political economy of trade integration and interest group alliances was fleshed out by an American political scientist, Ronald Rogowski, in the 1980s. This section discusses ideas presented in his seminal book *Commerce and Coalitions*, which shows how the factor proportions model yields powerful insights into globalization and the unfolding of history.

Best understood as a description of long-run tendencies, the factor proportions model suggests that opening trade helps domestic owners of the abundant factor—whether land, capital, or labor—as well as companies that intensively use the abundant factor. In effect, after allowing trade, foreign sources increase demand for the locally abundant factor which is relatively inexpensive and often used in exporting industries, thereby bidding up its rental price. In the above example, free trade helps the 19th century American landowners and the agricultural sector. The opposite is true for holders of the scarce factor: they feel threatened by free trade because it is cheaper to rent their factor abroad. Production in their sector will shift overseas under free trade, and inexpensive imports could injure their livelihoods. For owners of scarce factors, it makes sense to demand protectionism and fight trade. In the early-19th century United States, capital was relatively scarce, so industrialists, trying to build up a budding manufacturing sector to compete with Great Britain, demanded tariffs on imports.

As illustrated in the table below, any economy can be classified according to whether capital and land are abundant relative to labor. A backward economy is primitive and developing, meaning there is little capital per worker. An advanced economy is mature and industrialized, so that the capital-to-labor ratio is high. And keep in mind that land interests are rural, while capital holders are mainly situated in urban areas.

Economy	High land-labor ratio	Low land-labor ratio
Advanced	Abundant: Capital & Land	Abundant: Capital & Labor
	Scarce: Labor	Scarce: Land
Backward	Abundant: Land	Abundant: Labor
	Scarce: Capital & Labor	Scarce: Capital & Land

On the eve of the first great globalization boom, which began after the Napoleonic Wars and lasted until World War I, the United States would be represented in the lower left quadrant, signifying backward frontier economies that are full of land. (This quadrant also covers the rest of the Americas at that time.) In these societies, rural agricultural interests generally favor free trade but urban industrial and labor interests do not, leading to an urban-rural cleavage. This scenario is illustrated by the "Tariff of 1828," which increased the price of imported goods and marked the high point of American import tariffs prior to the Civil War. Southern agricultural interests were vehemently opposed, calling it the "Tariff of Abominations." However, favored by Western and Mid-Atlantic states, the tariff contributed to the growth of the American manufacturing base. From 1833 to the Civil War, the Whig Party (which was superseded by the Republican Party) supported modernization, protectionism, and the growth of manufacturing; it was the party of Northern business interests and the professional class. They were opposed by the Democratic Party, which was dominated by large-scale Southern farmers, urban labor, and immigrants. Interestingly, the Whigs backed railroads, canals, public education, and national banking, believing that in the long run, these policies would promote American industrialization and economic growth. They were right. Trade, growth, frontier expansion, and the rapid development of the nonagricultural sector during the mid-19th century played a decisive role in the ascendance of the North and West. With its relative power declining, the agrarian South was defensive, and in opposition, the North and West moved closer together politically. Southern states started to secede in late 1860, shortly after Abraham Lincoln's election. The Northern Union possessed an overwhelming resource advantage, and by the summer of 1865, just weeks after Lincoln's assassination, the Confederacy was defeated and the Civil War was over.

Now consider backward economies that are land poor, in the lower right quadrant: they are abundant only in labor. Much of Eastern Europe—such as Poland, Romania, and Bulgaria—provided a good example until recently. Today, Bangladesh, India, and the Philippines are all developing nations with a low land-labor ratio. In these economies, labor supports free trade while capital and landowners are more likely to band together in favor of protectionism. Instead of an urban-rural conflict, there exists a class struggle between poor workers and commercial interests. This dynamic is one reason why socialism has continued to survive in India. Germany's experience during the second half of the 19th century is a good illustration of shifting alliances that accord with the factor proportions model. In the middle of the 19th century, the German economy was backward, with plenty of labor but a relative scarcity of capital. Workers supported free trade and industrialists sought protectionism. Landowners (called the "Junker") favored free trade, given Germany's successful exporting of agricultural products. However, by the 1870s, American grain was underselling German grain in every market; with a new railroad system and cheap land throughout the United States, it was impossible for Germany to compete. In response, German capital owners and landowners formed a successful protectionist alliance (called a "marriage of iron and rye"), made all the more urgent due to the onset of the Long Depression in 1873. Germany continued to industrialize, and by the 1890s, it was advanced, with ample capital and higher wages. Now in the upper right quadrant of the table above, German industrialists became more free trade-oriented after the turn of the century, in tune with workers. Spain, by contrast, stayed backward throughout the 19th century and beyond, as labor constantly fought against capital and landowning interests.

During the early-to-mid-19th century, nations rich in capital and labor—represented in the upper right quadrant—were concentrated in the developed regions of Western Europe. Great Britain was the global leader in industrial maturity, trailed by Belgium and Switzerland. There were urban-rural social divides in all three nations. As world trade took off in the 1820s, Britain was at the forefront, with urban capital and labor united to repeal protectionist policies supported by rural landowners, most notably the Corn Laws. Capital and labor ultimately won that battle, as the Corn Laws were abolished in 1846, ushering in an era of free trade and robust economic growth. In response to new foreign competition, the British agricultural sector upgraded its technology and capital, and was able to thrive for several decades until a torrent of cheap American foodstuffs swamped global markets. Belgium's mid-19th century history paralleled Great Britain, albeit with a lag. Supported by industrialists and urban labor, the Liberal party succeeded in winning free trade by 1861. They were opposed by the Catholic party, which was dominated by rural landowners and Flemish labor. Both Belgium and Switzerland were free trade- and export-oriented during the second half of the 19th century, policies which supported economic growth and further industrialization. The sway of labor grew as well, so that universal male suffrage was achieved in both nations by the early-20th century. Lagging behind Belgium and Switzerland, France's 19th century capital accumulation and modernization was uneven. French manufacturers and landowners in backward regions opposed free trade, although by mid-century urban workers, financiers, and industrialists in wealthy districts around major cities such as Paris and Marseilles supported it.

Prior to World War I, the United States and Canada appear to be the only nations that were capital and land abundant yet scarce in labor (in the upper left quadrant). The United States did not achieve advanced status until about the turn of the 20th century, while Canada took a little longer. After a bout of protectionism during the Long Depression, American business interests called for free trade, and tariffs diminished after 1900. Since the United States had become an industrial juggernaut, Canada was worried about American competition and consequently kept import tariffs high on American goods (while easing tariffs on European imports). The case of pre-Bolshevik Russia illustrates an additional category that is not shown in the above table, namely, economies rich in land and labor but short of capital. Russia quickly built railroads after 1850 so that foodstuffs grown across its large landmass could be transported and sold in foreign markets. Between 1860 and 1880, Russian grain exports tripled, and from 1850 to 1900, the Russian population doubled. However, the Russian czarist government held firm to industrial interests and urban development, enforcing policies that squeezed both land and labor and contributed to famines during the 1890s. Land and labor remained in opposition to the government, and after 1900, peasant revolts and urban strikes became more common, leading up to the Russian Revolution of 1917 that resulted in a new communist government entrusted to uphold labor interests.

Factor Coalitions Across Globalization Eras

All the aforementioned examples are taken from the prewar period when—spurred by reduced transportation and communications costs—international trade and global economic integration was expanding. In such epochs, momentum favors the abundant factor, since it typically has more to gain from opening trade than the scarce factor has to lose. (Furthermore, even if tariffs remain constant, diminishing transportation costs will lead to increased trade volumes, benefitting owners of the abundant factor.) To capture the latent surplus from trade, abundant factor coalitions are expected to be aggressive in their support of free trade. In opposition, political alignments between scarce factors emerge; they are defensive and protectionist. As the case of post-serfdom Russia demonstrates, although abundant factors can be resisted for many years, they may well accumulate sufficient strength to prevail in the long run.

These forces are consistent with political developments during the 16th and 17th century globalization boom. Though lacking in land, leading economies like England and Holland possessed plenty of capital and labor. Conversely, the Americas were abundant solely in land. After settlers moved to the New World, they realized labor power was a critical engine for growth, but given its scarcity, landowning colonists often resorted to

forced labor such as slavery to maintain their economic and social dominance. Back in Europe, both the flourishing Dutch Republic and Britain
under the Tudors were dominated by an alliance of capital and skilled
labor, which eroded the power of the traditional landowning aristocracy.
In the lightly populated regions of Eastern Europe and Russia, trade aided
landowners, keepers of the sole abundant factor, serving to support the
"Second Serfdom" that lasted into the 19th century.

Political dynamics were reversed during the 20th century interwar
period of declining globalization and autarky, when abundant factors were
on the *defensive*. International trade disintegrated, empowering scarce factors, first economically and then politically. In the United States, where
only labor was scarce, restrictive immigration acts were passed in the
1920s, and emboldened workers sought favorable reforms such as the New
Deal. Across the wealthy economies of Western Europe, land was the sole
scarce factor, so that agricultural and landed interests gained power. In
Germany, Italy, and Austria, these rural elites supported a rightward turn
toward fascism. In fact, almost all interwar dictatorships were founded on
pre-industrial sources of social power, such as the monarchy, aristocracy,
church, and military. Fascist movements became extremely dangerous
when the wealthy old aristocracy was able to align itself with the working
class. With mass appeal to the working poor, the Nazis were first enabled
by German agricultural interest groups. Once in power, they raised import
tariffs on food products, created agricultural cartels, and preached rural
values. The climate in Belgium was similar, though the Belgian fascist
party (called the "Rexists") did not ultimately prevail. Great Britain provides a stark contrast. Although its domestic factor proportions were
broadly parallel to Germany, British agriculture had negligible influence
by World War I, as British labor and capital came to dominate domestic
affairs during the 19th century globalization explosion. Consequently, a
reactionary turn in England favoring country landowners was simply not
feasible during the Great Depression.

Between the wars, across regions of Europe that remained backward—
namely the South and East—scarce capital and land formed alliances to
suppress abundant and defensive labor. A May 1926 coup in Portugal
would result in dictatorship; the Greek monarchy was reinstated in
1935; and in Spain, dictatorship followed a devastating civil war during

the 1930s. Political structures underwent upheavals in Latin America, which was land-rich but capital- and labor-poor. The power of the landed aristocracy declined, replaced by populist movements that supported urban interests and industrialization. Most of Asia was densely populated during the interwar era, with relatively little capital and land, sparking a dynamic favorable to commercial interests but potentially damaging to workers. Even in Japan, the wealthiest and most advanced nation in Asia, industrialization was not yet complete by World War I, and half of the work force remained in agriculture. Beginning in the 1920s, Japanese labor faltered while landed elites, business interests, and the military promoted imperialistic fascism.

Backward China—which, like Russia, contained powerful landed interests, a tiny middle class, and a docile bureaucracy—also endured tremendous turmoil between the wars. Not long after the 1925 death of Sun Yat-Sen, President of the post-imperial Republic of China, communist forces led by Mao Tse-Tung, representing peasants and workers, began waging war against the Kuomintang led by Chiang Kai-Shek, who favored status quo capital and landowning interests. The two parties continued fighting, though they were united in their opposition to the partial Japanese occupation from 1931 to 1945. By 1949, Mao and the communists had beaten Chiang and the Kuomintang, who were thereafter relegated to Taiwan. In neighboring Vietnam—also relatively full of labor but lacking in capital and land—communists fought against old elites and gained ground as postwar trade expanded, eventually becoming a socialist state after the 1975 capture of Saigon by the communist North.

The end of World War II ushered in another era of expanding globalization across much of the world. Among advanced economies after the war, land was not nearly as important to economic development as it once was. Agriculture's employment share, already low, continued to decline. Instead, led by the United States, the wealthiest economies were capital-abundant and full of new technologies. Some rebuilding economies had plenty of labor and industrial know-how, like much of Western Europe and Japan, where rapidly increasing trade volumes melded together coalitions of labor and capital in support of open trade as well as democracy. Aided by the election of socialist governments, trade unions became more powerful in prosperous European nations. In backward areas of Europe and Asia abundant only in labor, worker movements surged. On the other hand, in the relatively labor-scarce United States, where a ubiquitous fear of communism helped restrict the development of left-wing politics, organized labor never achieved quite the same degree of influence.

Beginning in the 1980s, the era of hyperglobalization brought about a renewed interest in market forces, integrated global capital markets, and minimal trade barriers. These trends favored advanced economy professional classes, especially propagators of commercial technologies and financial sector interests, such as those within the strongholds of New York, London, Tokyo, and Hong Kong. Human capital and physical capital are often abundant in the same regions; within these wealthy economies, the professional and managerial classes tend to align with capital in urban areas, supporting open trade and the spread of new technologies. Unskilled labor in wealthy economies—relatively scarce compared to international averages—has been defensive and less welcoming of these developments. In the United States, economic and political influence has shifted toward financial and commercial elites, resulting in an overall political drift to the right.

Globalization and Government Size

Without question, globalization has not diminished the size of governments. A century ago, government spending in industrialized nations accounted for less than a tenth of national income. For example, in the United States, federal spending was under 3% of income in 1900. National income taxes—in the relatively few places they existed—were much lower back then, and governments (especially in younger nations) used to rely more on tariffs for revenue. The situation today is very different. Government spending now accounts for almost half of national income in advanced economies. Even in the United States and Japan, countries with relatively small public sectors, about a third of national income is devoted to the state. The wealthier and better-developed a country is, the more of its national income is directed toward government spending. In other words, richer countries not only have better functioning markets, they also have larger governments, suggesting that markets and governments are complements, not substitutes. As emerging countries grow in the coming years, they will distribute more resources to their public sector to provide for infrastructure, education, health care, pensions, and defense. In many wealthy nations, the political influence of elderly pensioners will grow due to their relative abundance. In spite of the deteriorating finances of European sovereigns and the American federal government, it seems very unlikely that public sectors in these countries will shrink to levels seen a century ago. Communism may be dead almost everywhere in the 21st century, but the social welfare state is certainly not.

Empirical research by economists and political scientists has shown that openness to international trade is a key factor in explaining why governments have become larger in advanced nations. In fact, one important reason why the United States and Japan have smaller governments relative to other wealthy nations is that their economies are not as dependent on trade. At the other extreme, Scandinavian welfare states like Sweden and Finland have historically been very reliant on international trade. The demand for social insurance among voters explains much of this relationship. The more vulnerable workers are to the vagaries of external economies and the international business cycle, the more likely they are to demand government benefits like unemployment insurance and social security (at least in affluent economies that can afford such programs). These safety net provisions help ordinary workers face the downside risks inherent in economic globalization. They even act as substitutes for protectionist trade barriers. During the 1930s, when tariffs went up around the world, social safety nets were in their infancy in the wealthiest countries such as the United States. Today, instead of agitating for tariff barriers, struggling workers now receive government benefits during powerful economic downturns. In the absence of welfare state policies, it is likely that more extensive trade barriers would have gone up as a result of the Great Recession. Open economies also tend to be more industrialized and possess private sector institutions that are able to transfer risk away from workers. They have stronger labor federations, higher rates of unionization, and more collective bargaining; Germany provides a good case in point. Modern financial markets, offering life insurance and annuities, provide some risk mitigation that is commonly supported by the public sector.

Globalization affects the costs and benefits of a country's size. People usually think of nations as fixed objects, yet there are more nations now than ever before. After World War II, there were 74 independent countries in the world, whereas today, there are about 200. The four wealthiest nations on the planet on a per capita basis—Liechtenstein, Qatar, Luxembourg, and Singapore—are also among the tiniest, while the United States and Japan are the only wealthy nations among the ten most populous—which are, in order, China, India, the United States, Indonesia, Brazil, Pakistan, Nigeria, Bangladesh, Russia, and Japan. Is this only a coincidence, or is economic growth easier to achieve in small countries? Recent economic research has highlighted some of the size trade-offs that countries face, and how globalization affects them. Small nations benefit from having homogeneous populations that are less prone to internal conflicts. Political policies can be tailored to suit most of the population within a small country, facilitating efficient governance which promotes peace and growth. For tiny countries, international trade acts as a necessary lifeline. By globalizing, they can get away with staying small, because in a world of global supply chains, they only need to specialize in a few chain links to prosper. According to this reasoning, globalization can lead to separatism, which is consistent with the postwar evidence, as the number of nations has increased alongside growing globalization. On the other hand, if economies of scale are important to economic growth, larger countries are advantaged. They are able to provide public goods (like defense and infrastructure) more efficiently, and they also derive economic benefits from having a larger domestic consumer market. In the absence of international trade and globalized capital financing, it may be better to be a large country with a big diversified domestic market.

Brief History of Modern Warfare

The Prussian general and military theorist Carl von Clausewitz famously declared in his posthumous 1832 magnum opus *On War* that war is "a continuation of politics carried on by other means." Since Columbus set foot on New World soil, international wars fought by the most powerful nations have become less common and less lengthy. After the European population had recovered from the Black Death, the 16th and 17th centuries were replete with major wars between Spain, France, Portugal, England, and Holland. Military force and economic dominance were deeply linked in those mercantilist days. Among the European powers, labor was common but land was scarce, so the Crown could make gains by conquering new territories. Colossal battles between wealthy European nations subsequently declined during the 18th and 19th centuries—with the most glaring exception the devastating Napoleonic Wars from 1799 to 1815—as economies and populations expanded and overflowed to the New World. Under the peaceful century of the Pax Britannica, from the end of the Napoleonic Wars to the start of World War I, British naval dominance lowered the risks of trade and transport. World trade exploded, new technologies spread, and international wars were relatively brief.

Growing rivalries between the industrialized powers of Europe led to World War I and then World War II, initiating a new era of modern warfare by global powers. Battles became bloodier than ever with new technologies like machine guns, poison gas, and tanks. Although precise figures are difficult to pinpoint, there were over 10 million casualties in World War I. World War II featured even deadlier technologies such as long-range fighter planes, bombers, and nuclear weapons. It was the great-est atrocity in world history, resulting in over 60 million casualties. In just 6 years of conflict, about 2.5% of the world's population perished—half on the battlefield, half outside it—with mortality rates much higher for younger cohorts.

Since the end of World War II, no military conflicts have come close to matching its scale and lethality, and the volume of deaths caused by war has remained relatively low. The timeline above implies that—whether due to technology, economic growth, or globalization—warfare among major powers has drastically changed over the past two centuries. Rudimentary economic reasoning implies that the costs and benefits of fighting another powerful nation have shifted because of technology. Production technolo-gies have advanced enough to make land and natural resource scarcity less relevant, so the benefits of conquering a foreign power have declined. On the cost side of the equation, more powerful weapons have made war much more deadly, at least among great powers, implying that the potential costs of waging large-scale war have skyrocketed. Thus, as new technologies have made wars more lethal if they do break out, governments are less inclined to fight them. With global armed conflicts between wealthy nations more risky, fewer are fought. (Civil wars in small nations, discussed below, are a somewhat different story.) Of course, while there are limits to assuming rationality on the part of governments, advanced nations that possess the most formidable militaries seem to be the most rational.

Globalization and Warfare

Trade and globalization have influenced war, though perhaps not to the same extent as technology. During the Enlightenment era, when influential thinkers in the West destroyed the notion that kings had a divine right to rule, two 18th century philosophers, Kant and Montesquieu, argued that trade between nations naturally brought about peace. Kant believed that "Durable peace could be built upon the tripod of representative democracy, international organizations, and economic dependence." Trade and globalization make states dependent on each other and therefore less likely to fight a mutually destructive war. Quantitative economic research in this area is mounting and it is difficult to make definitive conclusions as yet. Nevertheless, empirical studies suggest that the number of violent interstate conflicts—among all nations, not just global powers—has stayed roughly constant over the past century. This includes the postwar period when the degree of trade openness rapidly increased around the world. Moreover, military conflicts have apparently become more localized since World War II. So it isn't clear at first glance whether Kant and Montesquieu were precisely right about the postwar globalization experience.

According to statistical evidence, when it comes to *bilateral* trade between two nations, increased trade does indeed reduce the likelihood of military conflict. Consider that the volume of trade between two partners is a measure of the opportunity cost of conflict: the higher their trade flows, the more incentive they have to avoid violence. This is consistent with Montesquieu's observation that "Two nations who differ with each other become reciprocally dependent; for if one has an interest in buying, the other has an interest in selling; and thus their union is founded on their mutual necessities." Yet other research suggests that *multilateral* trade openness has the opposite effect, increasing the likelihood of conflict. The theory is that countries which are more internationally integrated to global trade flows may be less dependent on trade with any single partner. When a potential conflict arises, they have less incentive to avert escalation by making concessions, so that in the end, greater multilateral trade openness can make countries more prone to war. One surprising implication is that bilateral trade flows reduce the probability that the two nations fight each other, but may increase the likelihood of conflict with third party nations.

Other research suggests that the postwar globalization boom actually increased the overall likelihood of conflict among countries that are close to each other (meaning, in other words, the multilateral trade effect has dominated the bilateral trade effect). This result is important because most interstate military conflicts today are local. They commonly stem from border or ethnic disputes, because populations that are more closely related share a greater set of common issues that can lead to major disagreements. This may also explain why the rate of violent interstate conflicts generally hasn't decreased since World War II. Moreover, since multilateral trade can be used to supply arms, strengthening multilateral trade routes to a given region may make war more likely. This is all the more relevant because the global arms trade disproportionately sends weapons from developed nations to the developing world. To offset the negative effects of globalization, regional trade agreements can strengthen trade relations among nearby nations facing the greatest potential for conflict. This conception was a driving force behind the "European Economic Community" (EEC), the forerunner of the present European Union. Enhanced trade links were established to try to ensure that France and Germany would never go to war again, as they had done three times in the preceding century.

Parallel research on civil wars sheds light on how globalization can lead to internal conflicts. Frequently relapses from previous conflicts, civil wars are much more likely to occur in countries with a large population of young uneducated males, and where one ethnic group outnumbers the rest. Within a given country, international trade raises the cost of a civil war, making it less likely to happen since violent conflict would place the gains from foreign trade at risk. But international trade can weaken economic dependence between groups within a country; during a civil war, each faction can turn to foreigners to trade for resources, including arms. Indeed, civil wars are more likely to be fought in regions rich in natural resources like oil and valuable minerals such as diamonds. The international statistical evidence indicates that since World War II, civil wars have become more frequent and much lengthier, lasting 4 years on average. And as mentioned above, there are more than twice as many sovereign nations today as there were at the end of World War II. Part of this tendency must be due to the fact that the great powers aren't as imperialistic as they once were. As Plato once said, "the number of citizens should be sufficient to defend themselves against the injustice of their neighbors." If dominant neighbors become less threatening, small nations are more likely to survive on their own—and thus, more likely to attempt to break free.

To generalize, consider again the benefits and costs of state size. Large nations benefit from economies of scale—related to infrastructure, police, and defense spending, for example—but they face costs when various populations don't agree on governance policies—due to, for instance, regionalism or ethnicity. Given the postwar decline in imperialist warfare by powerful states, small- or medium-sized nations may not achieve the same military economies of scale that they once did. Since the benefits of staying intact have faded, they're less fearful of breaking up, making civil war more likely. Trade could be one factor driving the trend, as it facilitates low-intensity civil wars by giving warring parties easier access to foreign resources. Globalization can also generate sudden slumps in national income that lead to domestic friction. Evidence indicates that in countries which export raw materials, civil war is more likely to break out when there are large drops in the international price of their primary commodities. This mechanism is particularly relevant to sub-Saharan African nations that are dependent on revenues from a few commodity exports. Uganda, a major coffee exporter, is an illustrative example; the world price of coffee fell before Ugandan civil wars that began in 1981, 1991, and 2002.

Conclusion

Globalization offers a menu of new options to citizens and governments: novel or cheaper goods to choose from; jobs for relatively inexpensive domestic workers; foreign buyers of domestic goods and resources; an expanding export sector; new sources of investment funds; access to foreign technologies; increasingly sophisticated industries, products, and services; integration into global supply chains; and larger state tax revenues. Yet globalization also comes with potential costs. It can lead to: new international competitive pressures; sectoral dislocations or "deindustrialization"; employment losses; capital outflows; domestic economic conditions increasingly dictated by international business cycles; massive swings in the value of domestic currencies; wealth windfalls for connected elites; immigration inflows and foreign cultural influences; and international restrictions and regulations.

Trade-offs are inevitable as modern governments attempt to integrate their economies globally while balancing the interests of domestic coalitions. Some scholars even argue that nations cannot have democracy, national determination, and economic globalization at the same time. For example, by maintaining a globalized democracy, a country necessarily gives up freedom to pursue certain goals of national determination and autonomy, such as full employment and capital restrictions; in recent decades, the United States and Canada are both examples. An autonomous democracy will closely manage its international economic integration, lest foreign economies dictate domestic outcomes; India is an example here. And a self-ruled globalized state governed by technocrats will have little room for democratic policies mandated by the public; China is one such example.

International economic integration strengthened from the end of World War II through the 1970s under the Bretton Woods system, which allowed for national determination and growing prosperity among rich nations. This framework helped shape a collective political will that was ever more accepting of globalization. After the economic turmoil of the 1970s, many states shifted to favor economic globalization at the expense of national determination and—to a lesser extent—democracy. Comprehensive state industrial policies and capital controls went out of favor, even though under globalized capital markets, financial difficulties in one country are more likely to spread to other countries, faster than ever before. With the late 1990s East Asian financial crisis, governments were reawakened to the dangers of liberalized capital flows. Developing Asian economies (most notably China) subsequently maintained high savings rates and accumulated massive sums of international reserves (mainly dollars), which facilitated investment and lessened the need for foreign debt financing, in a kind of self-insurance. But the massive surpluses also contributed to low interest rates in the United States and Europe, helping to generate a global credit boom that led to the most recent global financial crisis. In the coming years, a new balance will likely be struck in an emerging multipolar world, as nations reevaluate their place in the global economy and craft policies that respect the competing goals and interests unique to each economy, thereby regaining the support of citizens.

Further Reading

Acemoglu, D., & Robinson, J. (2006). *Economic origins of dictatorship and democracy*. New York, NY: Cambridge University Press.

Acemoglu, D., & Robinson, J. (2012). *Why nations fail: The origins of power, prosperity, and poverty*. New York, NY: Crown Publishers.

Alesina, A., & Spolaore, E. (2003). *The size of nations*. Cambridge, MA: MIT Press.

Baker, D. (2016). *Rigged: How globalization and the rules of the modern economy were structured to make the rich richer*. Washington, DC: Center for Economic and Policy Research.

Bernstein, W. (2013). *Masters of the word: How media shaped history*. New York, NY: Grove Press.

Chandler, A. (1994). *Scale and scope: The dynamics of industrial capitalism*. Cambridge, MA: Harvard University Press.

Downs, A. (1957). *An economic theory of democracy*. New York, NY: Harper and Row.

Frieden, J., Tomz, M., & Pastor, M. (2000). *Modern political economy and Latin America: Theory and policy*. Boulder, CO: Westview Press.

Huntington, S. (1968). *Political order in changing societies*. New Haven, CT: Yale University Press.

Huntington, S. (1991) *The third wave: Democratization in the late 20th century*. Norman, OK: University of Oklahoma Press.

Lipset, S. M. (1960). *Political man: The social bases of politics*. New York, NY: Doubleday and Company.

McCarty, N., Poole, K., & Rosenthal, H. (2006). *Polarized America: The dance of ideology and unequal riches*. Cambridge, MA: MIT Press.

Moore, B. (1966). *Social origins of dictatorship and democracy: Lord and peasant in the making of the modern world*. Boston, MA: Beacon Press.

Olson, M. (1982). *The rise and decline of nations: Economic growth, stagflation, and social rigidities*. New Haven, CT: Yale University Press.

Ostrom, E. (1990). *Governing the commons: The evolution of institutions for collective action*. Cambridge, England: Cambridge University Press.

Polanyi, K. (1944). *The great transformation*. Boston, MA: Beacon Press.

Rogowski, R. (1989). *Commerce and coalitions: How trade affects domestic political alignments*. Princeton, NJ: Princeton University Press.

Harvard Business School Case Studies

Andrews, M. *Effective revenue collection in Nomburo (or not)*, HKS441-PDF-ENG.

Badaracco, J. L., Jr., & Useem, J. *Exporting American culture*, 396055-PDF-ENG.

Cadieux, D., & Conklin, D. W. *The Great Recession, 2007–2010: Causes and consequences*, 910M08-PDF-ENG.

Chu, M. *Microfinance in Bolivia: A meeting with the President of the Republic*, 307107-PDF-ENG.

Colpan, A. M., & Jones, G. G. *Vehbi Koc and the making of Turkey's largest business group*, 811081-PDF-ENG.

Conklin, D. W., & Cadieux, D. *Hugo Chavez's public policy vision for Venezuela: Rooted in the past, doomed in the future?*, 906M59-PDF-ENG.

Conklin, D. W., & Cadieux, D. *Mekong Corporation and the Vietnam motor vehicle industry*, 907M74-PDF-ENG.

Conklin, D. W., & Cadieux, D. *The 2007–2008 financial crisis: Causes, impacts and the need for new regulations*, 908N14-PDF-ENG.

Daemmrich, A. A., & Kramarz, B. *Denmark: Globalization and the welfare state*, 709015-PDF-ENG.

Jones, G. G., & Ghanem, L. *Elia Nuqul and the making of a Middle Eastern business group*, 813052-PDF-ENG.

Jones, G. G., & Lluch, A. *Ernesto Tornquist: Making a fortune on the Pampas*, 807155-PDF-ENG.

Koehn, N. F. *Abraham Lincoln and the Civil War*, 805115-PDF-ENG.

Mathis, F. J., Albqami, R. A., & Rogmans, T. *Foreign direct investment in the Middle East: Riyadh and Dubai*, TB0269-PDF-ENG.

Mayo, A. J., Nohria, N., Mendhro, U., & Cromwell, J. *Sheikh Mohammed and the making of 'Dubai, Inc.,'* 410063-PDF-ENG.

McCraw, T. K. *Labor movement between the wars*, 391257-PDF-ENG.

McKern, B., Meza, P., Osayande, E., & Denend, L. *The business environment of Nigeria*, IB90-PDF-ENG.

Musacchio, A., Werker, E., & Schlefer, J. *Angola and the resource curse*, 711016-PDF-ENG.

Rangan, V. K. *Corporate responsibility & community engagement at the Tintaya copper mine*, 506023-PDF-ENG.

Trumbull, G. *Creation of the European Union*, 703032-PDF-ENG.

Vietor, R. H. K., & Comin, D. *South Africa: Stuck in the middle?*, 711084-PDF-ENG.

Werker, E., & Beganovic, J. *Liberia*, 712011-PDF-ENG.

Zuckerman, E., & Feldstein, J. *Venture capital in Israel: Emergence and globalization*, SM88-PDF-ENG.

CHAPTER 6

Poverty, Progress, and Critics of Globalization

Introduction

At the very end of the 20th century, massive protests surrounded a WTO conference during the infamous "Battle of Seattle." These loud voices condemned the treatment of poor nations ostensibly beholden to Western corporations and international financial organizations (such as the IMF). Protesters saw the spread of globalization as tantamount to exploitation of the developing world. They believed it benefitted a small class of insiders at the expense of powerless citizens. Fans of globalization—many of them economists—responded by elucidating the virtues of international economic integration, which include enhanced economic opportunities and poverty alleviation in the least developed nations.

Today, over a decade later, the debate has shifted. Following the global financial crisis, critics—who were ultimately unsuccessful in arresting globalization—protest the power of global capital even more vociferously. Yet they are forced to acknowledge that economic growth in emerging markets has been brisk over the past decade, drawing tens of millions out of extreme poverty. China has achieved rapid growth based on an idiosyncratic program of carefully managed liberalization reforms allowing it to globalize piecemeal. Meanwhile, proponents concede that globalization entails important costs such as lower job security. There also exist severe macroeconomic risks, even for rich nations, when massive tidal waves of liquidity are allowed to travel across the world in the blink of an eye.

Given recent developments, globalization is now being questioned by many, and it isn't clear if the hyperglobalization era will continue indefinitely. Although world trade flows have recovered from the last global financial crisis, there has been a reversal of financial globalization;

cross-border capital flows today are approximately half their peak volume reached just prior to the crisis. The lingering weakness of the "eurozone" banking sector and European economy has contributed to this turnabout. The decisions of government policymakers remain difficult to predict, but the debate over globalization's merits will surely persist in the coming years. This chapter is a modest discussion of some of the most pressing criticisms of globalization, informed by contemporary economic research and international statistical evidence.

Foreign Direct Investment, Multinationals, and Growth

Research has shown that within emerging economies, foreign direct invest-ment (FDI) inflows generate economic growth in manufacturing sectors, at least among countries that possess well-developed financial institutions. In addition, FDI that brings new technology leads to higher local growth, as long as domestic human capital levels are sufficiently high. Therefore, as long as developing countries have sufficient absorptive capacities to make use of it, FDI can lead to local economic growth and help economies move up the value-added chain.

Multinational enterprises (MNE) are the conduit for most global FDI today. By definition, MNE are firms that control and manage commercial operations in more than one country. These MNE provide FDI by creat-ing new foreign firms, buying foreign companies, or forming cooperative ventures with firms already operating in foreign markets. A major compar-ative advantage of MNE is that they are able to transfer intangible assets—such as intellectual property or managerial capital—across borders and along vertically integrated production operations, often via FDI. MNE based in wealthy countries (such as Intel) commonly engage in FDI by moving certain stages of production abroad to cheaper locations, in a process called "vertical" FDI. However, few realize that most FDI actually occurs through "horizontal" FDI, when MNE move roughly the same production activities from their home to a destination market in order to save on trade and transportation costs. For example, when Toyota builds an automobile manufacturing plant in the United States, it is engaging in horizontal FDI.

Governments in emerging markets have become much more open in allowing MNE to enter over the past several decades, and ever since, the presence of MNE in emerging economies has exploded. Accounting for over two-thirds of global business research and development spending, MNE are important agents of economic innovation and productivity growth. To a great extent, they are the principal force behind the deepening integration of the global economy. They can attract foreign investment capital, new technology, expanded business networks, new prospects for domestic entrepreneurs, managerial capital and know-how, and training opportunities for local workers. On the other hand, MNE can also crowd out domestic firms, causing some to close, and conceivably reduce domestic employment through dislocations. In spite of the potential growth enhancing opportunities that MNE can offer, economists still debate whether MNE play an essential role in generating economic growth among developing economies. For instance, neither MNE nor FDI per se were indispensable to Japan's rapid growth in the 20th century, though Japan certainly made use of foreign know-how via licensing and subcontracting agreements, among other means.

Foreign Capital and Emerging Economy Labor Markets

Many antiglobalization activists argue that in developing economies, foreign MNE prey on the local population of unskilled workers by offering unacceptably low wages, horrendous working conditions, and unbearably long hours. More generally, some critics of globalization maintain that MNE operations and foreign capital flows into developing nations lead to declining labor market conditions for domestic workers. The political economy of this mechanism is that foreign organizations and domestic elites conspire to suppress the wages of unskilled local workers, weaken trade unions, and allow workplace exploitation and human rights abuses, especially in countries where the legal system offers workers little protection. The presence of MNE and foreign investment may generate negative health consequences, due to increased local pollution combined with a lack of effective health care. In short, these critics argue that foreign capital flows and FDI harm domestic workers in developing nations. The pecuniary benefits instead accrue to foreign capital holders, local business owners, and foreign consumers.

The other side of the debate—commonly advanced by economists—holds that in poor nations, MNE and foreign investment stimulate economic growth, increase domestic labor demand, and drive wage growth. They also bring new technologies and managerial know-how, which are both likely to spillover onto the local area over time. Foreign investment and production can increase local tax bases, providing revenue for public education, health care, and industrial investment. Wages are often low in exporting sectors, though they are typically higher than in the informal sector or other local industries. Factory work conditions in poor countries may be unpleasant, yet they are no worse—and often better—than the alternative local work options. Finally, although it is difficult for MNE to monitor the behavior of all their contractors, pressures coming from consumers in wealthy nations have sometimes led to reforms that benefit workers in developing nations. Research shows that these consumers are often willing to pay a premium for products made under good work conditions.

Both sides of the debate can agree that "sweatshop" conditions exist inside many business operations in developing nations, and there may be abjectly poor work environments within MNE or their subcontractors, especially among textile and apparel manufacturers. In one famous example from the 1990s, Nike began monitoring their shoe production contractors in Indonesia after Indonesian newspapers ran stories describing clear violations of local labor laws, such as workers being paid less than the minimum wage. The episode dragged on for over a decade and was a public relations nightmare for Nike, an American company which had always relied on outsourcing shoe production so that the cost savings could be spent on marketing and advertising. The United States government even pressured Indonesia to address local labor abuses, and they responded by increasing the minimum wage. Although regulating international labor standards has proven difficult to achieve, American and European governments have long pressed developing nations to strengthen human rights and environmental protections when they appear to be lacking, sometimes by threatening to revoke favorable trade policies.

But is Nike (circa 1990) representative of other MNE that operate or subcontract in poor nations? This is a critical issue because FDI is the largest source of external finance for many developing economies—twice as large, on average, as foreign aid gifts and 50% larger than remittances—and the stock of global FDI now totals more than $20 trillion. Economists have attempted to measure how MNE and FDI affect local labor markets in developing nations. Empirical research shows that in developing countries, workers employed by MNE or their subcontractors are paid significantly more on average than other domestic workers in comparable employment. This may be partly due to a tendency (all else equal) for higher quality laborers to work at MNE or their affiliates; such individuals are more productive and earn more, too. Higher wages could also be paid by MNE to induce greater effort and productivity among local workers. It is important to note that alternative employment in developing nations is often in agriculture, which offers meager wages and unpleasant work conditions.

FDI in developing countries has traditionally taken the form of newly constructed establishments exhibiting technologies that are not widely available in the recipient country. Research suggests that in facilities supported by FDI, workers generally earn higher wages. The premium is even greater for skilled workers. In part, this is because FDI flows to higher paying domestic industries and larger firms in developing countries. Operations within these production sites are more sophisticated and demanding than at other local employers, so they pay rather well. Other evidence suggests that FDI leads to relatively greater demand for skilled and educated workers within the local area, driving up their wages. This makes sense if these workers are needed to manage or supervise multiple unskilled laborers, possibly with the help of additional training. Such a mechanism can also raise the level of local labor market inequality in emerging economies. In recent decades, relatively more FDI has originated in cross-border mergers and acquisitions. Some evidence shows that when foreign groups take over domestic operations in developing countries, wages increase slightly, though work conditions do not necessarily improve, on average.

Foreign Investors and Respect for Local Worker Rights

One common contention is that MNE and foreign investors seek out poor countries that do not respect human rights or labor standards, including the right of workers to establish unions. In such regions, the reasoning goes, MNE are able to pay as little as possible for sweatshop labor output, beefing up their bottom line. Yet according to surveys of MNE managers, in determining where to locate production, labor costs are less important than many other factors—namely infrastructure, political stability, labor quality, and the legal system. Research indicates that foreign investors prefer high-quality regulation and are not attracted to developing countries that do not respect worker rights. Nations that are politically stable and respect worker rights are presumably more attractive to foreign investors, because they are more likely to enforce foreign ownership rights and contracts, given their stronger legal structures. For example, American investment flows to developing nations favor democracies and are deterred by child labor utilization, in spite of higher labor costs. Likewise, nations that respect human rights are more likely to attract FDI. Since foreign investors have many options to choose from, it may not be surprising that (all else equal) they generally prefer stable, nonautocratic political regimes respecting worker rights, human rights, and the rule of law.

Evolution of Foreign Investment

Some analysts have pointed out that the behavior of MNE and foreign investors has undergone a historical shift over the past century. Through World War I and II, world powers backed by military force conquered backward regions rich in raw materials, or alternatively, set up local institutions designed to extract them. By the mid-20th century, following World War II and numerous independence movements, foreign corporations had become intent on establishing ties with local governments to protect and control valuable natural resources. Decades later, it became increasingly feasible for MNE to move production offshore to emerging economies. The advantage was not only cheaper labor, but also access to foreign consumer markets. Emerging nations wishing to attract more foreign investment have been able to signal their commitment to liberalization policies by joining international trade agreements such as the GATT or trade organizations such as the WTO. By the 1990s, students and activists in rich nations were determined to publicize the behavior of MNE that violate labor standards, take advantage of child labor, or utilize unethical subcontractors abroad. Today, many American companies advertise that they only buy products from foreign suppliers which respect environmental regulations and worker rights.

One ever-present concern is whether governments in resource-rich emerging regions are willing and able to negotiate favorable terms with extractive MNE and then use the funds for effective developmental programs to help their middle and lower classes. For example, China is currently trading infrastructure investment funds for African natural resources, though it isn't clear that African governments are getting as much in return as they could be, and more importantly, whether the funds are being efficiently utilized for projects that benefit the public at large. Resource extraction usually doesn't stimulate as much local job creation as other types of exporting industries (like textiles) and tends to last only as long as the resource itself, so the employment effects of foreign investment in mining, for instance, have frequently been disappointing.

When expensive raw materials are exported in large quantities, demand for the domestic currency by foreign purchasers can lead to currency appreciation, which harms other exporting industries such as manufacturing. Called the "Dutch disease," this process is named after an episode from the 1960s and 1970s when the Netherlands found natural gas deposits in the North Sea. Gas exports caused the Dutch currency to appreciate, making goods from their manufacturing sector more expensive and therefore less competitive as exports. Fortunately, countries that have experienced oil and mineral booms are more likely to benefit from the wealth than become cursed by the political and social instability it sometimes brings, according to new research. In Africa today, foreign money and influence will hopefully be used to build stronger institutions and enhance economic development, so that comparative advantages can shift from the export of raw materials to human capital-intensive procedures.

Foreign Capital, Globalization, and Poverty

FDI has come to trump all other types of financial flows to developing countries, even debt. It has been instrumental to economic growth in many countries, including Ireland, Singapore, Malaysia, Thailand, and China. More countries clamor to attract it than ever before. It seems reasonable that greater FDI, which often leads to growth, has the potential to reduce poverty, since economic growth should raise the incomes of the poorest, even if not proportionately. Growth and poverty reducing effects may come from several mechanisms. FDI spreads foreign technology and other best practices from abroad, which increases productivity and allows emerging economies to catch up faster. Foreign firms that bring investment tend to focus on labor-intensive goods; they are often larger, more productive, and more likely to produce higher quality goods than are domestic firms. These changes tend to drive up the wages of unskilled workers. Foreign investment also generates a larger tax base that can be used for social programs benefitting the poor and destitute (although this mechanism depends on good governance, which is commonly lacking in developing countries). Conversely, FDI can lead to difficult labor market adjustments and dislocations, which disproportionately harm unskilled workers in emerging economies.

In practice, FDI inflows tend to come with other policy changes (such as opening trade and financial market liberalization), so it is difficult to isolate its effect on growth and poverty reduction. Nevertheless, cross-country evidence suggests that FDI is correlated with diminished poverty and increases in local wages. Studies indicate that in a number of developing countries, FDI has spurred local employment and poverty reduction, especially when it is used to develop labor-intensive industries. For example, it has driven export growth and diminished poverty in Indonesia and Mexico. FDI has been less successful in improving the situation of local workers: when it is concentrated in extractive industries (such as oil) that typically employ a small set of skilled workers; where there is little capacity for the investment to create local spillovers, due to a lack of human capital, infrastructure, or economic development; or where local governments have not bargained effectively with foreign investors to extract maximal benefits for domestic workers and organizations. Research indicates that in Latin America, FDI has crowded out domestic investment in the past. In some instances, FDI has probably harmed developing host economies on net, and in others, such as oil- and diamond-abundant Angola, the economic benefits have been unevenly distributed at best.

Overall, FDI has the potential to bring benefits to emerging economies in many situations, though based on its historical record: it has brought negative dislocation spillovers at times; it has proven less effective when entering sectors reliant upon import-substitution programs; some regions simply do not have sufficient absorptive capacities to benefit from FDI; and it has not always been managed fairly or efficiently by local governments and foreign companies. The effects of FDI in developing countries differ from opening trade, which can benefit workers in exporting sectors yet hurt workers in import-competing industries (as in the cases of Colombia and India in the 1990s). By contrast, FDI is likely to increase employment and wages (both directly and indirectly) in exporting and import-competing sectors, thereby reducing domestic poverty. For example, without foreign investment and know-how, unsophisticated local industries may have trouble exporting to markets in the developed world, which are sometimes protected or subsidized, particularly in food products and basic manufactures. And while foreign capital flows to emerging markets can lead to financial market volatility, FDI is much less likely to contribute to financial crises—and better able to ride out market volatility—as compared to other types of capital such as portfolio investment in stocks and bonds. This is because FDI involves real investment in firms, and its mobility is severely limited by its dependence on local physical assets, infrastructure, human capital, supplier networks, and institutions.

Trends in Global Poverty

The incidence of poverty across the world has steadily fallen in recent decades. About half of the developing world population was under the World Bank poverty line in the early 1980s, compared to less than a quarter today. East Asia—dominated by China's huge population and low per capita income—used to have the highest poverty rate at over three quarters, but now fewer than one in six are below the poverty line. During the 1980s and 1990s, sub-Saharan Africa showed an increasing level of poverty, but since then it has progressively declined, so that less than half of the population now falls under the poverty line. According to the most recent data available, in spite of the recent global financial crisis, poverty incidence has continued to fall in the developing world. Relatively strong growth in China, India, and Brazil—combined with high commodity prices—has buoyed economies in the least developed regions, which continue to make their transition from low-wage agriculture to better-paying industrial and service activities.

Economic globalization has expanded as poverty has fallen, but has globalization played any role in poverty alleviation? Most economists believe that globalization has, on net, been a major contributor to declining poverty. For one, poverty has declined more in developing nations that have globalized than in those that have not. A growing consensus suggests that benefits to poor countries can be substantial, provided that international economic integration is managed carefully and strategically (with China as a case study in success). Policies of opening trade, allowing foreign investment, and liberalizing finance have given emerging economies room for new choices that can bring economic growth despite attendant costs (such as financial crises) which are sometimes colossal. Still, as the least developed nations shift to industrial and service production (following the past achievements of the Asian Tigers), expanding urban areas and a robust exporting sector can generate better job opportunities for millions.

Globalization, Pollution, and Public Health

In the language of economics, pollution is a classic "negative externality," meaning that its negative effects are commonly not "internalized" (or taken into account) by the party emitting it. Air pollution, groundwater contamination, and chemical waste are common negative externalities that are byproducts of industrial activity. International evidence on environmental quality and development suggests that there is a greater level of environmental degradation and pollution as the initial stages of economic development progress in a transition from agriculture to industry. In poor countries, generating income growth through industrialization is typically considered more important than controlling pollution.

At early stages of economic development, it is difficult to regulate environmental degradation due to a lack of well-defined property rights, insufficient legal remedies and technology, and public and private sector corruption. Yet environmental quality has a substantial impact on quality of life, so developing economies begin to trade off income for costly pollution reduction as they become wealthier. Once a certain level of development is reached, and a substantial middle class has emerged, political pressure for comprehensive policy interventions aimed at improving environmental quality is likely to expand in line with further economic growth. Emerging economies in the midst of their catch-up development (such as China today) often exhibit the worst environmental quality, and research indicates that as national income grows, the degree of environmental regulation increases. One possible exception to this pattern is the volume of carbon dioxide emissions (which make up the majority of global greenhouse gas emissions). Nonelectric automobile travel, coal-generated electricity, and other fossil fuel burning activities emit carbon dioxide. Carbon dioxide production generally increases with income up to a rather high level of national income. However, as economies become wealthier, they normally shift from industrial to service activity (which pollutes less), and they frequently implement technologies to reduce their environment impact.

Because greenhouse gas emissions contribute to global warming and climate change regardless of the source location, they are negative externalities at the global level. Unfortunately, instituting cross-border property rights is not feasible for this market. As a consequence, to reduce global carbon dioxide emissions, the best mechanism is to forge international agreements where nations multilaterally commit to costly emission reductions. One such attempt to extend economic globalization to environmental policy was initiated in the 1990s with the Kyoto Protocol, which set variable targets for most developed countries to either reduce or limit increases in their greenhouse gas emissions. Ratifying countries have had mixed success, with some managing to meet or exceed their targets (including many European nations and Russia) while others have not. The United States—formerly the largest net emitter of greenhouse gases before being overtaken by China, and still one of the highest emitters in the world on a per capita basis—signed it, never fully ratified it, and then withdrew from it in 2001. (Canada later withdrew in 2011.) Global carbon dioxide emissions have continued to grow over the past decade. Still, the Kyoto agreement helped to initiate international emissions trading, which has the potential to reduce global pollution efficiently through a pricing mechanism. This approach forces nations to internalize their pollution externalities, and it may facilitate other multilateral agreements in the future. Currently there is a major international push to substitute toward clean energy sources (such as solar and wind power) and alternative transportation (such as electric cars).

On the whole, globalization and trade have contributed to pollution and environmental degradation around the world. In China, economic development and the accompanying pollution wouldn't have been as rapid and severe in the absence of international trade. However, in China as elsewhere, pollution is a byproduct of industrialization and growth, and would have occurred even under autarky. The wealth derived from economic development can also be used to reduce environmental degradation and clean damaged land and waterways. Restricting pollution in developing countries has been a very contentious issue for decades (including during the Kyoto Protocol discussions). Growth in greenhouse gas emissions and other harmful pollutants is expected to come disproportionately from emerging economies in the future. Poor nations invoke their sovereign rights, arguing that they are simply following the same growth trajectories that other economies achieved decades before. Indeed, large-scale federal regulations in advanced nations were not implemented in force until the 1970s. Today, many developing countries export goods that are pollution-intensive to produce, so by restricting their allowable level of pollution, they may not be able to capitalize on their comparative advantages, and thereby suffer lower growth.

The idea that sectors producing pollution-intensive goods tend to migrate to developing economies with laxer environmental standards is called the "pollution haven" hypothesis. It implies that the lack of environmental regulations in poor countries attracts dirty industries, and that by strengthening regulatory oversight, these economies would necessarily sacrifice output growth. Despite its intuitive appeal, empirical support for the pollution haven hypothesis has been mixed. There is some evidence indicating that countries with weaker environmental regulations tend to export more in pollution-intensive industries. However, pollution-intensive industries are often in heavy intermediate goods (such as metals and industrial chemicals) that are unattractive to export, and environmental compliance costs are typically only a small fraction of total costs, even in countries with stringent environmental protection. Other studies have found that FDI flows to China have benefitted the local environment by bringing cleaner, more efficient production technologies, and crowding out inefficient domestic firms. Scholars are concerned that in the future, least developed nations may boldly attempt to spark growth by acting as a pollution haven for China, India, and other middle-income nations trying to lower their own domestic pollution. Still, countries open to international trade have been found more likely to agree to multilateral environmental protocols, and by attracting foreign investment, they are better able to implement new technologies to reduce environmental degradation.

Globalization and Disease Transmission

Diseases have been spread along trade routes since ancient times. One prominent example from the past century is the Spanish influenza epidemic that began in 1917 and lasted until 1920, infecting over a quarter of the world's population. It is estimated to have killed up to 50 million, making it deadlier than World War I. More recently, Acquired Immune Deficiency Syndrome (AIDS), caused by Human Immunodeficiency Virus (HIV), is believed to have originated in African primates before its transmission worldwide. It was first recognized as a new disease in the early 1980s. Since then, it has caused over 25 million deaths.

Other pandemic viruses have caused widespread fear but resulted in far fewer fatalities. Severe Acute Respiratory Syndrome (SARS) is a viral respiratory disease that killed almost 800 people in 2002 and 2003 after an outbreak originated from Hong Kong. The Avian Influenza (or Bird Flu) continues to kill humans sporadically, though only several hundred deaths (disproportionately in Asia) have been reported as yet. The West Nile Virus has killed a hundred Americans on average each year since 2000. However, less than 1% of the infected show any severe illness, and most show no symptoms at all. In 2009, humans picked up an influenza strain through contact with pigs in Mexico, called Swine Flu, which was quickly spread and resulted in at least 15,921 deaths within a year.

On a brighter note, economic growth has brought better nutrition and sanitation, while vaccines, antibiotics, and other pharmaceutical breakthroughs have reduced the incidence of illness and death. The spread of modern health technologies has led to greater life expectancy in almost all countries. Over the past two centuries, the average global life expectancy at birth more than doubled, from about 29 years to 68 years. Throughout the developing world, life expectancy has slowly continued to converge to wealthier countries. In Africa, life expectancy today is more than 50 years, higher than it was in wealthy countries a century ago.

Population Growth, Natural Resources, and Commodity Prices

World population broke seven billion in 2011, and the majority of the world (about 60%) now lives in Asia. Almost all population growth today comes from developing countries, and the rate of growth is the highest in Africa. Many developing countries are undergoing the demographic transition, where public health improvements lead to lower mortality rates (which increases population) followed by reductions in fertility rates (which decreases population). In the long run, once countries are developed, the result is often a fertility rate below the level of replacement—at slightly over two children per woman—which, if not offset by increased migration, can lead to a drop in population. This is precisely what has happened in Japan and Germany, which are both experiencing slight population declines.

Demographic research shows that fertility rates in Africa and Asia have been falling for decades, and that the global population growth rate has already begun to slow. The most recent official projection by the United Nations proposes that the world population will reach 9.3 billion by 2050 and then add fewer than a billion more over the following 50 years. Of course, predicting population levels decades into the future is an imperfect science, not least because so much depends on national political policies and social attitudes. For instance, China's population growth has slowed relative to India, primarily due to the enactment of differential policies such as one-child rule fertility restrictions. Changing views toward marriage and the family have also led to significant drops in birth rates in Spain, Portugal, and Italy.

Many environmental scholars worry that population growth will put excessive strain on global resource supplies and exacerbate climate change. Globalization plays some role here. In its absence—that is, under autarky—economic development and population growth would likely be slower, and the world's natural resources would not be extracted and utilized at the same rapid rate as they are now. On the other hand, public health technologies such as contraceptives have been spread around the world, leading to lower fertility rates, and hence, slower resource depletion. As poor nations become wealthier, their consumption of agricultural products, energy, metals, and concrete will become higher. The most prominent example is China, which has been growing faster than advanced economies by a wide margin.

Global commodity prices began rising steeply in the early 2000s after slumping in the 1980s and 1990s. The change was largely driven by economic growth in emerging economies, particularly China. As a response to the commodity boom, investment in agriculture, energy, metals, and other raw materials has picked up, which will help accommodate future commodities demand. However, the increased supply of commodities may not be enough to keep pace with demand if emerging economies continue to develop rapidly. Many analysts believe that new technology has made it easier to industrialize quickly, implying that growth in the least developed nations could accelerate in the near future. In one unfortunate scenario, natural resource prices could remain high in the long term if drought conditions become increasingly common due to global warming and weather instability around the world. (This has occurred of late in Australia, Mexico, and the American Midwest.)

In 1980, the issue of population growth and natural resource supply came into the public eye in the United States. Biologist Paul Ehrlich and economist Julian Simon made a famous wager. Ehrlich was a pessimist who thought that population growth would soon lead to disaster, with astronomically high commodity prices in the near future. Simon believed that markets—due to the dynamic innovation and efficiencies they wring out of production—would be able to supply basic materials in sufficient quantity to keep up with global economic development and population growth. The bet was simple: Ehrlich chose five commodities—chromium, copper, nickel, tin, and tungsten—that he believed would go up in price over the next decade. By 1990, the price of all five metals had declined after adjusting for inflation, and Ehrlich mailed Simon a check, conceding his defeat.

What is fascinating to observers today is that if they had agreed to the same bet in 2000—or if it had run for 31 years, not 10 years, beginning in

1980—Ehrlich would have won due to the great run up in commodity prices after 2002. Compounding the risk of high food prices, many analysts are predicting that water shortages are going to become more likely. People in wealthy nations take clean water for granted, yet in much of the world, water supplies are dangerously inadequate because of shortages, poor quality, and inadequate distribution and disposal systems. Over a tenth of the global population lacks access to clean drinking water, and more than a third of the world lives in areas without access to proper sanitation. Driven by proper price signals, innovative supply, sanitation, and distribution technologies may be able to ease pressures.

Walmart, Low Prices, and Globalization

In the late-19th century, mass-market retailers Sears Roebuck and Montgomery Ward reached American consumers with mail order catalogues, taking advantage of railroads as their main channel of distribution. Appealing to small town residents in underserved consumer markets, they offered a massive selection of goods at low prices. After World War II, shopping malls and discount department stores popped up across the United States, driven by suburban sprawl. One such discounter, Walmart, started in 1962 with a single store in Rogers, Arkansas. Its founder, Sam Walton, realized the potential in opening large low-cost retail stores in small Southern towns. His business strategy was successful, and by the 1990s, Walmart had become a very profitable national chain. Walmart is now the largest private employer and largest retailer in both the United States and the world. To this day, it has continued its expansion internationally into Mexico (as Walmex), Japan (as Seiyu), and India (as Best Price). The experience of Walmart illustrates many of the issues raised by critics of globalization.

Walmart is known for its low prices, which is why customers keep coming back. Although Walmart has maintained low net margins of under 4% over the past decade, it has become progressively more profitable due to its mammoth sales volume, which continues to expand. Walmart has been a leader in implementing retail store information technology and the efficient control of inventory, logistics, and distribution. It has also been aggressive in pursuing cost savings and forging new supply chain relationships across the world. Some studies suggest that Walmart saves the average American household a substantial amount of money each year, partly because the presence of a Walmart lowers the prices that local competitors charge. Although the exact amount of savings is difficult to pinpoint, Walmart's role as consumer products importer and distributor has been an important factor in lowering the cost of living since the 1990s, particularly among low-income populations which can now afford DVD players and large screen televisions. In terms of productivity growth, Walmart has contributed to greater retail productivity in the United States and around the world, both directly (through its normal operations) and indirectly (through imitation by competitors).

Still, the company has its many critics. They believe Walmart has been far too aggressive in keeping operating costs low, especially when it comes to human resource practices. These critics maintain that Walmart pays unreasonably low wages to retail employees, with inadequate health insurance benefits. (Large retailers have been criticized on similar grounds for nearly a century.) Among Walmart's largely female workforce, the average employee is paid no more than about $20,000 each year. Some of Walmart's competitors—such as Costco, which has far lower employee turnover—pay their workers more and give them more training, too. Historically, Walmart has taken a firm antiunion stance, sometimes closing stores after employees voted to unionize. Over time, such hard-line tactics by a large industry powerhouse may have increased the overall bargaining leverage of employers throughout the American retail sector. Empirical evidence suggests that a Walmart opening drives several general merchandise stores out of business on average, yet the overall effect within a region is not large, given that there are about 200 such stores in a typical county. Other studies have shown that the local employment effect of a Walmart opening appears to be small or negligible. There is also evidence that the presence of a new Walmart—which can be considered a type of amenity—increases housing prices within a mile of the store.

At the local level, the opening of a new Walmart can be extremely controversial. In some regions, local governments have subsidized new Walmart locations through tax exemptions and funds for job training and infrastructure. However, in other areas, usually large cities, Walmart has met stiff resistance from local residents after announcing its intentions to open a store. At the national level, Walmart has devoted an increasing amount of time and money to lobbying for free trade policies, given its heavy utilization of low-cost foreign suppliers. At the same time, detractors have argued that Walmart's monitoring of foreign suppliers is deficient; for example, some Walmart goods containing wood may have been produced with illegally harvested timber from China, Russia, and Brazil. Amidst a growing chorus of criticism from corporate watchdog organizations over the past decade, Walmart has responded by altering some of its business practices. The company has been concerned about its tarnished reputation, which was apparently hurting sales. As the Walmart CEO publicly admitted in 2005, the "critics are sometimes right." Walmart is now one of the top corporate charitable cash contributors, and it is currently engaging in a large-scale program to reduce all greenhouse gas emissions associated with the manufacture, distribution, and usage of their products. Like many other corporations in recent years, Walmart is attempting to manage its reputation and build brand equity by enhancing the social responsibility of its practices before actively publicizing the changes.

Globalization and Labor Unions

The first thing to understand about trade unions is that their prevalence varies widely around the world. In Sweden, Denmark, and Finland, nearly 70% of the workforce is a member of a union, and many nonmembers are represented by unions in collective bargaining agreements. In these three countries—collectively part of the "Ghent system" with Belgium and Iceland—unions distribute welfare payments (including unemployment insurance benefits), and workers have an incentive to join them. At the other extreme, just over 10% of American workers are union members, and the union membership rate is less than 20% in New Zealand, Japan, and South Korea. In continental Europe, public policies and large-scale employment agreements frequently cover employees at nonunion establishments. France, a country with rigid labor markets and a strong socialist history, is an instructive data point: less than 10% of French workers are union members though 90% of the workforce is covered by collective bargaining agreements. While membership rates are a proxy for the general bargaining power of unions in a society, coverage rates are a better measure of union reach in providing basic employment protections and income benefits. Due to extensive centralized collective bargaining practices, coverage rates tend to be much higher than membership rates in most of continental Europe. A number of European countries also have "works councils," giving workers at larger companies the right to influence certain organizational decisions.

The experience of American labor unions provides an interesting case study in industrial relations. The labor movement in the United States—a labor-scarce country with no feudal tradition—has never been particularly strong. American unions reached their peak years of influence from the mid-1930s—when the National Labor Relations Act was passed—through the mid-1950s. Union membership rates then started to decline, falling steadily from about 35% following World War II to about 12% today (which is the same level as the early 1930s). The change was driven by falling membership rates in the private sector, which employs about five times as many workers as the public sector. Whereas private sector membership rates exhibited a gradual decline, public employee rates actually exploded upward in the 1960s—when legal restrictions on public sector unions started to ease—and have remained at slightly under 40% since the late 1970s. Some economists believe that American business was relatively unpopular in the public eye back when unions were powerful, but an antiunion backlash began in the 1980s, when many middle-class workers were struggling and the public began to question why only the unionized should be afforded exemplary protections. Another peculiarity is that labor bargaining is relatively decentralized in the United States, so very few nonmembers have their terms of employment covered (or represented) under a collective bargaining agreement.

Many American commentators have attributed the decline in unionization to trade and technology. The idea is that manufactured imports from low-wage countries have put downward pressure on wages for many Americans, which (along with global capital mobility) has increased the bargaining power of large private employers in the United States, especially in the manufacturing and retail sectors. On top of that, technology has stoked the demand for highly skilled professionals who know how to utilize it, without helping other groups quite as much. However, what's fascinating is that the international data do not square with this story. Among advanced nations that have been broadly subjected to the same forces of globalization and technological progress as the United States has, there is tremendous variation in union membership and coverage rates, implying that the degree of union influence has diverged. Consider Canada, a country similar to the United States in many important ways. In 1960, union membership (and coverage) rates were both about a third in the two neighboring nations. But since then, the rate has stayed approximately the same in Canada. In other wealthy English-speaking market democracies (like the United Kingdom, Australia, and New Zealand), union membership rates started to decline in the 1980s.

Such patterns demonstrate that political factors are fundamental to understanding the prevalence of unions across countries. Within affluent regions where political systems are similar, unionization rates are broadly comparable. In the Ghent system nations, union pervasiveness is the highest, and it has stayed the same or even increased over the past 50 years. In Continental European market economies—which fall in between Ghent system nations and liberal free market economies like the United States—union membership rates have remained constant (as in Italy) or fallen somewhat (as in Switzerland, France, Germany, and Holland). Union coverage has fared better; in Austria, for example, coverage actually increased in spite of dramatically falling membership rates. The same pattern occurred in Spain in the late 1970s (after Franco), although in Portugal, both membership and coverage declined (after Salazar). As the empirical evidence shows, wealthy nations that trade more tend to have a higher union prevalence, in part because unions help cushion the impact of the global business cycle on local workers. In this respect, there is a positive relationship between globalization and unions. This correlation doesn't appear to have been driven by technology adoption, either. For instance, the United States and Japan are technologically sophisticated economies that have been in the vanguard for decades. But the same can be said of Scandinavian economies, where—contrary to the United States and Japan—unions are very powerful.

In the developing world, collective bargaining systems are weaker and unions play a smaller role. Perhaps this isn't surprising, since poor nations have relatively fragile political institutions, and most workers remain in the informal sector where governments have trouble monitoring employment practices. Because labor market institutions like unions and collective bargaining arrangements reduce wage dispersion among comparable workers, one consequence of weaker unionism is relatively greater wage inequality in emerging markets. Although international empirical evidence is lacking, critics of globalization argue that capital mobility can lead to greater workplace insecurity in poor and developing countries, diminishing unionism and labor protections. On the other hand, workers can clearly benefit from globalization and capital mobility: as developing nations become richer through trade and foreign investment, political institutions can be stabilized and suitable labor market regulations can be formulated, including collective bargaining. As developing economies grow, their citizens are likely to call for greater political control and sovereignty, including new labor market institutions that could potentially conflict with export-based growth policies requiring low wages. These scenarios involve a rebalancing favoring democracy and national determination over economic globalization, and China is a case in point: workers there are now demanding greater protections, and unions could help bring about major democratic reforms someday.

Rise of Globalized Finance

Following World War II, the Bretton Woods system provided the foundation for international finance throughout the industrialized world. It coordinated currencies by instituting pegged (yet adjustable) exchange rates which the IMF was tasked with overseeing. The value of each currency was fixed against the American dollar, and in turn, the dollar was worth $35 per ounce of gold. Some have called the subsequent quarter century a "golden age of controlled capitalism": under Bretton Woods, another depression did not occur; Europe was able to rebuild successfully; exchange rates were stable; and inflation was relatively low. However, tension within the currency system built throughout the 1960s, as American macroeconomic policy, military commitments, and balance of payments deficits led to the dollar becoming overvalued. In 1971, the United States—fearful of a run on its gold supply—suspended the dollar's convertibility into gold. By 1973, most major world economies had stopped setting their currency's value to a fixed rate against others—meaning that currencies within the system started to "float." The Bretton Woods system of pegged exchange rates was over, and luckily the adjustment did not cause a major financial crisis. Still, oil prices rose steeply in the 1970s, contributing to inflationary pressures, and the decade was characterized by economic instability, relatively low growth, rising unemployment, and high inflation—a state of affairs commonly termed "stagflation." International capital mobility increased in some advanced nations during the 1970s (such as the United States, Germany, and Switzerland), though the overall degree of mobility remained fairly limited, consistent with the designs of the Bretton Woods founders.

The 1980s marked a turning point. At the start of the decade, the Federal Reserve ramped up interest rates to unprecedented levels in an effort to end double-digit inflation. Although this strategy led to a severe recession, it successfully curbed inflation, and the American economy soon stabilized. Capital mobility increased as burgeoning political trends around the world supported the integration of global financial markets. Even emerging economies—which had traditionally curtailed inflows of foreign capital through taxes, legal restrictions, and prohibitions—became more likely to lift capital controls. Following decades of support, governance based on strong social welfare states and robust regulatory regimes fell out of favor in a backlash movement in many regions. Instead, the public became more sympathetic to market-oriented approaches to growth and governance, with politicians pledging lower taxes, new privatization, less regulation, the curbing of unions, and enhanced globalization. This movement was symbolized by Margaret Thatcher's election as Prime Minister of the United Kingdom in 1979, followed by Ronald Reagan's 1980 victory to become President of the United States. It even extended to India and China, two countries that were far from free market sanctuaries (both then and now). They initiated distinctive liberalization programs that were usually inconsistent with contemporary prescriptions from Western economic specialists.

Deeper international financial integration programs persisted throughout the 1990s and afterward. The IMF and World Bank commonly advised struggling lower- or middle-income countries to follow a set of structural adjustment policies commonly referred to as the "Washington Consensus." This paradigm was derived from the prevailing conventional wisdom among Washington D.C. policymakers involved in foreign economic development issues. In practice, the Washington Consensus advocated market-oriented measures that included trade liberalization, liberalization of inbound FDI, competitive exchange rates, fiscal discipline, privatization, deregulation, and secure property rights. Critics have suggested that such policy recommendations were too simplistic and did not give enough weight to crisis avoidance or the challenges in jumpstarting recessionary economies without fiscal stimulus. The policy prescriptions were embraced after many Latin American economies suffered through devastating debt crises and recessions in the early 1980s triggered by a combination of high borrowing, oil price shocks, and rising interest rates in the West. However, the country originating these prescriptions for financial and economic soundness—the United States—did not appear to follow them. With growing budget deficits and a consistently negative balance of trade in the 1980s and 1990s, the United States began borrowing from international capital markets on a massive scale.

It remains very controversial whether Washington Consensus policies provided any advantage to developing countries in many instances. This picture is further clouded by the fact that some critics have publicly conflated the original Washington Consensus policies with additional "neoliberal" prescriptions such as monetarism or a minimal state. And although most financial economists maintain that the benefits of globalized financial markets have largely outweighed the costs—at least when capital inflows are reasonably well managed—this issue also remains contentious. The evidence suggests that capital inflows (such as FDI) to emerging economies can help them grow, at least once they have achieved a minimal level of development. On the other hand, when financial markets are global and capital controls are weak, the result can be increased financial instability, particularly in countries with weak or inconsistent macroeconomic policies or inadequately regulated or capitalized financial systems; for one, it is easier for crises to be sparked and then spread across borders when there are no controls in place. A prominent case in point is the Asian financial crisis of the late 1990s. Earlier in the decade, Thailand, Indonesia, Malaysia, and the Philippines dropped their capital controls in an attempt to attract FDI. They were successful in drawing international capital, but a large proportion of it was in the form of short-term, highly liquid flows known as "hot money," which could easily be withdrawn if investors lost confidence. This is exactly what happened in early 1997, when anxious investors, reacting to a rapidly deteriorating Thai real estate and financial sector, began to withdraw funds in local currencies for dollars. The panic quickly spread and local currencies crashed, leading to severe recessions. It is also clear that international financial integration contributed to the recent global financial crisis.

Elites, Concentrated Power, and Globalization

In the United States, the financial sector's share of the total economy has steadily grown since World War II, more than trebling in that time. From the 1940s through the 1970s, financial and banking occupations were unexciting, with unexceptional compensation, and graduates from elite universities did not gravitate toward Wall Street. But starting in the 1980s, finance began to hire more skilled workers, paying them generously. This decade was the beginning of a boom period in complex corporate financing and the proliferation of new financial products. Financial deregulation and newly globalized capital markets brought fresh opportunities, and highly skilled individuals—armed now with personal computers—were most able to take advantage of them. Financial sector compensation rose, particularly among professionals working in investment banks and hedge funds. Since the 1970s, tremendous financial sector growth also occurred in other major advanced nations such as the United Kingdom, France, and Germany. Many analysts believe that the financial sector of the industrialized world now holds excessive economic and political power. Given its practical function of allocating capital to other sectors of the real economy, critics argue that its size is too large to be justified. The challenge is to craft new rules and regulations that will keep the financial sector functioning without another major crisis in the years to come. New regulatory frameworks are expected to stabilize capital allocation, preventing excessive risk-taking as well as too-big-to-fail levels of financial concentration.

The current discussion about the proper role of finance is closely related to a broader debate about the power of global elites. During the age of hyperglobalization, a select group of executives and equity owners capitalized on new opportunities that technology and globalization presented. Many view the resulting wealth accumulation as fair and natural, while others—citing financial sector deregulation such as the 1999 repeal of the Glass-Steagall Act—contend that the gains were induced through political influence peddling. Informational disparities seem to be part of the problem. Finance is largely a kind of information brokerage, and as it has become more complex, the gap in knowledge between leading financial professionals and the general public has widened. Such a disparity can be used by insiders for their benefit, by selling flawed products to the public, or by lobbying for favorable laws. More generally, as advanced economies become more complex, it is natural that the division of labor becomes more specialized—experts are needed to make decisions, so their overall influence has increased. Yet, as many American commentators now insist, difficulties arise when a sufficiently large portion of the specialized elite professional class is incentivized to behave in a recklessly self-interested manner that is overly focused on short-term gain. In fact, in the years leading up to the Great Depression, the American financial sector was full of highly skilled, highly paid professionals, but after President Franklin Delano Roosevelt took office in 1933 and pushed through new regulatory measures, finance became staid, with less potential risk (and reward) for bankers.

The political problem, in sum, is how to align the interests of elites and insiders with the rest of society. To the long-term detriment of some economies, adequate solutions are not always found. In the cautionary tale of medieval Venice, the sustained rise in wealth brought about by new foreign trade opportunities produced excessively concentrated political power and contributed to the republic's long-term decline. Beginning in the 10th century, Venetian merchants grew wealthy by pursuing long-distance trading and shipping opportunities. For over two centuries, political power wasn't tied to heredity, and Venice's sophisticated institutions and innovative financing systems allowed its economy to flourish. But in the early-14th century, a small group of ultra-wealthy merchants used their power to restrict political participation and trade opportunities to a privileged elite, based on family heritage. Land-poor Venice—for centuries a business-minded haven from agrarian feudalism—now possessed a governing class of hereditary nobility. The resulting "plutocracy," which led to political rent-seeking and inadequate entrepreneurialism, weakened Venice's maritime power. Over the subsequent centuries, Venice lost its lead as the greatest banking center in Europe, and it was never again such a dominant force, although it did remain quite wealthy.

Concern that well-connected elites possess excessive influence and power isn't novel; this very issue drove many individuals to move from the Old to the New World. The primary author of the American Declaration of Independence, Thomas Jefferson, was deeply worried about the potential political influence of a "moneyed aristocracy" of financiers, arguing that "banking establishments are more dangerous than standing armies." Accordingly, he favored an economy of independent, small-scale farmers. Throughout the 19th century, Americans remained worried that northeastern banks held too much sway over the rest of the nation. State banking regulations helped to keep the financial sector decentralized, and before the Federal Reserve was founded in 1913, the United States had been without a central bank for three quarters of a century. In the early-20th century, a major progressive movement swept through the United States, pressing for political rights (such as women's suffrage) as well as enhanced business regulations (such as child labor laws). Today, another massive populist political outcry of that size and reach isn't likely to take place, though a political and economic rebalancing, which includes new regulations and accountability measures, seems to be occurring in the United States and Europe.

The forces of globalization can encourage the concentration of power, but they can also promote institutional dynamism and change. Although it is difficult to reform political cultures overrun with rent-seeking, globalization can act as a long-run catalyst by forcing competition through trade and mobility. In other words, inefficient states fall behind in a globalized world, giving their citizens and leaders an incentive to initiate reforms. In developing countries—where oligarchies are more common—globalization has spread the concepts of market economies, democracy, and human rights, which can help chip away at the power of corrupt rulers over time. England's history during the Middle Ages shows it to be a forerunner in bestowing modern rights of liberty, property, and due process upon its citizens. The 1066 "Norman Conquest" of England by Scandinavian and French forces contributed to changes in governance and economic dislocations that were unpopular with the natives, leading to marked hostility toward the monarchy, and a century and a half later, the weak King John, in his struggle against rebellious barons, acquiesced to the 1215 "Magna Carta" (or Great Charter), which limited his power. Then as now, capital tends to flow to regions which treat it well, so global financial integration can prompt states to modernize and provide protections to investors and other property holders. And the creative destruction of capitalism can not only wipe out old fortunes, but also generate new wealth to support reforms. These are just a few of the currents that will impact regimes in the future, as the world shifts to a multipolar system exhibiting a wider, more varied orbit of political influence.

Growth, Happiness, and Globalization

Economists commonly equate happiness (which they technically call "utility") with financial well-being. This is obviously a simplification, and the empirical evidence indicates that there is more to the story. Back in the 1970s, American economist Richard Easterlin uncovered the first major empirical finding about happiness, known as the "Easterlin paradox." His research indicated that wealthier citizens within any given country were more likely to report themselves as being happy. So far, so good. The paradoxical finding was that this positive relationship did not hold up when comparing nations: there was no correlation between a nation's income and the average happiness of its citizens. Moreover, Easterlin found that in the 25 years following World War II, Americans became richer, but not happier, on average. Based on recent research, Easterlin contends that in both rich and poor countries, there is no long-run relationship between happiness and income, implying that economic growth does not ultimately make citizens happier. (Still, Easterlin has never denied that *short-run* fluctuations in income have a positive effect on happiness.) His theory is that the happiness of an individual depends on their income and circumstances relative to others, and that over time, people adapt to changes in income and living standards.

Easterlin's results remain contentious. New findings from psychology indicate that people in different countries do not fully adapt to their level of prosperity, and other studies—analyzing nations over the span of a decade or more—have provided stronger evidence that income does indeed have a positive long-term effect on happiness. Some critics question the validity of self-reported happiness, which may be susceptible to cultural biases and therefore fragile. Along these lines, precisely how happiness is measured appears to make a difference. Besides self-reported happiness levels, other measures include overall life satisfaction and "best possible life" queries (where respondents are asked to compare their life today versus the best possible life they can imagine for themselves). It turns out that income tends to be most correlated with best possible life measures and least correlated with self-reported happiness, with life satisfaction in the middle. This may be because people believe that having more money would allow them to improve their lives in tangible ways, while it is less clear that their momentary level of happiness is directly related to long-term income. Afghanistan is a case in point; recent survey evidence shows that although Afghans are surprisingly happy, they do not indicate they are living their best possible life, for obvious reasons.

After several decades of research, it is clear that life satisfaction in poor countries increases with national income (especially up to middle-income levels), and that poor people in poor countries become more satisfied with their lives (and less stressed out) as they are able to buy necessities. In fact, new research shows that people around the world tend to have similar notions of a good life, and they consider financial resources to be an important part of life satisfaction. Higher incomes and economic growth bring greater self-reported life satisfaction levels across most nations, and life satisfaction is the highest in rich countries. On the other hand, ultimate happiness depends on other factors that are largely nonfinancial, such as spending time with family and friends, having good health, being satisfied with work, and being married; it turns out that these factors are actually more important to happiness on a day-to-day basis. Other work has shown that business cycles influence happiness, as people are happier when inflation and unemployment are low.

Globalization can affect happiness in a number of ways. Although—as Easterlin would point out—economic growth does not guarantee happiness, globalization and trade can spur growth in the least developed nations. By bringing many out of extreme poverty, globalization has almost certainly raised overall world happiness, and has the potential to do the same for many more. Since the marginal effect of income on happiness seems to decline as people become wealthier, the gains to the poor in poor countries should be greater than any adverse effects on rich country workers (as according to Stolper-Samuelson). However, if globalization isn't managed well, it can lead to employment dislocations and financial crises in those same countries, which disproportionately harm the poor and diminish their happiness. Moreover, as economies develop, they are better able to provide education and health care for their citizens, and research shows that better educated and healthier individuals are reported to be happier, even after holding income constant. As nations become wealthy, they erect social welfare states, and new findings have shown that social insurance makes people happier on average. For example, the generosity of unemployment benefits is related to happiness, among both the unemployed and employed. Politics matter: citizens living in countries with less corruption and more freedom report being happier. And individuals in more equal societies tend to be happier, which partly explains why egalitarian Scandinavian countries score the highest on national happiness around the globe.

Conclusion

The above topics are amenable to economic and statistical analysis, though other controversies are more difficult to scrutinize through traditional research methods. For instance, it is challenging to quantify any losses in utility from the global "monoculture"—dominated by Western and American products—that has crowded out native cultures in some regions, and the spread of the Western diet has contributed to higher obesity rates around the world. On the other hand, there are benefits to cultural assimilation—namely, the proliferation of human rights and democracy—and modern food supply chains have the potential to stop wastage, eliminate food poisoning, and feed more people at a lower cost.

It's even possible that in evaluating the effects of globalization, the importance of intangibles ultimately outweigh the tangible, material benefits and costs. To wit, the greatest piece of good fortune to come from globalization may be its role in fostering peace through trade. In Europe, the common currency project of the euro has been a symbol of this transformation. Globalization also continues to spread the tools of economic growth to backward regions around the world. This suggests that the moral case for globalization is strong, as it can sustain peace among powerful nations and reduce poverty in developing countries. Learning from past failures, as long as countries manage their liberalizations effectively with carefully crafted policies—understanding that one-size-fits-all policy prescriptions are rarely optimal—they should be able to employ the forces of globalization to the long-run benefit of their citizens.

Further Reading

Bartels, L. (2008). *Unequal democracy: The political economy of the new gilded age.* Princeton, NJ: Princeton University Press.

Chandler, A., & Mazlish, B. (2005). *Leviathans: Multinational corporations and the new global history.* Cambridge, England: Cambridge University Press.

Chang, H.-J. (2012). *23 things they don't tell you about capitalism.* New York, NY: Bloomsbury Press.

Cowen, T. (2004). *Creative destruction: How globalization is changing the world's cultures.* Princeton, NJ: Princeton University Press.

Deaton, A. (2013). *The great escape: Health, wealth, and the origins of inequality.* Princeton, NJ: Princeton University Press.

Easterly, W. (2007). *The white man's burden: Why the West's efforts to aid the rest have done so much ill and so little good.* Oxford, England: Oxford University Press.

Frey, B. (2010). *Happiness: A revolution in economics.* Cambridge, MA: MIT Press.

Frieden, J., Lake, D., & Broz, L. (2010). *International political economy: Perspectives on global power and wealth.* New York, NY: W. W. Norton and Company.

Galbraith, J. L. (1958). *The affluent society.* New York, NY: Houghton Mifflin.

Graham, C. (2010). *Happiness around the world: The paradox of happy peasants and miserable millionaires.* Oxford, England: Oxford University Press.

Harvey, D. (2007). *A brief history of neoliberalism.* Oxford, England: Oxford University Press.

Klein, N. (2002). *No logo.* New York, NY: Picador.

Klein, N. (2008). *The shock doctrine: The rise of disaster capitalism.* New York, NY: Picador.

Layard, R. (2006). *Happiness: Lessons from a new science.* New York, NY: Penguin.

Luttwak, E. (2000). *Turbo-capitalism: Winners and losers in the global economy.* New York, NY: Harper Perennial.

Moore, M. (2003). *A world without walls: Freedom, development, free trade and global governance.* Cambridge, England: Cambridge University Press.

Putnam, R. (2000). *Bowling alone: The collapse and revival of American community.* New York, NY: Simon and Schuster.

Rodrik, D. (1997). *Has globalization gone too far?* Washington, DC: Institute for International Economics.

Rodrik, D. (2016). *Economics rules: The rights and wrongs of the dismal science.* New York, NY: W. W. Norton and Company.

Sen, A. (1999). *Development as freedom.* New York, NY: Random House.

Singer, P. (2002). *One world: the ethics of globalization.* New Haven, CT: Yale University Press.

Stiglitz, J. (2003). *Globalization and its discontents.* New York, NY: W. W. Norton and Company.

Stiglitz, J. (2007). *Making globalization work.* New York, NY: W. W. Norton and Company.

Wolf, M. (2004). *Why globalization works.* New Haven, CT: Yale University Press.

Wolf, M. (2010). *Fixing global finance.* Baltimore, MD: Johns Hopkins University Press.

Yergin, D., & Stanislaw, J. (2002). *The commanding heights: The battle for the world economy.* New York, NY: Touchstone.

Harvard Business School Case Studies

Abrami, R. *Worker rights and global trade: The U.S.-Cambodia bilateral textile trade agreement,* 703034-PDF-ENG.

Alfaro, L., Dev, V., Allibhoy, F., & Spar, D. L. *Botswana: A diamond in the rough,* 703027-PDF-ENG.

Bose, I., Banerjee, S., & Robbe, E. V. *Wal-Mart and Bharti: Transforming retail in India,* HKU845-PDF-ENG.

Conklin, D. W., & Cadieux, D. *Transformations of Wal-Mart: Experimenting with new retail paradigms,* W11056-PDF-ENG.

Diermeier, D. *Wal-Mart: The store wars,* KEL658-PDF-ENG.

Hannan, M., McMillan, J., Podolny, J., & Warren, M. A. *World Trade Organization and the Seattle talks,* IB41-PDF-ENG.

Jones, G. G., & Brown, A. *Thomas J. Watson, IBM and Nazi Germany,* 807133-PDF-ENG.

Jones, G. G., & Reavis, C. *Multinational corporations in apartheid-era South Africa: The issue of reparations,* 804027-PDF-ENG.

Jones, G. G. *Brazil at the wheel,* 804080-PDF-ENG.

Jones, G. G. *Multinationals as engines of growth?,* 803108-PDF-ENG.

Konrad, A., & Mark, K. *Staffing Wal-Mart stores, Inc.,* 904C06-PDF-ENG.

Neeley, T. *Language and globalization: 'Englishnization' at Rakuten*, 412002-PDF-ENG.

Pill, H., & Sprague, C. *Uganda and the Washington Consensus*, 798047-PDF-ENG.

Pill, H. *Mexico: Reform and crisis—1987–95*, 797050-PDF-ENG.

Pill, H. *Recycling problem: International bank lending in the 1970s*, 796131-PDF-ENG.

Plambeck, E., & Denend, L. *WalMart's sustainability strategy*, OIT71-PDF-ENG.

Ramanna, K., Lenhardt, J., & Homsy, M. *IKEA in Saudi Arabia*, 116015-PDF-ENG. https://cb.hbsp.harvard.edu/cbmp/product/116015-PDF-ENG

Spar, D. L., & Burns, J. *Hitting the wall: Nike and international labor practices*, 700047-PDF-ENG.

Subramanian, S., Dhanaraj, C., & Branzei, O. *Bayer CropScience in India: Against child labor*, 910M61-PDF-ENG.

Teagarden, M. B., & Schotter, A. *Blood bananas: Chiquita in Colombia*, TB0245-PDF-ENG.

Wells, L. T., Jr., & Sprague, C. *Background and agreements on foreign direct investment*, 796148-PDF-ENG.

Werhane, P., & Mead, J. *Abbott and the AIDS crisis*, UV1157-PDF-ENG.

Werker, E. *Foreign direct investment and South Africa*, 707019-PDF-ENG.

Epilogue (2013)

Economists … are the trustees, not of civilization, but of the possibility of civilization.

—John Maynard Keynes at his retirement toast
from the editorship of *Economic Journal*, 1945

Inspired by the sentiment above, the preceding six chapters have explored economic concepts that should be helpful to businesspersons operating in today's deeply interconnected global economy. To recap: the process of truly global economic integration stretches back some 500 years to the discovery of the New World, its pace quickening over the last two centuries (see Chapter 1). To understand the process of long-run growth as economies develop and globalize, the neoclassical growth model—with a special focus on the role of human capital and technology—is an invaluable framework (see Chapter 2). Comparative advantage and the factor proportions model provide key insights into the structure of international economic specialization and the global division of labor (see Chapter 3). The impact of globalization on local labor markets depends on the level of economic development within a nation, including its stock of human capital (see Chapter 4). Domestic political coalitions often have sharply divergent views on whether their economy should liberalize and integrate internationally (see Chapter 5). And although its benefits are broadly appreciated, there are many critics who point out that globalization has frequently encouraged environmental degradation and exacerbated social inequities (see Chapter 6). Right now, these criticisms are all the more evident because during the recent era of hyperglobalization, the gyrations of the global economy ended up overwhelming the capacity of international institutions to accommodate change.

Core, Periphery, and Convergence

Over the past two decades, new technologies providing personal computing power and effortless global connectivity have become available to a substantial fraction of the world population. Spurred by these modern information and communications technologies—as well as FDI and a richer appreciation for market-driven growth strategies—the *periphery* has been able to catch up with the *core* at a rapid pace. Imitation, replication, and coordination are fundamental to this process.

While today's pace is new, the interplay between core and peripheral economies stretches back to pre-modern times. Historians have long debated why the Roman Empire fell in the 5th century AD, but one undisputed cause is the growing strength of barbarian forces northeast of imperial borders along the Rhine and Danube Rivers. At the beginning of the first millennium AD, Roman commanders concluded that the backward regions of Europe dominated by Germanic tribes—constituting the poor undeveloped periphery of that era's economy—were not worth conquering. Yet the population and wealth of the external tribes multiplied over the subsequent centuries, leading up to the great raids on Roman territories by Hun and Gothic armies in the 4th century. With mounting archaeological evidence, some historians argue that the barbarian forces only grew to such strength—with modes of economic production that were ever more sophisticated and diversified—because of their repeated trade and contact with the Roman core economy, which fueled technology transfer and imitation. Thus, Rome's success contributed to its downfall, as backward regions near the imperial border began to catch up, indicating that globalization's reach extends well before the Middle Ages.

The rapid convergence of many developing economies today generates further trade integration, making conflict less likely (even if the outbreak of war remains unpredictable). Technology and expertise from advanced economies spills over onto emerging economies in this process. With each passing year, knowledge becomes more important to national competitiveness, and land less so. As opposed to the Roman practice of paying tribute to Germanic armies threatening to invade as a containment strategy to keep the peace, wealthy nations today give free aid to the least developed economies partly out of altruistic motivation, given the immense differences in living standards. Altruism is less relevant to China's development, which was driven by a sharp change in ideology that allowed for market reforms and foreign trade. China's rapid ascent would not have been possible without globalization: the Chinese leveraged an enormous pool of cheap domestic labor and bargained for access to foreign technologies and know-how. Many contend that China had long laid claim to the world's grandest civilization, with the exception of the past two centuries when it pursued deglobalization.

In the coming years, emerging markets will provide growth opportunities for established products and businesses. Residents of many developing countries will enjoy rising living standards as their economies converge toward those of wealthy nations. Walmart and other likeminded distributors will undoubtedly supply them with the finer goods of middle-class life. Each successful businessperson's story is different, but it is often the case that tapping into expanding consumer markets leads to greater profitability than other strategies. As financial traders say, the trend is your friend. Taking advantage of momentum can lead to outsized gains, and emerging markets are a potential source of exceptional sales growth.

Advanced economies on the technological frontier will continue to drive innovation, with fits and bursts of productivity growth coming from unexpected sources. Much attention has been paid to sluggish American real wage growth, but there is cause for optimism in the United States. There may well be a forthcoming revival of American manufacturing, as tradable sector work shifts from China back to the United States, given rising Chinese labor costs and enormous American productivity advantages. China is new to the club of middle-income countries, and to become as rich as leading economies, it must carry out decades of social transitions and policy reforms. No matter how successful they are in the near term, other developing countries (such as Vietnam) cannot become China redux, for the simple fact that China's size and history make it truly unique.

State of Globalization Today

Governments around the world are now adjusting policies in the wake of the last global financial crisis that began in 2007. It threatened to grind the financial system to a halt, setting off a new global depression. Some reforms have been enacted so far, yet the world's financial infrastructure remains largely intact. With so many complex financial products in existence, an underlying compensation structure that is arguably incompatible with prudent risk management, and an overall lack of transparency, many economists believe that additional restructurings are necessary because taxpayers remain exposed to excessive systemic risk. There is also the sobering fact that modern economic crises are highly contagious. Despite these enormous policy challenges, the governments of rich nations—including those within the EU—appear committed to the globalization project.

Even if serious conflict between global powers were to break out again, the contemporary Western mindset stands in great contrast to ideologies of the interwar deglobalization period from 1914 to 1945 (which very few alive today experienced as adults). The instability of that era was shaped by the interests of reactionary elites whose power had long been on the wane yet were still highly influential. In wealthy nations of the West today, the power of archaic aristocratic elites has expired. Few prevailing coalitions call for a robust deglobalization—as the reactionary aristocrats and socialist labor leaders of yesteryear did—much less with a compelling message that appeals to ordinary citizens. Some analysts argue that the void has been filled by the titans of the contemporary information economy, some of whom head MNE. Critics insist that too many of these moguls are dangerously adept at rent-seeking, dubious "shadow banking" practices, and other activities with potentially adverse social consequences.

The current debate about economic policy doesn't concern the merits of capitalism versus socialism as it did throughout much of the 20th century, when great tragedies were manufactured by anti-capitalist totalitarian rulers such as Stalin and Mao. Today's debate, reflecting a pragmatic state of mind, is much narrower: how best to create a sustainable market-based global economy that has the support of participating citizens and can adapt in the face of serious threats such as global warming. In fact, the greatest threat to long-run prosperity may be "anthropogenic" (meaning human-caused) climate change. The quality of the global environment is a public good, so maintaining it requires a concerted multilateral effort. Yet due to the absence of preemptive collective action, greenhouse gas emissions have escalated, threatening to wreak environmental devastation (even if the full set of consequences has not been firmly established at this time).

Shifting from fossil fuels to clean energy sources will be very costly, and given the deteriorating fiscal situation of many wealthy nations, funding clean energy investment is problematic. Combating climate change would likely slow international trade flows, because under current technologies, the shipping and transport of goods relies on fossil fuels. At least there is a growing recognition of global warming stemming from mounting evidence that polar ice caps are melting, sea levels are rising, extreme weather events are increasingly common, and the world's food supply chain is threatened. Some degree of political progress has been made over the past several years. For instance, as part of the 2010 "Cancun Agreement," 193 nations consented to the goal of keeping global temperature increases under 2°C (as compared to temperatures before the "Industrial Age"), and to date, over 90 nations have made voluntary pledges to reduce their emissions for 2020.

The governance of the international economy is currently under heavy scrutiny. At the same time, the public lacks faith in corporations, politicians, and regulators. Given the present age of disarray, some commentators have made comparisons to the global economy's last great period of transition: from approximately 1973 to 1983, the United States and other affluent nations shifted from *reglobalization* supported by the Bretton Woods style of controlled capitalism to free markets and *hyperglobalization*. A new framework has not yet emerged; the extent of cross-border economic integration could diminish, though a true *deglobalization* seems unlikely. Western economists still favor free and open trade, recognizing that the gains from globalization—while incrementally diminishing—have been considerable in the aggregate. As usual, much depends on politics, which are fickle, and capable leadership.

Over the last several decades, analysts of all political persuasions have frequently argued that economic growth and globalization have eroded social cohesion within nations. After the long stretch of economic expansion from 1983 to 2007, advanced nations such as the United States are experiencing growing pains as they debate political and social reforms designed to provide greater equality of opportunity and stabilize the quality of life for middle- and working-class citizens. The "old-age dependency ratio"—defined as the number of elderly per working age citizen—is set to increase substantially throughout much of the world, including the United States, Europe, Japan, and China. The economic drag caused by the aging of prosperous societies will strain public sector budgets for years to come. Luckily many leading scientists working in biology, clean energy, and

nanotechnology are optimistic about new breakthroughs that could catalyze productivity growth.

Over a billion people have been lifted out of poverty since 1980, and
the worldwide poverty rate now falls by at least one percentage point every
year. Globalization has played no small role in this transformation. Brazil's
recent development has demonstrated that an open economy can see both
growth and a diminishing gap between rich and poor. Under the savvy
political leadership of Presidents Cardoso and Lula da Silva—and owing
much to the global boom in commodities—Brazil stepped up expendi-
tures on education and welfare, which spurred growth and reduced poverty. With an economy now larger than the United Kingdom's, Brazil has
disproven the fatalistic adage that it is "the country of the future and always
will be." Africa's economic prospects have brightened. Foreign investment
has soared over the past decade, partly due to a mining boom, and the
quality of governance in many countries has improved. The continent still
has a long way to go, as most Africans live on less than two dollars a day,
and education, infrastructure, and basic services such as electricity and
water remain inadequate.

Even as globalization has helped to reduce poverty in the poorest
nations and generate immense wealth, its impact on the world economy
can be destabilizing and anxiety-inducing. The world is still in the midst of
political uncertainty, heightened financial turbulence, and transition to a
multipolar orientation, with relatively less power centered in the United
States and Europe, the latter a weak link in the recovery from the last global
economic crisis. As of mid-2013, the eurozone economy is well into its
second year of recession, marking Europe's longest postwar slump, with no
vigorous recovery in sight until the debt crisis is resolved. EU leadership
has repeatedly vowed the euro will be saved, reflecting their belief in the
value of pan-European political and economic solidarity. Today's overwhelming degree of economic interdependence means that globalized
nations simply have too much to lose from separatism, which would dramatically reduce living standards, giving them all the more incentive to
avoid conflict (or paralysis) by assenting to reasonable consensus policies
of international governance and trade.

Further Reading

Banerjee, A., & Duflo, E. (2012). *Poor economics: A radical rethinking of the way to fight global poverty*. New York, NY: PublicAffairs.

Barofsky, N. (2012). *Bailout: How Washington abandoned Main Street while rescuing Wall Street*. New York, NY: Free Press.

Chinn, M., & Frieden, J. (2012). *Lost decades: The making of America's debt crisis and the long recovery*. New York, NY: W. W. Norton and Company.

Eichengreen, B. (2011). *Exorbitant privilege: The rise and fall of the dollar and the future of the international monetary system*. Oxford, England: Oxford University Press.

Freeland, C. (2012). *Plutocrats: The rise of the new global super-rich and the fall of everyone else*. New York, NY: Penguin Press.

Heather, P. (2012). *Empires and barbarians: The fall of Rome and the birth of Europe*. Oxford, England: Oxford University Press.

Johnson, S., & Kwak, J. (2012). *White House burning: Our national debt and why it matters to you*. New York, NY: Pantheon.

Khanna, R. (2012). *Entrepreneurial nation: Why manufacturing is still key to America's future*. New York, NY: McGraw-Hill.

Koo, R. (2009). *The Holy Grail of macroeconomics: Lessons from Japan's Great Recession*. Hoboken, NJ: Wiley.

Luttwak, E. (2012). *The rise of China vs. the logic of strategy*. Cambridge, MA: Belknap Press.

Mahbubani, K. (2013). *The great convergence: Asia, the West, and the logic of one world*. New York, NY: Public Affairs.

McCormick, M. (2001). *Origins of the European economy: Communications and commerce AD 300–900*. Cambridge, England: Cambridge University Press.

Moore, M. (2009). *Saving globalization: Why globalization and democracy offer the best hope for progress, peace and development*. Hoboken, NJ: Wiley.

Moss, T. (2011). *African development: making sense of the issues and actors*. Boulder, CO: Lynne Rienner.

Pisano, G., & Shih, W. (2012). *Producing prosperity: Why America needs a manufacturing renaissance*. Boston, MA: Harvard Business Review Press.

Radelet, S. (2010). *Emerging Africa: How 17 countries are leading the way*. Washington DC: Center for Global Development.

Rodrik, D. (2011). *The globalization paradox: Democracy and the future of the world economy*. New York, NY: W.W. Norton and Company.

Roett, R. (2011). *The new Brazil*. Washington DC: Brookings Institution Press.

Schlesinger, A., Jr. (1986). *The cycles of American history*. New York, NY: Houghton Mifflin Company.

Stiglitz, J. (2010). *The price of inequality: How today's divided society endangers our future.* New York, NY: W.W. Norton and Company.

Harvard Business School Case Studies

Abdelal, R., & Tarontsi, S. *Natural gas,* 713020-PDF-ENG.

Abdelal, R., & Tuthill, K. *Romney vs. Obama and U.S. energy policy,* 713050-PDF-ENG.

Alfaro, L., & White, H. *Brazil's enigma: Sustaining long-term growth,* 713040-PDF-ENG.

Alvarez, J. B., & Johnson, R. *Doug Rauch: Solving the American food paradox,* 512022-PDF-ENG.

Alvarez, J. B., Riis, J., & Salmon, W. J. *H-E-B: Creating a movement to reduce obesity in Texas,* 512034-PDF-ENG.

Burgelman, R. A., & Schifrin, D. *Nissan's electric vehicle strategy in 2011: Leading the way toward zero-emission,* SM189-PDF-ENG.

Ceranic, T., Montiel, I., & Cook, W. S. *Sierra Nevada Brewing Co.: End of incentives,* NA0156-PDF-ENG.

Clendenen, G., Thurston, P. W., Zhao, F., & Kidwell, S. *Coal, nuclear, natural gas, oil, or renewable: Which type of power plant should we build?,* NA0007-PDF-ENG.

Daemmrich, A. A., & Musacchio, A. *Brazil: Leading the BRICs?,* 711024-PDF-ENG.

Hawarden, V., & Barnard, H. *Danimal in South Africa: Management innovation at the bottom of the pyramid,* 910M99-PDF-ENG.

Hoyt, D. W., & Reichelstein, S. *REI's solar energy program,* BE17-PDF-ENG.

Khanna, T., & Palepu, K. G. *Emerging giants: Building world-class companies in emerging markets,* 703431-PDF-ENG.

McKern, B., & Denend, L. *The business environment of Brazil: Navigating the financial crisis,* IB96-PDF-ENG.

Musacchio, A. *Brazil under Lula,* 707031-PDF-ENG.

Musacchio, A. *Inequality in Brazil,* 711086-PDF-ENG.

Palepu, K. G., & Bijlani, T. *Bharti Airtel in Africa,* 112096-PDF-ENG.

Pill, H., & Vogel, I. *John Maynard Keynes: His life, times, and writings,* 702092-HCB-ENG.

Rao, H., & Elkin, G. *Chez Panisse Foundation: Scaling up a delicious revolution,* HR33-PDF-ENG.

Reinhardt, F., Casadesus-Masanell, R., & Nellemann, F. *Maersk Line and the future of container shipping,* 712449-PDF-ENG.

Rice, C., Zegart, A., & McMurdo, T. L. *Political risk in the Kaesong Industrial Complex,* IB103-PDF-ENG.

Scott, B. R., Potvin, S., & Adams, A. *Capitalism and democracy in a new world*, 706030-PDF-ENG.

Zerio, J., & Conejero, M. A. *Brazil's waste: A big emerging market*, TB0231-PDF-ENG.

Postscript (2017)

There is nothing permanent except change.
　　　　　　　　　　　—Heraclitus (5th century BC)

The year 2016 offered two bombshell elections with twin results no one had anticipated: Great Britain collectively decided to exit the European Union, and Donald Trump was voted President of the United States. Although electoral margins were extremely slim, British and American citizens were expressing frustration with hyperglobalization, notably its failure to provide widely shared economic benefits to those disconnected from wealthy high-tech hubs such as London, New York, and San Francisco. A strong case can also be made that ostensibly non-economic factors—such as irritation with pluralism, open borders, and weakened national identities, particularly among older voters—were the primary forces underlying election results. Today in February 2017, some prominent Western politicians (such as Marine Le Pen in France) are actually calling for deglobalization. More than a few analysts have argued that 2016 marked the end of the postwar "Pax Americana" era—lasting roughly a lifetime—and a new period involving the readjustment of trade and immigration policies may be afoot.

In the United States, Europe, and elsewhere, the crux of the political and economic conflict revolves around labor. Aggravated workers are able to vote (unlike capital itself, even if wealthy capital-owners do retain a disproportionate influence on the political system). As compared to interest rates, wages, and earnings—meaning the returns to labor—have a much larger impact on human well-being across a broad cross-section of any society. Middle-to-lower-income workers—who now take Walmart for granted—have helped fuel a populist backlash against globalization, which so many concluded was a free-for-all. Historians enjoy analyzing parallels with the last great populist revolt against globalization that occurred in the late 19th century, paving the way for an extended period of progressive reform. Even among elites, there is a growing awareness that inequality within rich nations presents a persistent social problem that may require an enhanced "social contract." A desire for new solutions appears to be spawning a vigorous debate at last, even if labor economists have been analyzing income inequality in exhaustive detail for over 30 years.

Finding the right policy balance properly reflecting national interests is difficult to achieve within Western democracies because domestic coalitions have sharply divergent interests, just as the Stolper-Samuelson theorem implies. In contrast, autocratic governments (such as the Communist Party of China) have an easier time coordinating and implementing sweeping reforms. The United States now appears to be in the process of reevaluating its industrial policy, yet economists are skeptical that momentous changes will prove beneficial in the long-run given the law of comparative advantage, to say nothing of political traps such as rent-seeking. When it comes to struggling "Rust Belt" labor markets, the empirical evidence shows automation is far more important than free trade in explaining why the number of jobs in the US manufacturing sector has been declining (a pattern Germany also experienced). And if the flow of immigrants—who are disproportionately younger—is restricted, there will be fewer working age contributors to Social Security pension funds, which is economically unhelpful due to the demographics of an aging society, among other reasons.

Contrary to the scathing political rhetoric, economic research demonstrates that globalization has had only a moderate effect on wage inequality within the United States and other affluent Western nations. Technological change has been a far more important force driving inequality, and when it comes to national economic health, subpar productivity growth is the dominant concern. While globalization as measured by trade intensity has stalled, the volume of cross-border electronic data flows has actually continued to grow at an increasing rate. Technological progress cannot be stopped, and it is unlikely that international economic integration will unravel. Yet with the political uncertainty that lies ahead, many urgent questions are impossible to answer at this date: Will the post-Brexit EU hold steady, or gradually break apart? Will the populist wave rise, merge with a new progressive movement, or simply bomb out? Will a worldwide neo-Silk Road Pax between China, Europe, and the United States emerge in due time—or remain just a chimerical notion? What's clear is that the economics—and politics—of globalization are more important than ever to understanding international business and world events.

Further Reading

Atkinson, A. (2015). *Inequality: What can be done?* Cambridge, MA: Harvard University Press.

Bessen, J. (2015). *Learning by doing: The real connection between innovation, wages, and wealth.* New Haven, CT: Yale University Press.

Bourguignon, F. (2015). *The globalization of inequality.* Princeton, NJ: Princeton University Press.

Bremmer, I. (2016). *Superpower: Three choices for America's role in the world.* New York, NY: Penguin.

Ferguson, N. (2014). *The great degeneration: How institutions decay and economies die.* New York, NY: Penguin.

Ford, M. (2015). *Rise of the robots: Technology and the threat of a jobless future.* New York, NY: Basic Books.

Goodwyn, L. (1978). *The populist moment: A short history of the agrarian revolt in America.* Oxford, England: Oxford University Press.

Hofstadter, R. (1955). *The age of reform.* New York, NY: Random House.

James, H. (2012). *The creation and destruction of value: The globalization cycle.* Cambridge, MA: Harvard University Press.

Judis, J. (2016). *The populist explosion: How the Great Recession transformed American and European politics.* New York, NY: Columbia Global Reports.

King, M. (2016). *The end of alchemy: Money, banking, and the future of the global economy.* New York, NY: W. W. Norton and Company.

Lindert, P., & Williamson, J. (2016). *Unequal gains: American growth and inequality since 1700.* Princeton, NJ: Princeton University Press.

Milanovic, B. (2016). *Global inequality: A new approach for the age of globalization.* Cambridge, MA: Harvard University Press.

Müller, J.-W. (2016). *What is populism?* Philadelphia, PA: University of Pennsylvania Press.

Piketty, T. (2014). *Capital in the twenty first century.* Cambridge, MA: Harvard University Press.

Shipman, T. (2016). *All out war: The full story of how Brexit sank Britain's political class.* London, England: William Collins.

Smick, D. (2017). *The great equalizer: How main street capitalism can create an economy for everyone.* New York, NY: PublicAffairs.

Stiglitz, J. (2015). *The great divide: Unequal societies and what we can do about them.* New York, NY: W. W. Norton and Company.

Stiglitz, J. (2016). *The Euro: How a common currency threatens the future of Europe.* New York, NY: W. W. Norton and Company.

Wolf, M. (2014). *The shifts and the shocks: What we've learned—and have still to learn—from the financial crisis.* New York, NY: Penguin.

Index

Absolute advantage, international
    trade, 68–69
Absolute convergence hypothesis, 47
Acquired immune deficiency
    syndrome (AIDS), 169
AIDS. *See* Acquired immune
    deficiency syndrome
American labor markets, 112–115
Anglo-Dutch War, 11
Avian Influenza, 169

Balance of trade, 2
Bang for the buck, 43
Big-push model, economic
    development, 100–103
Bilateral trade, 151
Bird Flu. *See* Avian Influenza
Black Death, 4, 5
Bretton Woods system, 177, 178
British cotton industry, 13–14
British industrial revolution, 19–21
Business opportunities, 53–55

Canton system, breakdown of, 16–18
CAP. *See* Common agricultural policy
Capital-abundant country, 76–78
Capital-deepening, 45
Capital-to-labor ratios, 46, 47
Cassa del Mezzogiorno program, 104
Centralized economic planning, 57
Chinese intellectual property
    enforcement, 53
Chinese labor markets, 118–122
Cobb-Douglas style production
    function, 43
Cobden-Chevalier Treaty, 28
Commerce and Coalitions (Rogowski),
    140
Commodity prices, 170–172
Common agricultural policy (CAP),
    89–90

Comparative advantage, international
    trade, 68–69
    evidence on, 73–74
Concentrated power, globalization
    and, 180–183
Conditional convergence hypothesis,
    47
*Considerations Upon the East India
    Trade* (Martyn), 14
Constant returns property, 44
Convergence, 46–49
Corn Laws, 26–28, 143
Cost of capital, 44, 53
Cultural Revolution, 58

Democracy
    and economic growth, 131
    globalization and, 132–135
Disease transmission, globalization
    and, 169–170
Diversification, economy, 105–106
Dutch Golden Age, 8–9

Easterlin paradox, 183
Easterlin Richard, 183
East Indies trade, 7–8
Economic development, 105–106
Economic growth
    business opportunities, 53–55
    convergence, 46–49
    democracy and, 131
    growth across continents, 58–60
    human capital, 49–51
    intellectual property rights and
        growth, 52–53
    neoclassical growth model, 41–45,
        46, 47, 49, 51, 53, 54, 55,
        58, 62
    productivity across nations, 55–56
    productivity slowdown puzzle,
        56–57

socialism, 57–58
steady-state equilibrium, 45–46
technology, science, and growth,
    51–52
Economy labor markets, 159–161
Economic policymaking, China, 120
EEC. *See* European Economic
    Community
Elites, 180–183
An Essay on the Principle of Population
    (Malthus), 20
European Economic Community
    (EEC), 152

Factor coalitions across globalization
    eras, 144–147
Factor proportions model, 75–77,
    108, 133, 140
FDI. *See* Foreign direct investment
Foreign capital, 159–161, 163–165
Foreign direct investment (FDI),
    158–165
Foreign investment, evolution of,
    162–163
Foreign investors, 161–162
Free trade, support for, 138–139
French and Indian War, 12

GATT. *See* General agreement on
    tariffs and trade
GDP. *See* Gross domestic product
General agreement on tariffs and trade
    (GATT), 35–36
Ghent system, 174, 176
Glass-Steagall Act, 181
Global commodity prices, 171
Globalization
    extensions, international trade,
        74–75
    government size and, 147–149
    growth, happiness and, 183–185
Globalized finance, rise of, 177–180
Global poverty, trends in, 165–166
Gravity model, international trade,
    83–84
Great Depression, 29, 32–34
Great Leap Forward plan, 58
Great Recession, 115, 136, 137

Gross domestic product (GDP), 58,
    59
Growth across continents, 58–60

Habakkuk hypothesis, 81–82
Heckscher-Ohlin model of trade, 75
HIV. *See* Human immunodeficiency
    virus
Hot money, 179–180
Human capital, 49–51
    international trade, 79–82
Human immunodeficiency virus
    (HIV), 169
Hyperglobalization, 36, 138, 147
Hypothetical constant returns, scale
    economy, 43

IBRD. *See* International Bank
    for Reconstruction and
    Development
IMF. *See* International Monetary
    Fund
Import-substituting industrialization,
    87
Indian labor markets, 122–125
India's poverty rate, 124
Industrialization and population
    growth, 107
Industrial policy, 103–105
Industrial revolution technology,
    diffusion of, 23–24
Infant industry protection, 87–89
Instruments of trade policy, 89–90
Intellectual property rights and
    growth, 52–53
International Bank for Reconstruction
    and Development (IBRD), 35
International Monetary Fund (IMF),
    35, 178
International trade
    absolute and comparative
        advantage, 68–69
    basic instruments of trade policy,
        89–90
    distributional issues, 77–79
    economic theories of, 67–92
    evidence on comparative advantage,
        73–74

external increasing returns and geography, 86–87
factor proportions model, 75–77
gains from trade, 71–73
globalization extensions, 74–75
gravity model, 83–84
increasing returns and trade, 84–86
infant industry protection, 87–89
Leontief paradox, 82–83
technology and human capital, 79–82
trade-offs in, 90–92
wine and cloth, 69–71
Intolerable Acts, 1774, 12
Iwakura Mission, 19

Japan's rapid industrialization, 18–19

Labor-abundant country, 76–78
Labor markets
    American, globalization, 112–115
    Chinese, globalization and reforms, 118–122
    Indian, globalization and development, 122–125
    Mexican, globalization and industrialization, 115–118
    theory of globalization, 107–108
Labor unions, globalization and, 174–177
Leontief paradox, 82–83
Lewis two-sector "dual" model of development, 98–100
License Raj, 123
Local worker rights, 161–162
Long depression, 28–30
Low-hanging fruit, 43
Lucas paradox, 54
Luddites, 79–82

Magna Carta (Great Charter), 183
Malthusian trap, 20
Managerial capital, 55, 106–107
Manila Galleon Trade, 6
Marriage of iron and rye, 142
Mercantilism, 87
    age of, 10–11
Mercantilist World view, 2–4

Mexican labor markets, 115–118
Ming and Qing Chinese economy, 15–16
Ministry of International Trade and Industry (MITI), 104
MITI. See Ministry of International Trade and Industry
MNE. See Multinational enterprises
Modern economic globalization
    Adam Smith, David Ricardo, and the Corn Laws, 26–28
    age of mercantilism, 10–11
    British cotton industry, 13–14
    British industrial revolution, 19–21
    Canton system, breakdown of, 16–18
    Dawn of the 20th Century, 30
    Dutch Golden Age, 8–9
    East Indies trade, 7–8
    Great Depression, 32–34
    historical background, 4–5
    hyperglobalization, 36
    India, China, and Europe, 14–15
    Industrial Revolution technology, diffusion of, 23–24
    Japan's rapid industrialization, 18–19
    long depression, 28–30
    mercantilist World view, 2–4
    Ming and Qing Chinese economy, 15–16
    The New World, 5–7
    19th century globalization, boom and divergence, 24–26
    reglobalization, 35–36
    Rise of Great Britain, 21–23
    slave trade, 9–10
    United States of America, 12
    World War I, 30–32
    World War II, 34
Modern warfare, history of, 149–151
Mongol Peace, 1
Multilateral trade, 151
Multinational enterprises (MNE), 158–162

NAFTA. See North American Free Trade Agreement

National Labor Relations Act, 175
NATO. *See* North Atlantic Treaty Organization
Natural resource curse, 134
Natural resources, 170–172
Navigation Act (1651), 13
Neoclassical growth model, 41–45, 46, 47, 49, 51, 53, 54, 55, 58, 62, 74, 76, 77, 79, 82, 97–99
  assumptions, 44–45
  production function, characteristics of, 42
Neo-mercantilist, 3
Norman Conquest, 182
North American Free Trade Agreement (NAFTA), 116, 117
North Atlantic Treaty Organization (NATO), 35

OECD. *See* Organization for Economic Cooperation and Development
Offshoring practice, 80
On the Principles of Political Economy and Taxation (Ricardo), 27–28, 69
Openness, trade, and growth, 62–64
Organization for Economic Cooperation and Development (OECD), 116

Patent Act, 1836, 53
Pax Britannica, 24
Pax Mongolica, 1
Peasants Revolt of 1381, 5
Physiocrats, 26
Political coalitions, 140–144
Pollution, economics, 166–169
Pollution haven hypothesis, 168
Population growth, 170–172
Porter hypothesis, 82
Poverty, 163–165
  trends in, 165–166
Poverty traps, 100–103
Price convergence, 25
Productivity across nations, 55–56
Productivity slowdown puzzle, 56–57

Progressive income taxes, 132
Public choice analyzes, 91
Public health, economics, 166–169

Regulation demand, winners and losers, 135–138
Residual total factor productivity, 55
Restructuring, economic, 105–106
Rexists, 145
Ricardo, David, 26–28
Rise of Great Britain, 21–23

SARS. *See* Severe acute respiratory syndrome
Scottish Enlightenment, 26
Severe acute respiratory syndrome (SARS), 169
SEZ. *See* special economic zones
Silicon Valley of India, 86, 123
Silk Road, 1, 2
Slave trade, 9–10
Smith, Adam, 26–28
Smoot-Hawley Tariff, 32–33
Socialism, 57–58
Special economic zones (SEZ), 118
Spice trade, 7
Spillovers, 50, 81
Stamp Act, 1765, 12
Statute of Laborers, 1351, 5
Statute of Monopolies, 1624, 53
Steady-state equilibrium, 45–46
Stolper-Samuelson theorem, 78, 108, 135, 136, 140
Sugar Belt, 6–7
Swine Flu, 169

Take-offs, economy, 100–103
Tariff of Abominations, 141
Tea Act, 1773, 12
Technology, international trade, 79–82
Technology, science, and growth, 51–52
Townshend Acts, 1767, 12
Trade liberalization, 135
Trade-offs, international trade, 90–92
Traditional Ricardian model, 73, 74
Treaty of Nanking, 17

Walmart
    globalization and, 172–174
    low prices, 172–174
Warfare
    globalization and, 151–153
    history of, 149–151
Washington Consensus policies,
    177–179
Wealth of Nations (Smith), 2, 14, 26,
    27, 68–69, 71, 72

Wine and cloth, international trade,
    69–71
World Bank, 35, 178
World Trade Organization (WTO),
    36
World War I, 30–32
World War II, 34
WTO. *See* World Trade Organization

Yersinia pestis bacterium, 4

OTHER TITLES FROM THE ECONOMICS COLLECTION

Philip Romero, The University of Oregon and
Jeffrey Edwards, North Carolina A&T State University, Editors

- *Eastern European Economies: A Region in Transition* by Marcus Goncalves and Erika Cornelius Smith
- *Health Financing Without Deficits: Reform That Sidesteps Political Gridlock* by Philip J. Romero and Randy S. Miller
- *Central and Eastern European Economies: Perspectives and Challenges* by Marcus Goncalves And Erika Cornelius Smith
- *A Primer on Non-Parametric Analysis, Volume I* by Shahdad Naghshpour
- *A Primer on Non-Parametric Analysis, Volume II* by Shahdad Naghshpour
- *The Modern Caribbean Economy: Alternative Perspectives and Policy Implications, Volume I* by Nikolaos Karagiannis and Debbie A. Mohammed
- *The Modern Caribbean Economy: Economic Development and Public Policy Challenges, Volume II* by Nikolaos Karagiannis And Debbie A. Mohammed
- *How the Information Revolution Remade Business and the Economy: A Roadmap for Progress of the Semiconductor Industry* by Apek Mulay
- *Money and Banking: An Intermediate Market-Based Approach, Second Edition* by William D. Gerdes

Announcing the Business Expert Press Digital Library

Concise e-books business students need for classroom and research

This book can also be purchased in an e-book collection by your library as

- a one-time purchase,
- that is owned forever,
- allows for simultaneous readers,
- has no restrictions on printing, and
- can be downloaded as PDFs from within the library community.

Our digital library collections are a great solution to beat the rising cost of textbooks. E-books can be loaded into their course management systems or onto students' e-book readers.
The **Business Expert Press** digital libraries are very affordable, with no obligation to buy in future years. For more information, please visit **www.businessexpertpress.com/librarians**. To set up a trial in the United States, please email **sales@businessexpertpress.com**.